*Developmental Editing*

# Developmental Editing

## A HANDBOOK FOR FREELANCERS, AUTHORS, AND PUBLISHERS

## Scott Norton

THE UNIVERSITY OF CHICAGO PRESS   *Chicago and London*

SCOTT NORTON is developmental editor and project manager for science at the University of California Press.

The University of Chicago Press, Chicago 60637
The University of Chicago Press, Ltd., London
© 2009 by The University of Chicago
All rights reserved. Published 2009
Printed in the United States of America

20  19  18  17  16                                7

ISBN-13: 978-0-226-59515-3 (cloth)
ISBN-10: 0-226-59515-3 (cloth)

Library of Congress Cataloging-in-Publication Data

Norton, Scott.
    Developmental editing : a handbook for freelancers, authors, and
publishers / Scott Norton.
        p.   cm.
    Includes index.
    ISBN-13: 978-0-226-59514-6 (cloth : alk. paper)
    ISBN-10: 0-226-59514-5 (cloth : alk. paper)  1. Developmental editing—
Handbooks, manuals, etc.  I. Title.
    PN162.N67 2008
    070.4'1—dc22

                                                2008026886

# CONTENTS

# PREFACE

I'm not proud of how I got my start in developmental editing. It was back in the early 1980s; I was about to graduate from college—and nervous about my prospects for finding a job with a bachelor's degree in English—when my Medieval Lit professor said, "Hey, I think I've got a way for you to make some cash." He'd noticed that my essays were well constructed and said he could get me freelance work that paid the princely wage of $15 per hour, so long as I could generate long, detailed outlines.

I could outline with my eyes shut. The underfunded Catholic grade school of my youth had been short on reading materials and long on memorization; English lessons consisted of interminable drills in diagramming sentences and, in the upper grades, outlining essays. The memory of Sister Rita still hovers over me when I edit: cheeks distended beyond her white-linen wimple the better to quiver with rage, arm lifting her disciplinary weapon of choice, a wooden paddle dubbed the Board of Education.

So I found myself—a recent graduate of Trenton State College—spending my days in the magnificent gothic main library of Princeton University, creating outlines for books that would never be written. At first, I didn't realize that this was the case: I knew only that I was creating book proposals for a man who styled himself a "book producer" and that I didn't need to expend much effort insuring the outlines against plagiarism because, as he said, "once we hire an actual author, they will do what they want anyway." The purpose of each proposal was to enlist the financial support of a corporate sponsor. When I entered the high-ceilinged, wainscotted halls of Firestone Library, I went straight to the Popular Interest section and pulled out a half-dozen books on the assigned subject of the day, digested their tables of contents, and scratched out on a yellow legal pad an outline that combined all their topics, then added a veneer of superficially "fresh" perspective. After that, I'd return to the storefront office—suspiciously empty of furniture but wearing its Nassau Street address prominently on its awning—and crank out a five-page introduction to the outline, which itself ran ten or fifteen pages.

From such thin air I created a guide to cosmetics, a baby book, a dog-grooming manual, and various personal finance management books that were clearly beyond my own paupered experience.

My boss was an excellent salesman. He extracted six-digit advances from his corporate sponsors and actually put a nonfiction book or two on the *New York Times* bestsellers list (or so went the legend). His problem was follow-through. As the advances grew larger, he got caught up in selling bigger concepts for more front money and became less interested in actually producing the books. Authors were not found for many contracts, and a lone keyboardist—who in memory seems lashed to her Quadritek typesetting machine twenty-four hours a day—chain-smoked and churned out galleys for the books that did come to fruition. Five months after my arrival, we employees were called one by one into his barren office and laid off. He was filing for Chapter 11 status.

Looking back, I recognize that these inauspicious beginnings were excellent training for a real job in book publishing. Since joining the staff of the University of California Press in 1995, I've done developmental plans for over fifty manuscripts on subjects ranging from Japanese history to Marilyn Monroe, the civil rights movement to natural history, and I've used my facility with outlining to help many fine authors improve manuscripts that have genuinely enriched their fields of study. I can only hope that Sister Rita is looking down on me and saying, "That's more like it."

Most of us enter into book publishing with a romantic idea of the Editor that matches the equally inaccurate notion of the Author as tortured genius. We aspire to a vocation that is equal parts benefactor, acolyte, and muse. Jackie Onassis was such an editor, evidently; decades earlier, Maxwell Perkins was another. In a 1947 essay, Perkins describes how a young Thomas Wolfe showed up at his home on Thanksgiving Day 1933 with "about two feet of typescript" and they "began a year of nights of work, including Sundays, and every cut, and change, and interpolation was argued about and about." The result was *Of Time and the River*. When the author humbly and "lavishly" thanked Perkins in a dedication, the critics sniped, doubting whether Wolfe could function as a writer on his own: "Wolfe and Perkins—Perkins and Wolfe—what way is that to write a novel." To salvage his reputation, Wolfe turned to another publisher—though, tellingly, he later named Perkins his literary executor.*

In this postmodern era, the Author is dead, television and cinema and the Internet are the dominant media, and the collaborative nature of all cultural production—books included—is a given. The Editor, too, is dead, having been replaced by a lowercase cadre of agents, acquisitions editors, production editors, freelance copyeditors, and marketing and sales directors pitching books to superchain bookstore buyers. But there remains the *function* of the Editor, hovering like a ghost over the proceedings (not unlike my own strict angel, Sister Rita). The Editor lives again whenever an agent persuades an author to broaden her thesis; whenever an acquisitions editor takes a manuscript home for the weekend to suggest rearrangements and cuts; whenever a production editor pays a copyeditor a few extra dollars to provide some missing connective tissue in an author's discourse. Among these partial reincarnations of the Editor, the one that concerns us is the Developmental Editor.

As near as I can tell, the job description of Developmental Editor came into existence around the middle of the last century when financial pressures on the Editor caused him (or her, more rarely back then) to focus on contract-signing goals at the expense of assisting authors in developing their books. Manuscripts were delivered with their developmental needs unattended, and staff were assigned to fix those problems before the texts went into copyediting and typesetting. Gradually, DEs became freighted with production tasks, taking over responsibilities once shouldered by the in-house copyeditor, page makeup artist, and typesetter. (Those jobs are mostly gone now, too.) DEs were reclassified as project managers or production editors, and developmental editing became a luxurious impulse rarely indulged.

Most staff DEs today work in professional, textbook, or reference houses and spend much of their time doing market research, working with curriculum developers, keeping abreast of new state laws mandating curriculum changes, and serving as traffic cops for the incessant flow of contributing authors' articles—though at the core of their profession remains a deep commitment to guiding and shaping the development of books. Another large contingent of DEs works with "subject matter experts" instead of authors to create documentation for everything from computer software applications to government procedures. A few in-house DEs hang onto their precarious positions in trade houses and at the largest university presses. But as outsourcing many aspects of book publishing—from copyediting to

---

*Maxwell E. Perkins, "Thomas Wolfe," introduction to Thomas Wolfe, *Look Homeward, Angel: A Story of the Buried Life* (New York: Scribner's, 1995), pages x–xii.

composition to publicity—becomes more pervasive, developmental editing has staged a comeback as a freelance career.

Today's freelance DEs tend to live away from the main publishing centers—anywhere that they can sustain a modest lifestyle and quiet working environment. Most have at least one advanced degree and have found that the strictures of teaching or in-house publishing jobs don't suit them; some are authors themselves. These DEs invest years of their lives in other people's manuscripts; they thrive on exercising their particular knack for putting themselves simultaneously in the author's and reader's places; and they take comfort in knowing that, as competition between publishing houses grows more vociferous under the fiscal pressures of parent media conglomerates, the demand for their skill set is on the rise.

✳

At cocktail parties, when the inevitable question about employment gets asked, my answer usually elicits one of four responses. The first is boredom—"Oh," followed by a quick change of subject. The second is guilt, typically expressed as "I really should read more." These folks right away start choosing their words more carefully; they hypercorrect their grammar, and sometimes take on a faint British accent. The third response is enthusiasm—"I have always wanted to be an editor"—that turns to disappointment when I explain that I don't edit fiction or poetry and that, in fact, my last project involved the life history of horned lizards, whose chief interest to the nonspecialist lies in their ability to squirt blood from their eyes to scare away predators.

But the response I like least is the droll, "An editor, are we?" It is the distress call of the Wounded Author. Whether the injuries are real or imagined, whether sustained last week or in early childhood, whether inflicted by a New York trade editor or a high school yearbook committee, hardly matters. This author has decided that all editors are useless meddlers. These encounters make me wish I were a horned lizard.

And yet, sympathy is an editor's stock in trade. During my own few years as a freelancer, my involvement with each author was profound—whether besotted or frustrated, I experienced all the throes of nineteenth-century epistolary relationships. Email was brand new and our use of it either flamingly rude or unbearably courtly. A few manuscripts proved unsalvageable—dry exercises produced for the tenure machine—but most were saturated with the authors' love of their subjects, whether awkwardly or deftly expressed. When asked, authors of the most arcane prose revealed a desire that their book "break out" to large audiences. They responded to coaching with gratitude, and if none of the books went on to win major prizes, their readers benefited significantly from our collaboration.

I have long since traded the loneliness of the freelancer's garret for the chaos (and reliable paycheck) of half a cubicle inside a publishing house. But as often as possible, I slap a Post-It on my computer screen that says "Working at Home," slide a manuscript into my bag, and return to my loft and a freelance state of mind. For a day or two, I let the phone ring, watch the emails pile up unanswered, and retire to a quiet existence of furious thinking and feeling. I engage in sustained acts of two-way empathy—toward these authors and their prospective readers. I become, in fact, the authors' first and most attentive reader, their first critic—and perhaps the only one who will offer his insights confidentially, while there's still time for them to make adjustments to the text.

It is into this intimate spirit of collaboration that I invite the readers of this handbook.

# INTRODUCTION

Many DEs have a process that is intuitive and organic. These editors are like the best cooks, who prepare a meal by seeing what they have in the fridge and cupboard, pulling out their spice racks, and creating as they go. But I'm hopeless in the kitchen without recipes, and my approach to developmental editing is meant for others who take comfort in the clarity and predictability of a written game plan.

The process of developmental editing is inherently complex and, unlike copyediting, cannot be demonstrated with brief examples. So I've adopted the strategy of creating extended narrative examples, which appear in an alternate typeface. Although fictitious and intentionally exaggerated, these "case studies" reflect the range of authors, clients, and developmental assignments experienced by myself and my colleagues over the past decade. They are meant to enlighten and entertain, and any resemblance to an actual person, project, or event is coincidental. Readers may skip the case studies and, inside of an hour, they'll have the gist of the entire process.

## What Developmental Editing Is

For our purposes, *developmental editing* denotes significant structuring or restructuring of a manuscript's discourse. The DE's role can manifest in a number of ways. Some "big picture" editors provide broad direction by helping the author to form a vision for the book, then coaching the author chapter by chapter to ensure that the vision is successfully executed. Others get their hands dirty with the prose itself, suggesting rewrites at the chapter, section, paragraph, and sentence levels. This hands-on approach is sometimes called *substantive editing* or *line editing*.

From this perspective, stylistic intervention alone is not "developmental."

To be sure, there are cases in which a manuscript's organization is sound but the tone so pervasively wrong that virtually every sentence must be recast. Severe as these problems of tone may be, they can usually be handled by a high-powered copyeditor—and those that can't are beyond the reach of editing, requiring instead the hand of a ghostwriter or coauthor. Nevertheless, most manuscripts with structural problems have stylistic lapses as well, and DEs are often asked to fix both kinds of problems, so stylistic intervention is discussed in chapter 9.

In the industry, opinions vary as to what constitutes "significant" restructuring. At the University of California Press in Berkeley, we define developmental editing as intervention that moves content from one chapter to another, or rearranges the lion's share of a chapter's contents within itself, but that falls short of writing new material. It's a tough definition to apply, because developmental editing almost always involves some writing, usually of transitional sentences at the beginnings and ends of passages. But when the freelancer finds herself interviewing the author in order to compose whole passages, she's crossed over to the realm of ghostwriting.

## Whom This Book Is For

This book has been written primarily for freelance DEs working on nonfiction trade books of substantive merit. Those already in the business will recognize the principles and techniques I demonstrate. Freelancers whose mainstay is project management or copyediting and who are somewhat intimidated by the prospect of doing developmental work will find, I hope, the process demystified and approachable.

This handbook also aims to assist in-house publishing professionals with their forays into developmental work. Acquisitions editors with aptitude and interest in development should benefit particularly, but production editors and marketing and sales staff may also find the book useful to the extent that it provides a vocabulary for describing how a manuscript falls short of its market's expectations and what can be done about the problem.

DEs in textbook, professional, and reference houses should be able to transpose my straightforward process onto their more detailed in-house flowcharts. Although no chapters in this book explicitly focus on technical editing, the process of conceptual development outlined here should also be useful to DEs of documentation projects ranging from grant proposals to corporate brochures, from primary-source legal publishing to complex financial statements, and from computer manuals to Web content.

Fiction editing is a specialty that has been written about well and widely by others (see "Further Reading"). Less attention has been paid to how editors of nonfiction may prompt their authors' use of fiction-writing techniques without undermining factual integrity. This handbook augments its discussions of key developmental stages with sidebars on creating suspense, balancing scenes with plot summary, and evoking character and setting.

Finally, this book is for authors who wish to improve their writing skills. Composing this book has heightened my awareness of the difficulties that an author must surmount when facing the blank page. Authors who read this book should find sympathetic and practical advice to help them overcome the obstacles in their own writing processes as well as to maximize the appeal of their manuscripts to prospective publishers.

## What This Book Covers

Although developmental guidance is most effective when a manuscript is first being drafted, DEs are only sometimes lucky enough to get invited into the process at that early stage. For this reason, this handbook emphasizes techniques for excavating valuable material—concepts, content, thesis statements, and structural and stylistic coherence—from completed drafts. Only the first chapter concerns a book proposal for a manuscript not yet written, and its methods for evaluating the goals of a book are crucial for any project, whether completed or not.

In CONCEPT (chapter 1), the sky is the limit: readers learn to brainstorm for the concept that will most compellingly animate a book proposal, taking into account the needs of audience and market and bringing the author's vision into focus. CONTENT (chapter 2) drags readers back down to earth to do a feasibility study. This chapter follows two lines of inquiry. First, are the author, publisher, and DE really up to the developmental task ahead? And second, does the completed draft have the "right stuff" to bring the desired concept to life?

In THESIS (chapter 3), readers learn to whittle the manuscript's concept down to a sharp thesis. They practice distinguishing theses from topics and culling the rehashed theses of other authors. Next, they learn to choose a main thesis from a handful of promising candidates and to create a working title that reflects the winning choice.

NARRATIVE (chapter 4) focuses on techniques for locating, and braiding into a coherent structure, narrative threads drawn from materials that are not necessarily obviously narrative in nature. It brings the DE and author to a crossroads at which they must choose between telling a story and making an argument (most manuscripts have both). It helps them to brainstorm various kinds of timelines, choose the most appropriate timeline, and finetune that timeline into a revised table of contents. In EXPOSITION (chapter 5), readers face the inverse challenge: finding a line of argument in material that has strong narrative tendencies. They learn how to use the tools of expository structure while brainstorming arguments, choosing from a variety of kinds of argument, and finetuning the main argument.

By this time, readers are ready to create a full developmental blueprint for the project. PLAN (chapter 6) provides a sample format for the document that will serve as the touchstone for DE, author, and publisher throughout the editing process. It prompts readers to flesh out the draft table of contents with draft chapter theses; it also provides strategies for planning limited interventions when a project's schedule or budget does not allow a full developmental edit.

Next begins the hard work of executing the plan. In RHYTHM (chapter 7), DEs learn how to establish an interesting rhythm in a discourse by rearranging passages, prompting authors for new passages, weighting chapters equally, and editing for pace. Yet when the rough carpentry of restructuring is done, there is still much sanding, trimming, and polishing to do. In TRANSITIONS (chapter 8), readers see how opening and closing transitions can be used to shift the tenor of a text's discourse. In particular, this chapter distinguishes between drawing conclusions and placing them; it demonstrates how moving a conclusion from one place to another can lead to entirely different effects.

With the structure in place, readers consider the color and texture of the prose. In STYLE (chapter 9), DEs learn ways to help authors achieve a pleasing integration of the elements that make up their unique voice in prose. A subcategory of style, DISPLAY (chapter 10) is the manner in which a book presents its face to the prospective reader. Particular attention is paid to subheads and the perils of epigraph use, but readers also learn how to look for opportunities to illustrate concepts and express data visually. Extra touches that can add luster to a project—sidebars, text boxes, and Web pages—are discussed under the Cajun idiom of *lagniappe*.

The sequence of discrete stages presented as chapters above is somewhat artificial. In practice, readers will find that some stages occur simultaneously, others recur frequently, and still others are inapplicable to specific projects. Even the order of the stages may change: for instance, experienced DEs may find that they prepare their developmental plans earlier than is advised here. There is no one way to perform a developmental edit: readers should adapt the techniques presented here to their own personal styles and discard advice that does not resonate. In editing, as in many endeavors, rules are made to be broken; but to break them well, we must first learn to master them.

# SOME GROUND RULES

The rules that follow could be applied, with obvious adjustments, to any partnership that relies on open communication and creative interchange. DEs, authors, and the publishers who chaperone their collaboration could all do worse than to review this list of principles regularly, the way twelve-steppers do their programs.

RULE 1: BE REALISTIC. Don't shoot for the moon if your author is not astronaut material. Set yourselves the most ambitious goal that you can realistically expect to reach, then evaluate whether that goal warrants the investment of time and money.

RULE 2: MAKE A PLAN. Don't say, "Let's get into it and see how it goes." An initial plan, however provisional, forces the involved parties to state their goals up front and describe how they imagine the process of collaboration will unfold. The initial plan flushes out a host of assumptions that can otherwise plague the project. It goes without saying that the plan will change—repeatedly—during the book's development.

RULE 3: ADDRESS LOGISTICS UP FRONT. In that initial plan, make explicit decisions about who will do what, by when, and in what order. Many times I have assumed a project was going smoothly only to discover, by impromptu phone calls, that author and DE were each waiting for the other to make the next move.

RULE 4: PROCEED WITH ENTHUSIASM. DEs, if the project doesn't truly engage your interest, don't accept the assignment. Authors, if the publisher's insistence that your manuscript needs development doesn't ring true, don't agree to the plan. Publishers, if you don't sense that both DE and author have bought into the developmental plan *con gusto,* don't bother—you'll end up sinking a lot of money into the job and reap marginal benefits.

RULE 5: LEAVE WELL ENOUGH ALONE. Focus on resolving problems that stand in the way of a manuscript's success. DEs, don't take out your frustrations as an underpublished novelist, scholar, or poet by attempting to contribute substantively to the book's content. Authors, don't keep rewriting passages that have been deemed successful; this constant revisionism will undermine the DE's efforts to bring the problematic passages into alignment.

RULE 6: REMEMBER THE READER. The silent partner in the developmental process is the audience, and the author, DE, and publisher may all have different ideas about who that reader is. The initial plan should include a readership profile, and collaborators should return to that profile regularly to ask themselves, "Are we still on target? Is the book shaping up to appeal to the intended audience?"

RULE 7: SET MILESTONES. The developmental plan should include concrete goals at regular intervals that will give both DE and author a sense of accomplishment. The first milestone should be an easy one that can be reached in two to four weeks—say, revising the table of contents, or writing a new passage to open the first chapter dramatically. Success in reaching the first few milestones will spur both parties onward; milestones at the halfway and three-quarters marks will keep both marathoners' chins lifted toward the finish.

RULE 8: BE TACTFUL. DEs, know that a book is the closest thing to a child that a human being can produce; don't say anything about the author's prose that you wouldn't say about her toddler. Authors, don't be so territorial about your discourse that you react in a knee-jerk fashion to ideas that hadn't occurred to you. Give all suggestions an honest and respectful hearing, whether or not you ultimately accept them.

RULE 9: BE CANDID. That said, don't allow tact to turn obsequious. If your collaborator doesn't understand a suggestion that you are making, restate your case more clearly and firmly. Sweeping issues under the rug will only accrue a lump of resentment that will ultimately impede communication.

RULE 10: LISTEN ACTIVELY. Get in the habit of repeating what your collaborator has just said back to her, paraphrasing her point to see whether you've heard it correctly. Verbatim parroting is no use; you must put her message into your own words to demonstrate that you've truly understood what she means.

RULE 11: BRAINSTORM TOGETHER. Make all key decisions with a brief, fervent brainstorming session conducted via phone or email or face to face. This habit ensures that all parties—DE, author, and publisher—are kept "in the loop" and have a sense of active participation. It also allows the collaborators to identify blind alleys at the outset rather than wasting days or weeks on an approach that will ultimately come to naught.

RULE 12: KEEP THE PLAN CURRENT. As brainstorming sessions give rise to alterations of the initial plan, update the written document and circulate it among author, DE, and publisher. This ongoing "secretarial" task can be tedious, but abandoning it halfway through the project, I've learned, can result in the project quickly veering off course. Either the publisher or the DE should perform this chore; most authors will find it too unnerving.

# 1 * CONCEPT * *Shaping the Proposal*

In today's world, crafting a sound proposal is the indispensable first stage in the process of publishing a book. Regardless of whether the manuscript has already been written or is only a gleam in the author's eye, publishers want to see a crisp proposal that clearly conveys the book's central concept and demonstrates how that concept will appeal to its target audience. For many authors, however, summarizing in a few pages a subject that represents years of research or personal experience can be a daunting exercise. DEs can help authors to find their central concepts, bring them into focus, and then shape them into proposals that will both sell their concepts and serve as useful blueprints for their entire manuscripts.

In this chapter, we consider how to choose a broad *main concept* before a manuscript has been written. This situation is ideal, because a vision statement evoking that concept can guide the author in choosing content and, eventually, closing in on a narrower central thesis. In the next chapter, we will hunt for a concept in a text that has already been drafted. In that case, a proposal will need to be developed retroactively for submission to prospective publishers.

Our case study takes us into the fast-paced world of agented trade publishing, where proposals often receive more attention than the manuscripts they eventually beget. It is the proposal that secures the royalty advances from which agents draw their commissions. Some agents are skillful at developing proposals, and a few—as in our story—engage professional DEs to do this important work. But the glut of submissions requires that they put most proposals aside if they're not already shipshape, so authors do well to consider hiring a DE on their own before shopping a proposal around to agents.

## Author Profile: The Veteran

Sometimes even experienced authors need help in shaping a proposal. Veterans may have several published books under their belts, but if they're writing about a new subject, for a new audience, or with a broad, synthetic perspective on a subject they've previously treated more narrowly, they can lose focus. Historians adept at interweaving the narratives of dozens of characters over centuries can become flummoxed by their own autobiographies; journalists who have covered political corruption fairly for decades may find that a particular scandal strikes a nerve, causing them to lose their reportorial balance. Often, an author whose previous book has been well received will be pressured to come up with a new project quickly and will dash off a sloppy proposal. Some of the worst books written are those that follow lauded debuts: the author has poured into the first book insights gleaned over decades of preparation, leaving no mature material for a quick second book.

Brace Phillips was aware of the pitfalls of proposal writing. During his three decades as pastor of Glad Tidings Free Evangelical Church in Thousand Hills, Kentucky, he'd produced several careful studies on narrow points of Christian doctrine. His day job was filled with the woes of his congregants: illnesses, infidelities, sorrows over children gone gay or drug-addicted or pregnant out of wedlock. But now he was committed to writing a big trade book, and it promised to be a bestseller—not because he was any great shakes, but because one of his parishioners had gotten himself elected to the White House. Nearly every day, the president implied that his political views had been nurtured by his religious upbringing, as if he had learned his bloodthirstiness and greed from the pulpit of Glad Tidings. But Brace had known the president when he was still wet behind the ears—had, in fact, baptized him in the Chattahootchienooga River. If anyone could call the leader of the free world on his hypocrisy, it was Brace.

Recently, the Lord had shown Brace that the success of his famous, if truant, parishioner would give him a national platform for speaking out on any issue he chose. The revelation had come in the form of a phone call from a publishing agent up in New York. But which message should he bring to the people? The agent had rejected his first draft proposal, saying that he was "trying to accomplish too much in one book." And she was right. He wanted to restore the separation of church and state so that sins like abortion, homosexuality, and drug use would be recognized as moral choices, not legal mandates. And he especially wanted to expose preachers of the so-called prosperity gospel as nothing less than pyramid schemers. If anything got Jesus steamed, it was judging others for their sins and making money on God. These church leaders of the Religious Right, and the politicians whose elections they secured term after term, were nothing but modern-day Pharisees.

The agent said she'd consult an editor with his proposal. Brace wasn't sure what to expect from this consultation, but he recognized that he needed help. Once the book was published, Brace would need even more help to deal with the media blitz: after years of welcome obscurity, he'd no doubt be interviewed on every television and radio network. He reckoned himself good talking-head material, if he did say so himself: handsome, gregarious, witty—and humble, as the old joke went. In the meantime, he waited and prayed.

## Client Profile: The Agent

Some authors are disinclined to trust agents. Why pay a commission to someone for brokering a deal that the author can surely make herself? If you've ever sold a house without engaging a Realtor, or gone to traffic court as your own lawyer, you know the answer: an agent is an expert guide in an impenetrable thicket of legalities. Because an agent's commission is tied to the size of the author's advance on royalties, the agent is sure to push for the largest advance and the best royalty deal; the better ones will also fight for larger print runs, bigger marketing budgets, and control over the design of cover and marketing materials. For these reasons, you'd think that agents would be anathema among publishers—but they're not. Although agents do have a tendency to raise the level of competition for desirable books, they save publishers many headaches by educating their authors about the business of publishing. The better agents develop reputations for literary taste, subject expertise, and author management: to use the argot of Hollywood, they are talent scouts, casting directors, and producers rolled into one.

During her thirty years in New York, Jenny Wishler had seen the independent houses gobbled up by the media giants, and those in turn swallowed up by international conglomerates. She had watched hundreds, if not thousands, of classic titles go out of print because their sales had dropped below unreasonably high thresholds. These days, Jenny could hardly afford to take on a manuscript with sales potential of fewer than 20,000 copies in hardcover. Occasionally, she did pro bono work in academic publishing, but too many of her days were spent dressing up perfectly good books with movie options or plans to cross-market the books with a parent company's other products.

For these reasons, the Brace Phillips book was an opportunity not to be missed. The inside scoop from a whistleblower in the top ranks of the Christian Right—this project had the dual advantage of salability and moral integrity. Unfortunately, the author could not decide which book he wanted to write, and other commitments left Jenny with no time to coach him through the process of birthing a healthy book concept. She was already spending her nights and weekends on the Pynchon tell-all autobiography. So she flipped through her Rolodex looking for a DE who could empathize with an author of liberal political values and conservative moral views. On the last index card, she came to Bud Zallis. A lapsed Catholic living in free-thinking San Francisco, Bud could be counted on to engage with this manuscript fully.

## Assignment: The Proposal with Too Many Concepts

Bud Zallis was an atheist who understood the desire to believe. As an editor, he was always looking for patterns of meaning in life's torrent of random events. Moreover, because his bread-and-butter client was Haphazard Grace—the San Francisco–based inspirational division of Haphazard House, the world's largest trade publisher—he had ample experience guiding preachers, prophets, and seers through the dark valley of book production. So when Jenny called at 7:30 A.M. about the Phillips proposal, he said, "Sure, send it along."

The email attachment arrived within minutes, and Bud read the proposal through twice with his first cup of coffee. On initial reading, he simply opened his mind to the author's thought process without judgment, going along for the ride. Bud considered himself an intuitive editor, and he wanted to listen with his gut before proceeding to diagnose any problems. On second pass, he began to atomize the author's plan, applying techniques he'd learned years ago in a class on developmental editing. His former instructor, Robert Worth—whom, come to think of it, Bud hadn't spoken to in a while—was the one who had encouraged this gut-first, head-second approach.

Jenny was right: as outlined, *American Pharisees* would be a schizophrenic, three-headed monster. First, the author implied a parallel between today's Christian Right leaders and the Pharisees of the New Testament. If the draft table of contents (example 1) was any indication, Phillips would spend a third of the book expounding on Scripture before discussing present-day parallels. Second, he wanted to float a highly original but legally fraught thesis that the Christian Right's web of financial networks is a Ponzi scheme, a pyramid plan for selling salvation. Third, he would rework a sequence of sermons he'd given in Thousand Hills, Kentucky, called the "Bible On" series, which addressed the pressing issues of the day in light of scriptural precedent.

A generous sampling of the unrevised sermons revealed something unmentioned in the proposal: the author had led an adventurous life before receiving the call to the ministry. He'd been scouted by professional football clubs before entering military service during the Vietnam War, serving in an elite intelligence squad so "top secret" it remained unnamed. He'd then gone into high-stakes

EXAMPLE 1. The unrevised TOC for the Phillips proposal. The author has tried to pack three books into one: each part has a different structure, and there's little to indicate how they relate to each other.

*American Pharisees: An Insider's View of the Christian Right*

Introduction: "This People Honors Me with Their Lips"
I.  Scriptural Foundations
    1. The Marks of a Pharisee
       Giving Lip Service (Mark 7:6)
       Teaching Human Tradition as Divine Precept (Mark 7:7)
       Using Religion for Personal Gain (Mark 7:11–12)
       Self-Righteousness: The Pharisee and the Publican (Luke 18:9–14)
    2. The Marks of a Sadducee
       Denying the Afterlife (Mark 12:18)
       Enforcing the Letter of the Law (2 Corinthians 3:5–6)
       Practicing Entrapment (Matthew 3:7ff)
    3. The Marks of a Zealot
       Confusing Church and State (Luke 20:24–25)
       Committing Acts of Terrorism (Josephus)
    4. The Marks of a Christian
       Loving God with Your Whole Heart (Deuteronomy 6:5)
       Loving Your Neighbor as Yourself (Matthew 22:39)
II. Economic Principles
    5. Is the Prosperity Gospel a Pyramid Scheme?
       Tithing and Abrahamic Wealth
       The Seed-Faith Principle
       Positive Confessions and Renewed Mind
       Losing Your Healing
       The Internet Bubble
       Affinity Fraud and "Anointed" Portfolios
    6. Do We Belong in Saudi Arabia?
       Democracy versus Free Markets
       Reaganism and Russia
       Religious Freedom in the Islamic World
       Supply-Side Jesus
III. Social and Political Ramifications
    7.  Does the Bible Speak to Today's Hot-Button Issues?
    8.  The Bible on Prayer in the Schools
    9.  The Bible on Women's Rights
    10. The Bible on Abortion: Thou Shalt Not Murder I
    11. The Bible on Sexual Fidelity
    12. The Bible on Gay Marriage
    13. The Bible on Drugs and Alcohol
    14. The Bible on Gun Control: Swords into Ploughshares
    15. The Bible on Capital Punishment: Thou Shalt Not Murder II
    16. The Bible on the War in Saudi Arabia
    17. The Bible on Greenpeace
Epilogue: "The Greatest of These Is Love"

security, bringing his spymaster skills to the corporate world, and was living in a multimillion-dollar home in Montclair, New Jersey, when he received Jesus as his lord and savior, quit his job, and moved his wife and three children to a midwestern seminary school. He wove these personal anecdotes into his sermons deftly, but modesty seemed to prevent him from building his own swashbuckling story into the proposed book's structure.

Bud answered the phone; it was Jenny. Could he do anything to improve the focus of the proposal—by next week? Bud said he'd give it a whirl and turned his attention to the considerations that face author, publisher, and DE at the beginning of any new project: concept, audience, market, and vision.

## Locate the Concept

Few pleasures are as great as the taste of a fresh idea. A new insight melts in the brain like chocolate on the tongue. Whether the insight is unprecedented in human history or news only to yourself doesn't matter; the first time a thought occurs is always magic. For an insight to be worth a whole printed book, however, an audience of significant size should join you in finding the insight fresh, if not revelatory.

CULL CONCEPTS FROM SUBJECTS. If you are an author or acquisitions editor, you can no doubt remember that "aha!" moment when you first thought of an idea for a book project. We call this insight a concept because it is the point of conception, the originary moment that gives birth to a book. Occasionally, an author stumbles across a subject that has never been written about before; in that case, the book's subject is itself novel enough to warrant publication. But most subjects have been written about before; in those cases, it is an author's special take on the subject that will make the book worth reading. This conceptual slant is one dimension of the author's *point of view* (see sidebar, "Point of View").

Suppose you want to write a book about the burgeoning charter-school movement in the United States. There are plenty of books on the market that already address the how-tos and wherefores; your concern is about how cyclical changes in the political arena tend to destabilize the funding and long-term development of these pioneer efforts in education. When you begin researching, you're not certain what prescriptions for improvement you will eventually offer. So your concept is expressed in broad terms, like this:

*Concept:* American charter schools need to be shielded from the effects of power shifts between Republican and Democratic administrations, in both the executive and legislative branches.

## Point of View

In a guide to fiction writing, point of view would merit a chapter of its own. In literary terminology, the phrase refers to the vantage point from which the reader watches the action in the text. Readers learn about characters internally by seeing things through their eyes, and shifts in viewpoint from one character to another often help to build suspense (see sidebar "The Art of Suspense," chapter 4). In classic literature, the vantage point of the narrator was that of an omniscient God or gods; this all-seeing, all-knowing perspective helped make sense of human experience and reinforced the dominant culture's moral values.

The vogue for omniscience continued to hold sway after the novel was invented, but when the Enlightenment began to undermine faith in the old verities, writers started to experiment with limiting their points of view. Henry James surveyed the action in his novels as a hovering ghost who would sometimes swoop down and inhabit first one character, then another, before returning to his post near the ceiling. This limited omniscience allowed James to exploit both the intimacy of characters' viewpoints and the moral authority of a god's.

In nonfiction, point of view is limited by another constraint: access to a real-life character's inner thoughts. Nonfiction writers cannot presume to speak for historical characters, much less God. Therefore, nonfiction authors have no choice but to default to their own points of view, in essence treating themselves as either godlike overseers or characters in their own story. If they inhabit other characters, they must couch these literary "possessions" in conditionals: King Henry VIII *might have* thought this, Kublai Khan *must have* felt that. The effect, if used liberally, undermines the authority of the author's voice.

Because of its awkwardness in nonfiction, this handbook downplays point of view as a literary device, considering it just one among many tools for organizing timelines and arguments (see chapters 4 and 5). Instead, we shall define the term more broadly to mean a mature, informed opinion toward a subject (which we call a "concept") or a topic (which we call a "thesis") that animates prose style (see chapter 9). For DEs editing nonfiction, the most common problem involving point of view is the lack of one.

This formulation leaves ample room for development of any number of sharper theses.

CULL CONCEPTS FROM THESES. Just as a book's concept differs from its subject, so too does it differ from its main thesis. A concept is a broad avenue of inquiry; a thesis is a precise inquiry resulting in a series of precise conclusions. In your book on charter schools, a thesis would look something like this:

*Thesis:* American charter schools can be shielded from the effects of power shifts in government only if funds for them are mandated and allocated at the school-district level.

This formulation is too narrow to serve as a guiding concept for an open-minded investigation—it jumps to a particular conclusion. Of course, a book's concept ultimately crystallizes into a sharp thesis, but in the early stages of development, a concept should be kept broad enough to embrace a number of possible theses.

BEWARE OF FALSE CONCEPTS. In Hollywood, a movie is ironically deemed "high concept" when its hackneyed theme has been given a fresh coat of paint with a clever gimmick. In *Ground Hog Day* (1993), Bill Murray's character wakes up on the same February 2 over and over again and gradually realizes that he's stuck in time. The premise seems promising until the viewer realizes it's been put in service of a trite love story with a triter moral, namely, that one can learn from one's mistakes if one makes them often enough. The film succeeds as light entertainment, but conceptual it is not.

This superficiality is not limited to mainstream media. With interdisciplinary studies all the rage in the academy, publishers have seen a spate of books by professors writing outside of their fields of expertise, often unadvisedly. A groundbreaking biophysicist writes about jazz because he loves the music, but his artistic insights are naïve; an art historian explores the masterpieces of Da Vinci from a scientific perspective and unveils a series of embarrassingly obvious correlations. These authors—original thinkers in their own fields—have mistaken the pleasure of personal insight for public revelation.

The problem with Brace Phillips's project was not that he lacked subjects or concepts but that he had too many subjects, and his attitudes toward them propelled his book in different conceptual directions. Because Bud was looking at a proposal and not a completed manuscript, his first impulse was to give Phillips the benefit of the doubt and assume that he would resolve these conflicts in the finished work. But Jenny and Bud both knew that a poorly conceived proposal often yields a poorly realized text. By revising and fleshing out the proposal now, they could increase its chances of producing a compelling and cohesive book.

Bud considered the first of the author's three potential concepts. Phillips seemed to be bogged down in Bible verses, making arcane distinctions among the scholarly Pharisees, priestly Sadducees, and political Zealots. Nowhere did the proposal explicitly state parallels between the religious factions of Christ's day and those of contemporary America. In short, the first of his potential concepts was underdeveloped; without clear direction from the author's perspective, it remained an inert subject.

The second of his potential concepts went to the opposite extreme. The author had not only seized on the concept of prosperity-gospel-as-Ponzi-scheme but evidently considered it a foregone conclusion. The proposal contained no discussion of the differences between Ponzi and pyramid schemes, for instance, much less between those and legitimate multilevel marketing schemes like Tupperware's. He didn't seem aware of the so-called Amway safeguards that serve as a litmus test for whether a financial organization is legal or Ponzi, though Bud had been able to learn of them in ten minutes of Internet surfing. If the first of the author's potential concepts was underdeveloped as a subject, this second was overdetermined as a polemical thesis.

Publishers would want this book to sell on the strength of its relevance to the upcoming election, and neither a scholarly disquisition on ancient Pharisees nor a diatribe against modern televangelists' financial shenanigans would serve that purpose. Which brought Bud to the third of the author's potential concepts, the inherent hypocrisy of the political platform of the Christian Right. The author's attitude toward the subject was clear: free will is the key to salvation through Jesus Christ; therefore, laws against "un-Christian" behavior are themselves un-Christian because they take away a citizen's choice to be sinner or saint. His grasp of this third concept was firmest because he'd already spent a lot of time researching it for his weekly sermons. Neither underdeveloped nor overdetermined, his approach to the subject was just right: capacious enough to embrace nuanced perspectives on a variety of political issues, yet directed enough to pack a conceptual wallop.

A fourth potential concept floated in the ether. In the central section of the proposed book, the chapter on the pyramid thesis was followed by a chapter on the free-market economy as a substitute for political democracy. The chapter titles asked, "Is the Prosperity Gospel a Pyramid Scheme?" and then "Do We Belong in Saudi Arabia?" as though the two questions were related, but the proposal did not address the linkage. Bud suspected the author would argue that Republican presidents' efforts to bring democracy to the Soviet bloc and to oil-rich Arab nations were really focused on opening up those regions as markets. Clearly, the Saudi war was a subject that would figure prominently in the election—but connecting those themes responsibly would require a sophisticated theoretical model that was not on the author's radar screen.

So the winner, it seemed, was behind door number 3, the doctrine of free will as an argument for separating church and state. Bud had located the most workable central subject and the author's attitude toward it—in other words, he had found the central concept. Now he needed to do some thinking about audience and market.

### Profile the Audience

Good authors are entirely absorbed in their material and assume that anyone else will find it equally enthralling. When this enthusiasm is contagious it is a great asset, but often there is a gap between the author's zeal and the audience's response. The primary task of publisher and DE is to help authors assess their material's appeal candidly and then tailor their proposals or manuscripts to meet the needs of their audiences.

BRAINSTORM AUDIENCE SEGMENTS. First, the publisher brainstorms all potential audience segments, large and small, core and tangential. A book on fly-fishing, for instance, may have some degree of appeal to freshwater anglers, saltwater anglers, boat anglers, jetty anglers, pier anglers, shore anglers, net fishers, handicraft enthusiasts interested in tying their own flies, and armchair anglers whose interest in fishing is purely romantic.

RESEARCH AUDIENCE SEGMENTS. Next, the publisher researches these audience segments demographically, noting age range, gender breakdown, regional affiliation, and so on. Are the folks interested in fly-fishing really true to stereotype, that is, middle-aged or older, mostly male, and hailing from landlocked regions of lakes and streams? Or has the catch-and-release movement broadened the appeal of fly-fishing to pro-environment youth? Have women taken up fishing as they have rock-climbing and other outdoor sports once considered the domain of men? Have saltwater anglers adapted this freshwater technique for use in inlets and bays?

DRAFT AN AUDIENCE PROFILE. Once these kinds of questions have been answered, the publisher can create a paragraph-long profile of the book's audience, and the DE can assess how well the proposal or manuscript appeals to that audience in its content and style. An irreverent tone toward "codgers on the pier" may increase the book's appeal to young X-treme anglers while alienating a core group of retirees. Instructions for tying twenty kinds of flies may delight the craft-minded, but the author will need to invest those details with poetic or philosophical significance to keep the armchair angler entertained.

ALIGN THE AUDIENCE PROFILE AND PROPOSAL. Usually, in their developmental plans (see chapter 6), DEs recommend some give-and-take between audience profile and book project. On the one hand, they prescribe adding some content to ensure that small audience segments are retained; on the other, they suggest excluding small segments whose interests are at odds with those of the larger audience. A DE may point out ways an author's tone alienates certain readers, or may encourage a certain "shock value" to draw readers into healthy public debate.

Jenny Wishler had already drafted a serviceable summary of the proposed book's audience:

*American Pharisees* will garner a broad readership across political, religious, and generational lines. The fringe element of the Christian Right will read it with great interest, if not enthusiasm; mainstream Republicans will find the book's message liberating and pragmatic as they navigate their civic lives in faith. The left will take issue with the author's conclusions even as they enthusiastically support his premise. Citizens who adhere to Judaism, Islam, and other faiths will find insights into the intolerance they experience in American culture. By challenging the present Christian political hierarchy to put faith, instead of money, where its mouth is, the author will draw the attention of young and old, man and woman, atheist and believer, activist and political junkie—in short, anyone who feels a personal investment in the national debate about the separation of church and state.

Well, that covered just about everyone on American soil. But was it realistic to expect all of these folks to plunk down $29.95 for a polemical tome? Were there any major demographics that would be turned off by the author's approach? Were there any elements that could be added to the proposal to solidify its appeal to certain audience segments?

Something in Bud's gut told him to delve deeper. His internal alarm had started beeping at the word "Judaism," so he went to an encyclopedia and discovered that, though their name has been mud in Christian society for two thousand years, the Pharisees are considered the forefathers of today's Reform movement in American Judaism. It was the Pharisees who shifted the religion's emphasis from temple to synagogue, blood sacrifice to learning, and retribution to justice; it was their teachings that laid the foundation for an educated, broadminded American Jewry. Jewish readers would know this immediately, and charges of anti-Semitism would overshadow the book's message. Bud could imagine Phillips dismissing this warning: "If Jesus called the Pharisees hypocrites, that's good enough for me." Bud doubted he could get the reverend to let go of the Pharisee conceit entirely, but he and Jenny would need to convince him to downplay its importance. And it had to come out of the title.

So much for the Jewish demographic. Bud also had doubts about this book's sermons appealing to a broad spectrum of young people and women. Yes, the Christian Right had seen a resurgence in popularity among the younger generation, including young women who embraced the traditional roles of housewife and mother. But this book hoped to reach beyond the converted, and to that end it seemed wise to play up the author's hipness. He was a dapper raconteur, with a penchant for anecdotes from his days as a college football hero and a spy. For example, in a homily on gun control he talked about what it felt like to have bullets whizzing by him in nocturnal forays across the North Vietnamese border. If Bud could get more of this author's derring-do into the proposal and the table of contents, the book would make inroads into the twenty-one- to thirty-four-year-old demographic, male and female.

Before he revised the agent's audience profile, Bud wanted to meditate a bit on the book's market potential. Something was still bugging him, and he couldn't quite put his finger on it.

## Evaluate Market Potential

If the audience is the group of people to whom a book addresses itself, the market is the place (real or virtual) where the book is sold to those people. When a new audience comes into being, a new market arises to meet its needs. When women swelled the white-collar workforce in the 1970s and early 1980s, feminist bookstores broadened their inventories, shelves for women's career issues appeared in the larger bookstores, and book displays aimed at women showed up in business supply stores. For most books, however, a market already exists, and the DE must understand the rules of that market's game to ensure that the manuscript develops into an excellent competitor.

SCOPE OUT THE COMPETITION. Any developmental plan must take into account competing titles. If existing titles are sparse, flawed, or out of date, then the new book will enter the market with little competition. If, however, the field is already crowded with well-received books, then the new book will need to stand out from the pack by virtue of its originality, comprehensiveness, persuasiveness, currency, or entertainment value. Some markets have a higher tolerance for redundancy than others—the cookbook market, for instance, seems limitless these days—but most titles must do battle with a few close competitors. A new book must match its competitors strength for strength and then go them one better.

GAUGE MARKET EXPECTATIONS. A book's success also rests largely on whether it conforms to the market's expectations regarding length, tone, depth of coverage, and the inclusion of key features. A how-to manual is expected to be short and casual in tone, a biography meaty and authoritative, a field guide complete and concisely phrased. A travel guide that lacks directions to key sites will be savaged in reviews, and a cookbook that skips over steps in recipes will be consigned to bookstores' bargain tables within months.

KNOW THE TITLE'S LIST POSITION. Finally, a DE's approach to a project should be informed by an understanding of its position on the publisher's list of books in print. The DE must know how the publisher intends to situate the book in the marketplace to ensure that the product fulfills the promise of the sales pitch.

*Frontlist* titles appear at the front of the publisher's seasonal catalog. Their content tends to be fresh but with an imminent expiration date; they sell briskly for a year or two and then fade quickly. The DE often needs to develop a frontlist title on an aggressive schedule, usually with some key marketing event (e.g., art exhibition, historical anniversary, or election day) imposing a firm deadline. Frontlist titles are often short and polemical, contributing to public debate of current affairs.

*Backlist* titles, which appear in the latter half of the catalog, tend to be more sober, reflective, comprehensive, and authoritative. Like great wines, they're not published before they're ready; the DE often enjoys a more open-ended schedule but must invest correspondingly greater effort in the revision process. Backlist titles tend to present a more balanced and nuanced point of view, remaining relevant for a decade or more.

Some publishers would quarrel with the distinction I've just made, saying that all titles start out on their frontlists for a specified interval of two, three, or five years before (a) going out of print or (b) moving to the backlist. This more egalitarian distinction is reassuring to authors whose books appear back-of-catalog; it also reflects how the two lists are handled in accounting practice. But it soft-pedals the reality that marketing dollars are apportioned in progressively smaller amounts from the front of the catalog to the back.

Most publishers would agree that the ideal book makes a big splash on the frontlist and then also has "long legs" on the backlist. Titles that achieve both goals on a modest scale are often referred to as *midlist*. These can be the hardest for DEs to manage because they may require deep restructuring of long texts on short schedules. Moreover, they may represent a compromise between the acquisition editor's ambitions and the marketing department's doubts—and a publishing plan with conflicted goals is rudderless.

Bud decided to go on a fact-finding mission to review the Phillips book's competition in his local bookstore. The election was still almost a year away, and already the shelves for both politics and religion were thick with face-out jeremiads by everyone from Al Franken to Rush Limbaugh. Among two dozen such titles (including eight by declared candidates), six were by leaders of the Christian Right, and three of those were by preachers. Good thing Phillips is well connected, Bud thought, though the president isn't likely to give him a blurb.

Perusing the tables of contents of these three closest competitors, Bud saw that Phillips already had a leg up: he was much more comprehensive in the array of political issues he covered. And, of course, he received his highest marks for originality—no one came close to the philosophy he espoused, melding left-wing platform with right-wing religious convictions. Bud noted that all three preachers wrote short books in large print at a sixth-grade reading level, presumably because they wanted to reach the broadest audience possible. Several of the professional Christian Righters, in contrast, wrote more theoretically, adding the luster of sophistication to their end of the political spectrum by offering heftier tomes with scholarly apparatus. Phillips compared favorably with both preachers and pundits: he had a knack for writing in clear, colloquial terms without relinquishing his intellectual strength or scholarly authority. Bud would take care to avoid messing with this winning formula.

Back at his apartment, Bud gave some thought to the agent's marketing pitch. Jenny's audience profile assumed that anyone interested in American politics would be immediately drawn to *American Pharisees*. Indeed, the subtitle, *An Insider's View of the Christian Right,* implied that the author was writing for the benefit of outsiders—those hankering for a behind-the-scenes look at the inner workings of a powerful cabal. But the author's focus in the table of contents was on preaching to *insiders,* letting believers know how they could better align their lives with the precepts of the Bible. In fact, Bud suspected that the subtitle had been cooked up by Jenny, who admitted as much in an email exchange.

Bud weighed the relative value of the Phillips project as frontlist blockbuster and backlist staple. If the book were to fulfill the proposal's frontlist promise, the author would have to broaden his tone to embrace Christians of varying degrees of fundamentalism. He could not wear his antagonism toward the prosperity gospel on his sleeve; rather, he would have to focus on his positive message of free will as the cornerstone of Christian culture. But the book also had real potential as an enduring backlist seller: the lessons it taught were timeless Christian values, and the social issues it addressed weren't likely to go away any time soon. If the text became dated, it could be revised and issued in a new edition a decade hence. Again, Bud made a mental note: retain the author's balance of polemics and authority.

## Bring the Vision into Focus

Once the book's concept, audience, and market potential have been identified, it's time to gather those discrete bits of information into a cohesive vision statement. If a manuscript already exists, the DE should skip this step for now and return to it after finding the text's main subject (see chapter 2). If the project is still at the proposal stage, a vision statement will provide a guiding light for DE, author, and publisher as they work together in the months (or years) ahead.

DRAFT THE VISION STATEMENT. The vision statement for a book project is not unlike the mission statement for any enterprise that marshals serious human and financial resources. The vision statement should summarize, in a paragraph or three, the book's goal—that is, what it hopes to achieve when it goes out into the world. It is a kind of snapshot of the book's concept, audience, and marketing strategy. A book on the history of Indian tribes in California may aim at documenting a way of life that has been mostly lost, or it may work to keep those practices alive and relevant: these two missions will result in very different books.

ANTICIPATE THE MAIN THESIS. When drafting the vision statement, the DE should keep in mind that the project's mission must align with its eventual main thesis. This point may seem obvious, but publishers know how often authors argue against their own cases, like overzealous lawyers. Biographers intent on portraying their subjects as unique characters may inadvertently evoke a stereotype; advocates for social progress may undermine their positions by focusing on obstacles instead of opportunities.

REMEMBER THE PUBLISHING TEAM. The DE should also remember that the vision statement serves as a touchstone for all members of the book's publishing team. If written well, it will find its way into key documents that guide the efforts of the acquisitions editor, managing editor, copyeditor, designer, proofreader, indexer, manufacturing coordinator, marketing managers, copywriter, endorsement (or "blurb") solicitor, publicist, and sales reps. Having everyone on the same page will greatly increase the chances of the book's success.

HONOR THE AUTHOR'S VISION. Finally, the DE must ensure that the vision statement represents the author's true point of view. If the publisher and author have incompatible agendas, the DE should withdraw from the project unless and until a single vision statement is agreed to by both parties. Even then, the DE should probably decline the assignment unless one party demonstrates a complete and genuine change of heart.

Bud got to thinking. Almost every day, the lobby of his apartment building in San Francisco received a blizzard of flyers and "free" newspapers. Most were menus for pizza delivery and Chinese takeout, but some were calls to march in front of City Hall against zoning changes, school budget cuts, and so on. At election time, the flyers shifted toward political endorsement, with many supplying

EXAMPLE 2. The final TOC from the Phillips book. Note how the subheads in chapters 1 and 2 provide the chapter titles for the rest of the book, integrating what had been the first and third parts of the unrevised manuscript.

*Beyond Lip Service: What the Bible Says about American Political Issues*

"convenient" checklists telling citizens how to vote on the bewildering array of candidates and state and local propositions. Which gave Bud an idea:

Most Americans hold Christian values and are socially moderate and fiscally conservative. They want the government to balance the budget and stay out of their personal lives but provide basic support for people in need. With the political landscape polarized between big-business Republicans and big-spending social Democrats, average Americans are looking for a sane political philosophy that marries their concern for the well-being of other citizens with their desire for the freedom to succeed materially and spiritually. Come November, they would like to carry into the voting booth a ballot scorecard filled out with the choices that Jesus would have them make.

*Beyond Lip Service: What the Bible Says about American Political Issues* will give voters that ballot card. One of the nation's most prominent spiritual leaders, with close ties to the president, author Brace Phillips provides sane, scriptural counseling on such current issues as gun control, abortion, gay marriage, capital punishment, and environmental regulation. In a reading of the Bible that will surprise both conservatives and liberals, he demonstrates that Christian values support the separation of church and state; he argues persuasively that attempts to criminalize certain kinds of sinful behavior have only resulted in a loss of free will, which is the essence of personal salvation. Using the parable of the Pharisee and the publican, he shows how modern leaders confound the letter and the spirit of God's law, allowing moneychangers into the temple and casting stones at the harlots of their day.

More than a polemicist, the author is an excellent storyteller. His sermons—many of which form the basis of this book—draw crowds from far and wide because of his reputation for tempering zeal with humor and candor. Once a college football star, an undercover agent in the U.S. military, and a high-stakes player in the corporate security industry, he illustrates spiritual principles with vivid tableaux from his remarkable and adventurous life. His willingness to bare his soul has won the hearts of young and old, man and woman, liberal and conservative alike. Readers will discover a visionary who is one of their own, a leader they can trust.

A little sappy, Bud thought, but a good start toward a vision statement. It managed to incorporate the author's trope of the Pharisee without emphasizing it overmuch, and it shifted the focus toward the publisher's main objective, to participate in the campaign debate. It avoided the Ponzi concept with its air of easy televangelist bashing, and it foregrounded the author's personal appeal as James Bond in a minister's collar. Finally, the new title steered clear of anti-Semitism as well as any perception of preaching only to the converted.

✳

Bud revised the remainder of the proposal and provided an alternate table of contents. Jenny liked it and said she'd just "tweak it a bit" before sending it out to publishers. As a "ghost" proposal writer, Bud was accustomed to never hearing another word about a project once he'd played his role. But Jenny emailed him when the proposal sold—for the astounding quarter-million-dollar advance she'd demanded.

The next Bud saw of the book was Brace Phillips's appearance on the *Today* show. The reverend exuded charisma from his flushed, bearded face to his stentorian voice. Gratified that Phillips had kept his suggested title and subtitle, Bud picked up a hardcover copy the next day and turned to the table of contents: it retained the structure of the one he had devised, but most of the chapter subheads were different (example 2). Bud had worked references to Phillips's personal narrative into the subheads—for instance, using the author's own professed love of the Beatles to retitle "The Bible on Gun Control" as "Happiness Is Not a Warm Gun"—but it seemed Phillips had preferred the repetition of "The Bible on . . . ," which had been the unifying element of the original series of sermons. In fact, he'd extended the use of this device to include several sections not originally written as sermons.

Bud left Jenny a voicemail congratulating her on the book's success. A week later, she returned the call and said that, yes, though the author had "loved" Bud's revision of the proposal, he felt that the original sermon titles ought to stick; he also had qualms about making the book seem too much about himself. She had asked Phillips whether he wanted Bud to help with the writing of the book itself, but the author had felt he could "take the ball and run with it."

Indeed he had. *Beyond Lip Service* helped shape public debate that election year: it was cited in speeches by both incumbent and challenging presidential candidates. Bud couldn't perceive an actual change in the outcome of the elections—at least, the candidates he voted for all lost—but there was some satisfaction in knowing he'd helped ensure that an important voice was heard.

All too often, authors are bewitched by the richness of their content into writing without a concept. Some explore difficult personal experiences; others become obsessed with a subject without knowing why. Before they realize it, an entire draft has been completed with still no concept in sight. Or they stumble upon their concept late in the manuscript, but the preceding text remains a tangle of switchbacks, detours, and dead ends. In these cases, the DE's job is to look for clues to a unifying concept, a central motivation, buried in an existing draft. Once the DE has gotten an author's gist, she or he can reorganize the text around that driving force. The DE doesn't strip the content of its richness; on the contrary, she or he unearths the relevance that underlies the details of the story or argument.

In this chapter, we learn how to analyze a manuscript with sprawling content to identify its *main subject*. Our goal is the same as it was in the last chapter: we are looking for the main subject so that we can transmute it into a main concept. The difference here is that, instead of a proposal with potential content leanings, we have a bewildering abundance of actual content to sift through.

Before DEs undertake this thorough excavation, however, they do well to scope out the motives of the key players. Remember: a successful developmental plan relies on the enthusiastic endorsement of three parties—author, publisher, and DE. If any one of these participants doubts the plan's efficacy or cooperates begrudgingly, the plan will fail.

Our case study thrusts a first-time author into the limelight of New York trade publishing. If the editor who discovers this project seems hungry, she is, literally: junior editors are among the lowest-paid workers in any white-collar industry.

## Author Profile: The First-Timer

An author's first book is a leap into the unknown. Some first-timers freeze, foot raised in mid-air, awed by the momentous step they are about to take. Others plunge blithely forward, assuming that their previous experience as contributors to journals, magazines, newspapers, government reports, edited volumes, or blogs has prepared them for whatever surprises sole authorship may hold. Most have no idea of the number of hours they are about to invest, not only in writing, but also in responding to recommendations by the acquisitions editor or expert readers, reviewing the copyeditor's changes, chasing down incomplete citations, securing permissions for quotations and illustrations, reading proofs, creating or editing the index, supplying contacts for media reviews and events, and doing readings and signings.

As far as Goldi Freimarke was concerned, his book had been finished since he'd written the last sentence. Now a potential publisher was asking for something called a point of view. But the essence of Goldi's life—and, therefore, his conceptual performance art—was that he embraced *all* perspectives. By blending in, he showed the world a chameleon's-eye view of itself. He was the medium, not the message; the conduit, not the content. And he'd held up a mirror to the face of America's most dangerous export, the commodified woman.

In the bathroom of his Berlin loft, Goldi examined his own face in a much grimier mirror: the stubble was coming back, but the contours of his cheeks remained feminine, like the soft protrusions of his diminishing breasts. The doctors had told him it would take months for the estrogen to reduce to its normal level, but he felt as though he would always remain part female.

He was tiring of the show. In America, while on his adventure as an "undercover woman," he'd felt larger than life, like the huge images he now projected each evening onto the two-story whitewashed wall of his studio space in the Friedrichschein District. The slides showed Goldi as a female office worker, housekeeper, Army recruit, backwoods lesbian, urban escort, biker chick, postulant nun—he'd had so many *lives* in the States, and now he was reduced to a whistle-stop on the tourist circuit. His show was highlighted by both Frommer's and Let's Go, and his sour, communal refrigerator even had a Zagat rating.

Once this book deal and television special were completed, providing a much-needed infusion of cash, he'd close down the nightly show. The next project—as yet a hazy constellation of yearnings in his psyche—would involve the science of gender more directly. For him, the gender experiment had been as much about science as art, but the Americans wanted him to remove his scientific material. They said 900 manuscript pages was too long, but he knew what they were really thinking—that his grasp of science was naïve, his aesthetic theories superficial. Cinching the belt of his frayed kimono, he decided, "They will not cut a word."

## Client Profile: The Big Trade House

Book publishing has always been a tough way to make a living. Whenever the economy hits a downturn, books are among the first consumer products to suffer. Between 1833 and 1907, no fewer than six Wall Street "panics" caused established houses to fold and provided openings for new ventures. This pattern continued through the twentieth century, with the two world wars and the Great Depression prompting dramatic changes in book content, format, and sales channels. Throughout its history, the industry has seen major houses swallow up smaller ones, with famous pioneers' surnames changing like dance partners. With the advent of media conglomerates, this consolidation has reached unprecedented proportions: a handful of global media firms, the so-called Big Five, now own the vast majority of book publishers, along with the lion's share of other media outlets.*

Today the book is in a trickier position than ever. After several centuries as the dominant form of recorded public expression, the book (along with its sister print forms, the newspaper and periodical) is being upstaged by movies, television, the Internet, mp3 players, and cell phones. Yet even in this volatile climate, where editors are forced to make publishing decisions based on the bottom line, the tradition of loving and nurturing books remains alive. For people endowed with editorial skills, there are plenty of industries in which to make more money, but none as satisfying. Despite its turbulence, publishing remains a vibrant culture of book lovers.

For Lainie Milano, her love of books was the only reason to put up with her job at Visigoth Publishing: the salary forced her to share a one-bedroom apartment with two other career women, and the long workdays were spent doing administrative tasks for her boss, Will Bentham. Lainie had already discovered several respectable midlist successes in the office "slush pile"—that stack of unsolicited manuscripts that buries the desk of the least senior staff member—and was quickly making a name for herself in-house with her eye for projects that mix social consciousness with the latest forms of entertainment. But the office was already top-heavy with senior editors, so she wouldn't be getting promoted any time soon—unless she could find a project to make a big enough splash.

*For American publishing history, see John Tebbel, *Between Covers: The Rise and Transformation of American Book Publishing* (New York: Oxford, 1987). For the Big Five, see Ben H. Bagdikian, *The New Media Monopoly* (Boston: Beacon, 2004).

Goldmund (a.k.a. Goldi) Freimarke was Lainie's key card to the executive elevator of upward mobility. She'd happened upon the author's slide show while on a backpacking tour of Europe, and after absorbing the entire five-hour saga, had cornered the latter-day Candide in the communal kitchen of his East Berlin loft. When she asked whether he'd be interested in turning his story into a book for the English-speaking world, Goldi had said, "Oh, but I've already written it." She left with the stack of typewritten pages in her pack, her essentials jettisoned, her walkabout abruptly cut short. Within days, Mr. Bentham had told her to "run with it" and helped her secure a letter of interest from PBS for a documentary to air on the book's publication date.

The only problem was, the manuscript was a mess: meandering, plagued with scientific data appropriated as artistic metaphor, and way too long. She'd asked Mr. Bentham for permission to edit the text during office hours, but he'd said he couldn't spare her. Then he'd offered her a consolation prize—the phone number of a good DE.

## Assignment: The Tome with Too Many Subjects

Hedda Miller had known Will Bentham since he was a fledgling editor at Stanford University Press. They had never met, but she knew how his mind worked from years of good-natured arguments over the phone. He said he didn't trust any other editor to poke holes in his projects. Now he occupied a window office overlooking Central Park, while she stayed put in her farmhouse filled with cats in Pennsylvania Dutch country. This time, his assistant Lainie was calling not to say "Please hold while I connect you with Mr. Bentham" but to offer Hedda a job.

Hedda had to admit, the story was enticing. Freimarke's use of a tiny digital camera and audio recording device while posing as a woman had all the intrigue of an espionage blockbuster. His true gender had been discovered on three separate occasions, and each time he'd narrowly escaped severe harm. And the honesty with which he chronicled the progression of his estrogen treatments— observing, in hauntingly clinical detail, their effects on his body, emotions, and social interactions—had the psychological complexity of a great memoir. To her own surprise, Hedda was entirely convinced of his improbable claim that he was "straight, one hundred percent heterosexual."

But there were problems. The author was a young German who had come of age in post-Wall Berlin, and his aspirations as an avant-garde artist thoroughly overwhelmed his central narrative. Raised in the Neue Kerngruppe commune, whose founders were eventually imprisoned for child abuse in 1993, Goldi believed that the concept of the "nuclear family" was the source of modern society's pathologies. Influenced by the dangerous actions of Chris Burden and the social documentaries of Mary Kelly, he began committing (and photographing)

EXAMPLE 3. The unrevised TOC for the Freimarke manuscript. The story of the author's journey is hidden behind the titles of performance pieces serving as chapter titles.

*Estrogen Situationist Documents*

| | | | |
|---|---|---|---|
| Introduction: | Empathy as a Performative Medium | Chapter 9. | The Chippendales Experiment |
| Chapter 1. | Vocal Chord Gender Sketches | Chapter 10. | Prayer as a Failure of Empathy |
| Chapter 2. | Interview with a Vamp | Chapter 11. | Lady Escort #1, #2, and #3 |
| Chapter 3. | Powder Room Improvisation | Chapter 12. | Jerry Springer Improvisation |
| Chapter 4. | Lesbian Body Sculpture | Chapter 13. | Lipstick on the Glass Ceiling (Social Batik) |
| Chapter 5. | Girl Talk (Covert Installation) | Chapter 14. | Abortion Clinic Body Shield |
| Chapter 6. | Electrolysis Meditation | Chapter 15. | Bridesmaid (Covert Happening) |
| Chapter 7. | Scrum #1, #2, and #3 | Conclusion: | Toward the Feminization of America |
| Chapter 8. | Anorexia as Empathy | | |

actions of his own, "happenings" that were transgressive by nature of their empathy. He snatched women's purses, inserted money, and returned them; he painted over graffiti-covered West Berlin walls with trompe l'oeil murals of bullet holes from World War II. On the five-year anniversary of the departitioning, he rallied hundreds of schoolmates to create a naked human wall in front of the Reichstag.

*Estrogen Situationist Documents* was the culmination of those performative experiments (example 3). Unfortunately, the text was bloated with Goldi's unique concoction of postmodern art theory and gender science. Visigoth wished to edit out this material—Lainie was working with PBS to simplify the material for a television special and wanted Hedda to do the same for the book. Whether Hedda could help would depend on two factors: if the gist of the story Visigoth wanted to publish could be extricated from the manuscript; and if all parties involved—author, publisher, and DE (that is, Hedda herself)—could agree on a shared vision for the project.

## Size Up the Author

Most of us think of ourselves as open to constructive criticism, but many of us are kidding ourselves. Some authors come to a publisher because of its reputation for editorial excellence and then kick and scream their way through the editing process. If a publisher and DE have agreed that a manuscript warrants development, the DE must determine whether the author is capable of collaboration. If the author does not embrace the plan with enthusiasm, there's no sense in attempting development.

To be fair, developmental editing is not easy on an author. If writing a book is like giving birth—investing all of one's inner resources in the creation of a living, breathing thing—then saying "yes" to developmental editing is like signing a consent form allowing one's newborn to go under the knife. DEs must expect authors to react defensively on behalf of their books' well-being.

ASSESS OPENNESS TO CRITICISM. Since most authors will say they're open to criticism, the DE must divine the author's true inclinations from subtle clues. Authors who, without prompting, articulate what's wrong with their text, or respond with eager recognition to the DE's diagnosis, are probably keepers. Authors whose motivations seem tied to the publisher's promise of a larger market with increased publicity or royalties may not have thought carefully about what they're getting themselves into. "I'm always interested in hearing other points of view" and similar noncommittal pieties may not augur well for developmental work.

ENGAGE IN INFORMAL DISCUSSION. The best way to size up a developmental candidate is to engage the author in informal discussion. The publisher can do this in writing and then submit the documentary evidence to the DE, or the DE can be given direct access to the author via telephone, email, or—best of all—a face-to-face meeting.

DISCUSS PREVIOUS PUBLISHING EXPERIENCES. Chatting about previous publishing experiences often provides the best clues: when a prominent cultural critic told me he once chewed out a magazine editor for "not making me look good enough" in print, I knew I had an author who would not obstruct the developmental process.

Lainie Milano assured Hedda that Goldi was open to substantive revision of the text. "He wants to be the Ken Burns of the counterculture movement—the next Michael Moore," she said. She couldn't put Hedda directly in touch with him in Berlin, but she did forward a link to his project's Web site, www.estrogensituation .com. Tall and skinny, with delicate features, he had the natural attributes of a talented drag queen, even through the pronounced five-o'clock shadow. His voice—which accompanied a video of him in his various disguises, interacting with famous and obscure American women—dug deep into his lowest register.

Several pictures were especially telling—photos in which the author himself did not appear. Inside an unkempt trailer, a grizzled biker lounged on a plaid sofa with crushed beer cans around him and gazed into the lens with disarming tenderness. Sandra Bernhardt, behind the curtain of a Broadway stage, the spotlight waiting for her entrance, cast a wry smile of complicity. A group of nuns in a cafeteria rocked with laughter, one clutching the rosary around her waist. Anti-abortion demonstrators outside a suburban clinic begged and threatened into the hidden camera, placards askew, tears streaming down their cheeks.

In each case, what made the photograph compelling was the viewer's realization that the subjects are utterly convinced of the photographer's female identity. How had he accomplished this feat? In bits of mp3 voiceover, he said that he was a sort of chameleon who had no interest in his own personality—for that reason, he instinctively transmogrified into what his subjects wanted him to be. Their desires—for a lover, an absent mother figure, a naughty sister—were projected onto him.

The Web site was not as compelling as it might have been, however, and for the same reasons that the manuscript was confusing. The portal was festooned with DNA strands and other scientific images. Photo sequences from his own work were intercut with Hollywood stills of iconic actresses, 1950s-style clip art of homemakers, and ghastly medical photographs of gender reassignment operations gone awry. The juxtapositions were jarring and perhaps even effective on a visceral level—but without the publisher's brief and the manuscript, Hedda wouldn't have been able to make heads or tails of the site.

Nope, thought Hedda, the prognosis was not good: this author showed all the signs of someone with a deep personal investment in those attributes of his manuscript that were its main defects. He might wish for the fame of a Ken Burns or Michael Moore, but could he really make the sacrifices necessary to broaden his appeal?

## Size Up the Publisher

An author or DE who considers developing a new book project should suss out the publisher's reputation and motives before making a commitment. After all, the publisher plays a key role in the success of any developmental plan. It is the publisher who makes the book happen with financial backing, production expertise, marketing savvy, and distribution networks. An acquisitions editor with a keen vision for the book may sometimes make the author's and DE's lives difficult, but the direction this editor provides will usually enlarge the book's audience. A good acquisitions editor is the author's advocate inside the publishing house.

STUDY THE PUBLISHER'S LIST. Become familiar with the publisher's list by studying its print or online catalogs. If the house has not published much in the project's subject area, it may not have sufficient in-house expertise to guide the developmental process. Word of mouth is often the best source of information about a publisher—join an authors' or editors' listserve and get the buzz.

ASK FOR A MARKETING LETTER. Publishers do not hesitate to ask for a curriculum vitae from an author and a reference list from a DE; they should not hesitate to provide the same themselves. Authors should ask for a letter from the marketing department that details the publisher's commitment to promoting the work once it's published via events, book signings, trade shows and conferences, flyers or brochures, display advertising, Web postings, and radio and television interviews. Of course, authors should have realistic expectations about the size of the marketing budgets their books can command. Many authors assume their publishers will pull out all the stops for every book they publish, only to be disappointed six months after publication. Often, the author brings a crucial component to the marketing plan with personal contacts that lead to readings, interviews, and public appearances.

REVIEW THE CONTRACT FOR SIGNS OF COMMITMENT. Standard book contracts are vague about details like publication schedule and format, production values, and print runs, and authors who insist on codifying these decisions in the contract may be shooting themselves in the foot. For instance, many authors require a "paperback clause" that commits the publisher to putting out a softcover edition in twelve or six months. If the book then remains in the public eye for longer, both publisher and author lose money by replacing the higher-priced hardcover edition before its sales have slowed. Worse, the paperback's unveiling may be ignored by book reviewers who feel that the public just heard about the book six months ago.

That said, authors (or their agents) do well to discuss publication scenarios with the publisher when negotiating a contract. Publishers should demonstrate eagerness to take authors' knowledge of their audiences into account. For a book about skiing, for instance, if the author feels that early fall publication will be key to the book's success, the publisher should offer a compelling argument to publish at any other time of year.

ASSESS THE MOTIVES FOR DEVELOPMENT. Even the best publishers can initiate a developmental plan for the wrong reasons, with painful results for all involved. Because DEs are unlikely to see the marketing letter or the contract, they should insist that the publisher express the goals of development in a written brief. Although a helpful starting point, this document may not be fully candid; DEs are advised to follow up with an informal client interview. Did the publisher pay a hefty advance at contract stage that it now realizes was a mistake? Is the author related to the publisher politically or otherwise? Does the acquisitions editor show interest in having the book "fixed" but not in the details of how the transformation will be accomplished? These are signs that a project may be marked for frustration and failure.

Clearly, Lainie Milano was a spitfire. Her style was a bit New Age meets Wall Street for Hedda's taste, but Hedda liked her chutzpah and trusted that she would follow through on any promises she made. What Hedda didn't necessarily trust was Lainie's judgment regarding this book: it was obviously a pet project, and those could sometimes lead even the most experienced acquisitions editors to make errors in judgment.

Visigoth Publishing was now an imprint of a large offshore media conglomerate, but it retained a strong reputation by jealously guarding its editorial autonomy. If this imprint was publishing *Estrogen,* then it would probably invest whatever resources were required to make the book a success in the United States. Lainie assured Hedda that the television package was "a done deal" and that her superiors (including her old friend Will Bentham) were fully behind efforts to broaden the book's appeal to the mainstream. Hedda wasn't privy to any documentation proving these claims, and this young editor's optimism made her wary; on the other hand, she knew that Visigoth usually invested its resources carefully.

Hedda's concern was that she might spend a lot of time and effort—several months of her life—on a book with an author who would reject every improvement she attempted. If the publisher didn't back Hedda up in these tussles, there was no use even starting down the road. Of course, there was also the hunger factor—a job Hedda had been expecting from another publisher had recently fallen through, and she still had property taxes to pay. She would collect her check whether or not the developmental editing was a success.

So far, Hedda had sized up the author as a liability and the publisher as an asset. Now it was time to step back and evaluate her own strengths and weaknesses as a potential member of the developmental team.

## Size Up the DE

Folks who call themselves developmental editors hail from a variety of backgrounds. Some have risen through the ranks as proofreaders, copyeditors, and production editors before taking the developmental leap (see sidebar, "How to Become a DE"). Others come from the opposite direction, starting out as salespeople, moving in-house as marketers, then segueing over to acquisitions before they realize that content, not contracts, is their métier. Still others have always known that development was what they wanted to do, and by dint of hard work and patience, have dragged themselves up the freelance ladder from corporate directories and technical manuals to nonfiction or fiction trade books.

Then there are those who once, during graduate school, helped a professor to polish her manuscript. These folks are often very intelligent and can be good writers, but their limited experience will not have exposed them to the full range of possibilities that are locked inside any manuscript. A good

## How to Become a DE

Once every few months, I'm asked to conduct an informational interview with a person considering a career as a book editor. We meet off-site at a nearby coffeehouse, and over my hazelnut Italian soda I break the bad news gently. It is this: the supply of qualified English majors is much greater than the demand for them in publishing, and applicants with book experience are favored over those without, no matter how many advanced degrees or decades of accomplishment in another field. Thus, the only way to become a book editor is to start at the bottom and apprentice your way up.

There are two career ladders, each with the same number of rungs. The *in-house track* has the obvious advantage of a steady salary with benefits. But it can be harder to rise in-house because of low turnover in the senior positions, and the in-house track involves much mind-numbing administrative work, even on the upper rungs. The *freelance track* requires entrepreneurial pluck; but once editors have impressed a key client or two, they never lack for work. Freelancers can move more quickly upward toward substantive editing, and most report greater job satisfaction because they spend all of their working hours actually engaged with text.

Here are the rungs.

LEARN TO PROOFREAD. Memorize the list of standard marks found under "proofreading" in *Merriam Webster's Collegiate Dictionary*, and bone up on grammar and bookmaking style by reviewing the resources listed in "Further Reading." Then take a proofreading test at a local publishing house. If you fail, ask to see the test so you'll know what you did wrong. Starting locally allows you to take the test on site or deliver it by hand, and publishers are more likely to engage the services of people whom they've met. If you're in an entry-level position in-house, you'll still be required to take the house test. Once you've passed it, you may be given some proofreading work during the day, but you'll mainly establish your proofreading chops by taking home freelance assignments.

LEARN TO COPYEDIT. Take a copyediting course. Even if you're an ace grammarian, you'll learn much about editorial convention that otherwise comes only with publishing experience. Also, listing the course on your resumé will distinguish you from those whose resumés clearly indicate that an editing career is a backup plan. Once you've passed a publisher's test, remind your contact via email that you're available for work—in-house editors are often reluctant to try a new freelancer, even one who has passed a test with flying colors. Make certain you do a flawless job on your first assignment, even if doing so means spending many more hours than the budget allows: a wowed staffer will speak highly of you, and soon you'll be getting more offers than you can accept.

If you're in-house, taking on copyediting assignments may be difficult while working full time. Instead, offer to copyedit in-house materials like copy for jackets and catalogs.

SHOW POTENTIAL. If you can find one, take a course in developmental or substantive editing. Signal your interest in such assignments by demonstrating a grasp of developmental issues in the projects you copyedit. *Do not overstep the bounds of a copyediting assignment and undertake developmental work without the publisher's express permission.* Instead, in the cover memo that should always accompany the copyediting jobs you return, let the client know that you noticed certain developmental issues, prescribe editorial solutions, and offer to do the work for an additional fee. The client probably won't take you up on that offer, but she may think of you the next time she has a job with developmental needs.

If you're in-house, the most direct way to enter the developmental fray is as the successful candidate for a position on the acquisitions staff. But you may also participate in project development as a production staffer or marketer: offer to read proposals and manuscripts at home, then write up reports that offer sound developmental advice (see chapter 6).

BE PATIENT. Whether you choose the in-house track or the freelance one, don't expect to be elbow-deep in developmental work overnight. Your first assignment will likely be to restructure an introduction or a single chapter in a manuscript that is otherwise solidly constructed. As a freelancer, keep updating your "List of Edited Works," and be sure to break out the developmental jobs under a separate heading. As an in-house staffer, be sure that your annual performance review documents your developmental accomplishments. Sooner or later, a big hairy job will come to you because nobody else wants it—and then you'll be on your way.

DE is an insatiable reader, but voracious reading habits do not guarantee developmental talent. Authors should insist on seeing evidence of a DE's level of experience.

Ultimately, though, authors must rely on the judgment of their publishers in the selection of a suitable DE. An author should beware of allowing the opinions of friends and loved ones to trump the better judgment of the publisher: often a stranger can see more clearly into the heart of an author's work and provide more useful help in achieving its fullest expression.

Most publishers administer copyediting and proofreading tests, but there's no way to test a prospective DE. The best an author or in-house editor can do is to ask for a list of books edited, references, and a sample or two.

REVIEW A LIST OF BOOKS EDITED. If the book list does not distinguish developmental edits from copyedits and project management, then this freelancer may be attempting to pull a fast one.

CONTACT PROFESSIONAL REFERENCES. When speaking with references, the publisher should ask not only about the success of the final product but how well the freelancer managed author relations and schedule.

STUDY DEVELOPMENTAL SAMPLES. If the samples provided have lingering infelicities of structure or style that reflect the stubbornness of the author, the DE should point them out without being asked and have a convincing explanation for why they remain in the published book.

Hedda was known for her relentlessly logical approach to developmental editing. Years ago, when she'd taken a night class on developmental editing out at the Berkeley Extension, the instructor, Robert Worth, had immediately pegged her as a science major. At that time, she'd expected to take up a career in biochemistry and work in a pharmaceutical company. But she soon discovered that she had a low tolerance for the politics of the laboratory and a strong interest in writing. Before long, she was on staff in the UC Berkeley biology department editing her professors' research findings. These scientists were her first clients when, after several years backpacking around the world, she returned to her hometown of Lancaster, Pennsylvania, and hung out her DE's shingle.

How would the avant-garde Goldi Freimarke take Hedda's rigorous brand of editing? He might see her as a middle-aged cat lady hopelessly out of touch with his generation. His constant references to techno music and neo-Goth blogs went over her graying head. There must be twenty-something DEs out there, she thought, who would get his current cultural references while possessing the skills needed to structure his manuscript. Of course, Hedda wasn't planning on sending her picture with the editing sample—but something about the opacity of his hip dialect made her feel *old*.

Still, she could remember what it felt like to be so young and transgressive. She and her old boyfriend Bud Zallis—now long since come out of the closet in San Francisco—had once drunk a few beers and scaled the north tower of the Golden Gate Bridge at 3:00 A.M. with their rock-climbing gear. They'd only gotten a third of the way up before the Marin police bullhorned them down. She could still feel the thrill of ascent, which stayed with her while they were booked and fingerprinted. The adrenaline hadn't lasted through 200 hours of community service of cleanup detail at Dog Beach, but a trace of it returned to her now.

Hedda reviewed her qualifications for taking this project on. She was fluent in German and had visited Berlin before the Wall came down. She had edited several manuscripts in gender studies for Duke and a transsexual's memoir for Temple. Some of the bloated texts she'd reduced to half their length had been as rambling and messy as this one. Finally, she was herself what Freimarke called a "genuine American woman" who had lived her life against the grain of cultural expectations. Surely she and this author could find some common ground.

## Create a Content Summary

A manuscript is not always about what it seems to be about. Completed drafts with structural problems often bury their most interesting content in a late chapter, or—more often—circle around their "real" subject without ever addressing it head on. DEs must follow this trail of bread crumbs to its end before they can know whether they have identified a book's main thrust. Thus, it is essential that the DE make a quick pass over the entire text before going further—skipping chapters and making assumptions about their content can lead to incorrect diagnoses of the text's ills. This pass results in a sheaf of notes and a concise content summary.

READ THE MANUSCRIPT THROUGH. On a fresh legal pad, the DE jots down the page number of each new subject change and discursive issue encountered, along with a telegraphic description. For a 500-page manuscript (double-spaced), these notes will fill at least ten pages of a legal pad. The DE need not worry about whether every nuance has been caught or every subject labeled consistently. The task at hand is to keep a diary of one reader's experience of the unedited text, making notes about every kind of problem found along the way, whether a missing transition or a lapse in tone (but ignoring mechanical defects such as misspellings). These notes will form the basis of all later restructuring (see chapters 3 through 8) and restyling (see chapters 9 and 10).

CATEGORIZE THOSE NOTES. Next, the DE evaluates these notes by categorizing the text's strengths and weaknesses. I usually circle an improvised abbreviation at the left margin of each notation, SUBJ for subject change, TRANS for transition problem, STY for style problem, TONE for diction problem, SYN for syntax error, TIME for chronology problem, DRAM for dramatic climax, EXC for excessive detail, and so on. Most manuscripts generate about a dozen abbreviations. With these allocations made, the DE can focus on the SUBJ notes and from them construct a brief summary of the book's content.

CONSTRUCT A CONTENT SUMMARY. If the author has successfully conveyed a main thesis, this summary may read like a short book review or abstract; if the author has too many or too few theses, it may simply sketch the text's raw content. Either way, this summary—no more than a few paragraphs long—will be recycled as part of the DE's developmental plan (see chapter 6).

Hedda pulled out a fresh legal pad and started taking notes. She knew that a manuscript's introduction is often its weakest element: usually written last, an introduction bears the weight of the author's ambitions to summarize the entire book and can become a boneyard for material that didn't find a resting place in the main text.

This project was no exception. Reading no further than the introduction, Hedda would have thought the book was mostly about the developmental effects of fetal testosterone on empathic brain function. True, the intro began and ended with the author's own story of growing up in the Berlin commune. But its substance pointed in a bewildering array of directions, including, for instance, recent neuroscientific proof of empathy among animals. Hedda could see possible links among all the subjects, but without the publisher's brief she would not have guessed where the narrative—if it could be called that—was leading.

Unfortunately, the text did not settle down much after the introduction. In chapter after chapter, shifts in subject were accompanied by shifts in tone, chronology, metaphor, and level of detail, so that Hedda's first attempt at assigning abbreviations was a mélange as confusing as the text it annotated (example 4). But as she read further, glimmers of the author's intentions began to shine through. The book's chapters fell into three parts, each covering a stage in gender transition: early transvestitism, then the first physical changes induced by hormone treatment, and finally the longer-term changes that precede surgery. (The author, the reader knew from the outset, would stop short of the knife.) The theme of empathy also progressed in three stages, from cultural fashion to biology to social roles.

By the end of the manuscript, the author's piecemeal approach had filled in enough holes in the puzzle that various narrative lines emerged. In fact, for all his McSweeney's-style flummery, he was a simple storyteller at heart. Hedda's content summary read like this:

The author grows up in a radical West Berlin commune, hitting puberty just as the Wall comes down. A child of the city's thriving counterculture, he quits high school to become an artist in a bombed-out East Berlin building. Most of the other squatters rail against materialism, but our young man—for reasons never made clear— becomes obsessed with Hollywood gender stereotypes. He also reads *Black Like Me,* John Howard Griffin's account of "becoming" a black man and traveling the South to experience racism; and he sees *Hedwig and the Angry Inch,* a punk-rock musical about a transgendered singer touring America's backwaters.

Realizing he wants to be the Griffin of gender, he panhandles the money to fly to Manhattan. There he meets with a surgeon, posing as a candidate for sex reassignment. A vocal coach teaches him to speak in a higher register, and lessons in etiquette cultivate in him feminine posture, gait, gestures, and social habits. His first trip to a busy public ladies' restroom is a success; he then lands a job with a temporary workers' agency. Gaining confidence, he joins a group of co-workers for drinks and meets a firefighter who first flirts with him and then punches him

EXAMPLE 4. Categorizing content notes for the Freimarke manuscript. The list goes on for a dozen pages. In this pass, the DE distinguishes notes identifying new subjects (SUBJ) from those identifying discursive problems.

**Introduction**

| | |
|---|---|
| SUBJ | 1—author's childhood in commune (strong beginning) |
| SUBJ | 3—amnio gender screening, political diatribe about |
| SUBJ | 7—empathy in animals "the primitive urge to create art"— huh? |
| TRANS/SUBJ? | 12—strange jump to "wrong body" trope in transsexual culture |
| SUBJ | 12—true hermaphrodite's story |
| EXC/SUBJ? | 18—intersex birth rate as key piece of info or too much info? |
| TONE | 25—author is parroting medical speak of interviewees |
| SUBJ | 27—against corrective surgery— ah, here's connex w/ trannies |
| SUBJ | 30—empathy as a performative medium |
| TIME/SUBJ? | 34—return to author's childhood commune as grown "woman" |

**Chapter 1**

| | |
|---|---|
| SUBJ | 36—*Black Like Me* as performance art before its time |
| TRANS | 42—how did we get from Griffin to panhandling? |
| SUBJ | 44—true art must lack "heuristics of passion" to record truth |
| SUBJ | 53—here, debuts his chameleon persona |
| SUBJ | 59—finagles interview w/ skeptical doc |
| TONE | 71—again, author slips into medical jargon; over his head |
| EXC | 82—too much detail re examining room; what's w/ the nurse? |
| SUBJ | 83—irony of doctor empathizing w/ author's false identity crisis |
| TIME | 95—rice-in-pantyhose boobs out of sequence |
| SUBJ | 97—author sees self as Hedwig "without the anger" |
| SUBJ | 100—ladies' room—author's first success at passing |

unconscious. Injured, the author lights out for the southern states, where he happens into a lesbian bar and convalesces in its hospitality.

In Georgia, the author begins hormone treatments, develops painful breast buds, gains weight, and experiences strange new emotions, most significantly empathy. He joins Dieters Anonymous, undergoes weekly electrolysis, and keeps up with his lesbian friends by joining their rugby squad. Incredibly, he lands a job as a local television reporter and covers a story about hormones causing men and women to breathe differently in sleep. This time, when he goes out "with the girls" to a Chippendales show, no one guesses his gender identity. A rugby pal who was once a nun gains him access to a convent; after ninety days, he and the abbess agree that he does not have a religious vocation.

His journey picks up pace, with weeks spent as a call girl, a guest on the *Jerry Springer Show*, the girlfriend of a Hell's Angel, and a legal aide. In Los Angeles, he helps win a ruling against gender reassignment of intersex babies. In Texas, he crosses a fundamentalist picket line to seek an abortion at a suburban clinic. The more violence he encounters, the angrier he becomes—like his heroine Hedwig—

and the more recklessly he enters volatile situations. The story ends at the famous coastal Hotel Del Coronado in San Diego, where our narrator is a bridesmaid. The outdoor wedding is replete with sexist themes, and when the bride's father asks our hero for a dance and then discovers his gender, all hell breaks loose. The author returns to Berlin, sets up his Web site and nightly slide shows, and receives starred reviews in American travel guides.

Reviewing this summary, Hedda realized that focusing on Goldi's story too closely would leave the text bereft of its central thesis: that it was possible to cultivate female empathy in a male-dominated society. The author's adventures demonstrated his thesis by example, but stripped of his expository musings, the story didn't hang together. As opaque and loopy as they were, Goldi's artistic theories were his motivation. He was the book's main character, and the audience needed to understand where he was coming from.

The tricky part would be to know how much of Goldi's exposition to restore without bewildering his readers and testing their patience. To do this, Hedda would have to revisit her subject categories.

### Find the Main Subject

Most texts with developmental problems suffer from a surfeit of subjects. First DEs must figure out what a manuscript is about; then they must consider what the revised text *should be* about. To do this, DEs weigh the publisher's content preferences—as stated in the written publisher's brief—against the subjects that engage the author's interest most deeply, those that best match the author's skill set, and those already featured prominently in the text.

This step is a crossroads: the DE must either conceive a vision for the project or bow out. This process extracts from whole manuscripts the equivalent of a proposal's vision statement. But whereas a vision can be summoned from a proposal with relative ease, a completed draft may hide its prize under tons of prose. Finding a manuscript's main subject means excavating much rubble to reach the book's spiritual core.

TALLY THE SUBJECT OCCURRENCES. The DE sifts through the ream of notes taken, reviews each SUBJ in light of the content summary, categorizes each SUBJ with a new code, and then begins a separate list of these subjects, recording all occurrences by page span. A manuscript on road rage might contain a mix of concrete and conceptual categories like STAT for statistics, PSY for driver psychology, HOR for the role played by hormones, ENG for engineered solutions to rage management in road planning, ENF for traffic enforcement, and so on. Usually, this process results in about a

| Introduction | | Chapter 1 | |
|---|---|---|---|
| EMP | 1—author's childhood in commune (strong beginning) | ART | 36—*Black Like Me* as performance art before its time |
| AGS, RTS | 3—amnio gender screening, political diatribe about | POV | 44—true art must lack "heuristics of passion" to record truth |
| ART | 7—empathy in animals "the primitive urge to create art"—huh? | POV | 53—here, debuts his chameleon persona |
| INT | 12—true hermaphrodite's story | TR | 59—finagles interview w/ skeptical doc |
| INT | 18—intersex birth rate as key piece of info or too much info? | EMP | 83—irony of doctor empathizing w/ author's false identity crisis |
| INT, TR, RTS | 27—against corrective surgery—ah, here's connex w/ trannies | ART | 97—author sees self as Hedwig "without the anger" |
| ART | 30—empathy as a performative medium | TR | 100—ladies' room—author's first success at passing |
| EMP | 34—return to author's childhood commune as grown "woman" | | |

dozen main subjects, and the tallied passages reveal three or four clear front runners.

SELECT A MAIN SUBJECT. Next, the DE must determine how these subjects correspond to the publisher's goals and the author's interests and abilities. Any subject that appeals to only one of these constituencies should be removed from consideration. So, too, should subjects that appeal to both publisher and author but have relatively slight treatment in the current manuscript. The best subject is one that supports the publisher's goals, exploits the author's enthusiasms, and is already well represented in the current draft. The winning candidate will not always be the hot topic that the marketing department pines for, but it may interest a large enough audience to warrant the project's development.

When DEs see that a manuscript cannot yield the book the publisher wants, they must not shrink from saying so. A DE who sugar-coats this bad news may end up saddled with the project, struggling to wrest from the text a book that just isn't there.

TRANSMUTE SUBJECT INTO CONCEPT. With the main subject identified, the DE can now turn it into a main concept by investing it with the author's point of view. Sometimes, DEs will be surprised to find that an explicit statement of the author's special take on the main subject had been right under their nose all along. Other times, DEs will need to draw out a point of view that is only implied.

Remember, at this stage we are looking for a broad concept, not a narrow thesis. Assessing the various thesis possibilities contained by a central concept is the focus of the next chapter.

Hedda went back and assigned new abbreviations, dissolving her SUBJ category into TR for transsexuality, RTS for gender rights, AGS for amnio gender screening, ART for the author's artistic theories, POV for his chameleon-like lack of a point of view, INT for intersex, EMP for women's empathy, and so on (example 5).

As she progressed, three codes—TR, ART, and EMP—began to surface most frequently. POV also proved a prominent code, but Hedda discounted it as a recurring non sequitur: clearly, the author did not lack a point of view, no matter how strenuously he claimed otherwise. Fringe subjects like intersexuality (INT) and amnio gender screening (AGS) did not recur. As new subjects came up, most fell into one of the emergent main categories. In chapter 5, electrolysis was a quintessential foray into empathizing with women's pain (EMP); in chapter 7, the suicide rates of post-ops fell under the heading of transsexuality (TR). Sometimes Hedda made up a new abbreviation—say, VIO for violence against women in chapter 11—only to conclude that it was actually a subcategory of an existing code, in this case women's empathy, or EMP.

On a clean sheet of paper, Hedda tallied the occurrences of each of her new subject categories by page span (example 6). No doubt about it, the front runners were transvestitism, art theory, women's empathy, and the irrelevant chameleon stance.

Having isolated the subjects that were the manuscript's strengths, Hedda turned to her other two primary considerations: the author's interests and the publisher's goals. In the end she was left with the conclusion that while all four of the text's main subjects were of abiding interest to the author (TR, EMP, ART, and POV), only two of these interested the publisher: the sensational topic of his foray into transvestitism and its sober justification as an exploration of women's empathy.

How, Hedda wondered, could she get Goldi to abandon his artistic theories and his self-invented persona? That's when revelation struck: far from being irrelevant, Goldi's chameleon shtick held the key to his motivations! Reviewing her notes, Hedda saw that each of his "Karma Chameleon" soliloquies implied a lesson learned from the adjacent experience. In the introduction, the issue of parents authorizing sex reassignment surgery for intersex infants evoked his own ambiguous identity. In chapter 8, when the author succeeded at passing as a woman during a Chippendales show, he felt disembodied, watching himself from a spot near the ceiling.

Hedda went back to the manuscript to review each chapter's POV and EMP

EXAMPLE 6. Tallying subjects in the Freimarke manuscript. Even before pages have been counted, the strings of spans clearly indicate which subjects dominate the author's discourse.

| Subject | Manuscript Pages |
|---------|------------------|
| TR | 27–29, 59–82, 100–101, 102–4, 236–38, 373–82, 453–62, 500–510, 521–50, 614–17, 694–701, 719–23, 740–47, 859–71, 905–9 |
| AGS | 3–7 |
| RTS | 3–7, 27–29 |
| ART | 7–11, 30–33, 36–43, 97–99, 190–96, 198–204, 229–35, 276–372, 420–28, 449–52, 551–60, 602–6, 618–21, 629–34, 661–66, 667–68, 728–30, 762–74, 809–15, 836–38, 899–902, 914–15 |
| INT | 12–17, 18–26, 27–29 |
| EMP | 1–2, 34–35, 83–96, 145–53, 171–89, 197, 205–28, 239–42, 243–75, 383–406, 407–19, 473–99, 511–20, 561–601, 702–18, 724–27, 775–78, 779–808, 816–35, 839–58, 872–98, 903–4, 910–13 |
| POV | 44–52, 53–58, 105–44, 154–70, 429–48, 463–72, 607–13, 622–28, 635–60, 669–93, 731–39, 748–61 |

passages. Over and over again, Goldi declared himself neutral out of one side of his mouth while celebrating the empathy of women (and deploring its absence from men) out of the other. Clearly, he needed the fiction of neutrality to provide him with the emotional distance to explore these connections consciously. And the more Hedda read, the more she saw that his ability to shape-shift psychologically was indeed a kind of artistic achievement—after all, weren't artists supposed to hold up a mirror to society? The nexus of POV, EMP, and ART was the book's center of gravity. She decided to call this newly forged central subject "ironic empathy." From there, Hedda leaped easily to the statement of a broad central concept:

The author explores American society as a "chameleon of gender," experiencing the battle between the sexes in his own mind and body and expressing it artistically as "ironic empathy."

This statement was lively enough to guide the editing process but broad enough to accommodate any number of precise theses. Although Hedda would normally identify a working thesis in her revision plan, she sensed that this sensitive author should not be bombarded with too many decisions at once.

With her breakthrough insight, Hedda could now propose a plan that would appeal to the author. Rather than coax him to suppress his theories, she would encourage him to put them into plainer words. And she'd cut back the self-psychoanalysis but leave enough intact to retain his artistic distance from his subjects. If she succeeded, Visigoth might just have a potential blockbuster on its hands.

The table of contents that Hedda proposed (example 7) hardly deviated from the author's. She switched chapters 2 and 3 so that his maiden trip to the ladies' room would precede his first falsetto interview; also, the original chapters 4 and 5 were out of order, with the wound-licking episode in the lesbian bar preceding the fight in the straight bar. But otherwise his narrative timeline was intact—Hedda had merely removed the jargon and promoted the author's homiest phrases as chapter titles. She decided he could open with a prologue devoted to his art theories and close with an epilogue featuring his "immodest proposal" to feminize the male population with hormone treatments.

The developmental plan went over with the author like a lead zeppelin. When she let Hedda know the bad news, Lainie soft-pedaled his objections, summarizing them in an email instead of quoting him verbatim. But the message was clear: he had no intention of abandoning the complexity of his postmodern pastiche for a straightforward "Hollywood-style plot line." Moreover, he'd taken exception to the assertion that his empathy was "ironic." Lainie said she and her bosses felt that Hedda had given the revision plan its best shot, so they were left with a decision: to pass on the project or publish it as is.

The television special was ultimately declined by PBS and ran instead on a music video station, where it reached its target demographic. The published book got some positive notices, but the only full-length reviews Hedda saw were in *Rolling Stone* and some local alternative-press rags; the mainstream media limited their coverage to short mentions that applauded the author's courageous experiment while deploring his confusing and "immature" writing style. Though Hedda took selfish pleasure in these criticisms, the victory was hollow: properly revised, the book might have had at least a touch of the cultural relevance of Griffin's *Black Like Me*.

Though she deemed it a failure, the project afforded Hedda one consolation. It had given her a potent experience of what Bud called his "aha!" moments. As DEs, she and Bud followed the same set of procedures they'd both learned in Dr. Worth's class back in the late 1980s. But whereas Bud had always maintained that his solutions to editorial problems were achieved in flashes of clarity that occurred while showering or driving, Hedda prided herself on unlocking a manuscript's secrets methodically, as if conducting a series of experiments. The Freimarke job had reminded her that those methods, however logical, could only provide a framework within which to be struck by inspiration. The moment she realized the connection between Goldi's chameleon persona and his empathy for women had been immensely satisfying. Like many an editor, Hedda would have to make do with the memory of a triumph to which she alone was witness.

**3** * T H E S I S * *Finding the Hook*

A thesis can serve purposes other than the sober statement of fact or belief. A thesis can beguile, inspire, enrage—whatever works to grab the readers' attention. It should promise readers an intellectual adventure; it should be at least a smidgen outrageous. A thesis is a gauntlet thrown down before readers, daring them to think back.

In the previous chapters, we focused on identifying a main concept. This concept, we learned, could be embedded in a proposal's vision statement or mined from the content of a completed draft. In both situations, we took care to keep the concept open and spacious so that it might embrace a number of possible theses. In this chapter, we narrow the author's investigation from a broad inquiry into the main subject to a precise inquiry into the *main topic*. In the process, we distinguish topics from theses, identify the multiple theses a concept contains, choose the *main thesis*, and fashion a working title to reflect it.

In our case study, the coauthors have done prodigious amounts of research yielding a number of compelling, but competing, theses. The DE must figure out which of these theses will best serve as a marketing hook that can garner the book positive reviews, air time, and, ultimately, sales. He makes this choice by focusing on the three characteristics of a strong thesis: point of view, originality, and relevance.

### Author Profile: The Coauthors

Some coauthors are like a long-married couple in which one spouse finishes the other's sentences. But most coauthors are not blessed with such telepathy, so they must create a division of labor that clarifies their respective areas of authority and responsibility. Some pairs divide up the book's table of contents by chapter; their battlefield is usually the joint introduction. On other projects, one author is assigned the role of writer and the other the role of content expert; this works best when the expert truly has no interest in the prose. Whatever the arrangement, their plan must include a procedure for resolving inevitable conflicts, whether by appealing to a third party or giving final authority to the author who penned the contested phrase. I've seen projects consigned to limbo for years by a spat that escalated to a full-scale cold war.

The coauthors had an understanding: Maria Sanchez-Collingwood was the anthropologist and had been assigned the role of writer; Jaime Dominguez was the sociologist who supplied, and crunched, the data. But the clarity of this division of labor did not stop Maria from feeling twinges of guilt when she agreed to meet with a developmental editor without Jaime's knowledge. Maria told herself that there was no sense in "upsetting" Jaime if the meeting yielded no results, but she knew the real reason for her secrecy: to give herself a chance to veto this move by the publisher. If Jaime liked the editor and she didn't, she'd feel usurped. Not that she wasn't open to suggestions for improvement—she wanted their book to be the best it could possibly be. But could a gringo editor really grasp what they were trying to say?

Both second-generation Mexican Americans, Maria and Jaime had met at graduate school and discovered, early on, a shared conviction that the plight of their ethnic community in the United States derived at least partly from a fatalistic subservience built into their Mexican cultural heritage. Like other academics in Chicano studies, they wished to liberate their people. But, while they held the American government responsible for its xenophobia and abusive policies, they were most concerned with helping *la raza* to find the inner strength to free itself. For them, César Chávez was a failed saint. What had undermined his experiment in passive resistance: religion? gender roles? family patronage?

Now, at the end of 2006, the fruits of fifteen years of careful ethnographic work were in danger of being deemed irrelevant. Back in spring, throngs of mostly Mexican immigrants had staged mass protests against legislation that would deny undocumented workers a path to citizenship. Millions of marchers, dressed in white shirts signifying peace and carrying American flags, had descended on the U.S. Capitol and the city halls of dozens of major cities. The spirit of César Chávez had finally risen in his people; but for how long? By fall, as a wall went up along a third of the U.S.-Mexico border and Congressional factions bickered about nine different immigration reform bills, the immigrant masses had fallen silent again. If their book was to contribute to the national debate among Mexican American leaders, they'd better move fast.

### Client Profile: The Small Trade House

In this era of corporate mergers, the independent book publisher is a living relic. Those successful imprints that have not yet been gobbled up by a media behemoth are likely to have a charismatic—and stubbornly independent—leader at the helm whose integrity inspires major authors to give her or him their minor works. The smarter of these leaders groom successors well in advance; the others take their houses with them to the grave. Usually, a handful of bestsellers on the backlist are the cornerstone of the house's financial solvency. The list tends to focus narrowly on a market niche in which the small house can compete against its major competitors as the "boutique" alternative: authors take lower royalties to see their books marketed more strategically and produced with higher quality in editing, design, and printing.

Tombolo Press had a highly regarded list in cultural studies and liberal politics. Unlike most independent houses, it had never been dominated by a single personality: control was exercised by consensus at weekly staff meetings. Its philosophy was aptly emblematized by the *tombolo*, a sandbar that forms a fragile link between a coastal island and its neighboring mainland. Most Tombolo offerings were attempts to bridge gaps in cultural understanding, and the proposal by Sanchez-Collingwood and Dominguez had promised just that. But when the acquisitions editor, Hayden Foster, presented the completed manuscript at the weekly meeting, his colleagues responded with alarm. The immigrant studies list was Tombolo's bread and butter, and several editors felt the book was a direct attack on the work of other authors on their list. The coauthors seemed to be taking potshots; they had too many points to make, and their arguments lacked control.

Hayden agreed that the text needed work, but he reminded his co-workers that Tombolo had a reputation for thinking beyond the pietisms of political correctness. For the past three seasons, the lead books had been debunkers of liberal myths: a tell-all about nepotism in the Green Party, a portrait of an Inuit village welcoming the oil industry onto its lands, and a look at the rise of the *fútbol mamá* in middle-class Mexico. Their readers, he argued—including their authors—valued this diversity of perspectives, which represented nothing less than a commitment to free speech.

Chastened, the staff agreed that Hayden could move forward with the project, on one condition: that he engage a DE to work with the renegade coauthors.

## Assignment: The Study with Too Many Theses

Dr. Robert Worth was the Bay Area's guru on developmental editing. He had created the DE department up at Covington, once a leading textbook publisher—a citadel on a hill that was now an ephemeral, fractured imprint of the international e-commerce giant Books-R-Us. After the buyout, Robert had taken severance pay and begun his own freelance concern, partly editing and partly training new DEs. The classes and seminars now occupied him almost full-time, allowing little time for actual editing. But he was sorely tempted to take on this project himself.

For starters, Robert had married a first-generation Mexican American and had witnessed, over the dinner table at family gatherings, spirited debates embracing the very viewpoints these authors expressed. Their study was broad in scope, encompassing communities of undocumented workers throughout the United States, in sectors ranging from agriculture to food service, domestic help, construction, health care, and various forms of menial labor. And their methods were sound, combining careful ethnography with empirical sociology in the form of a detailed questionnaire.

But their manuscript, for all its narrative richness, was a mess. They had too much to say on their subject, and many of their theses contradicted each other. On the one hand, they blamed the immigrants for buying into American materialism, on the other, for accepting a lower standard of living than that enjoyed by Anglo-Americans. They decried Mexican attitudes toward gender yet perversely admired individuals who manipulated Americans into marrying for green cards. They took a dim view of Mexico's distinctive brand of Catholicism, with its infusion of indigenous beliefs, but they mourned a loss of spiritual values in the younger Spanglish-speaking generation.

Their table of contents reflected these contradictory impulses (example 8). The result was an unsettling mix of advocacy and culture bashing, as if the authors were working through their feelings about their own childhoods. The Tombolo editors feared an outcry among their loyal readers, yet rather than cut the project loose, they preferred to try rehabilitating it. They felt the book could sell well if its wild themes were braided into a single strong thesis, a sturdy rope ending in a sharp marketing hook.

Robert reviewed his schedule. He was in a permanent state of overcommitment, and Tombolo needed a quick response. So he decided to recommend one of his two star pupils, Bud Zallis or Hedda Miller, both now well established in their freelance careers. Hedda would be better at corralling the text's myriad empirical facts into a cohesive argument, but Bud was the better storyteller, and, at its heart, this manuscript was the story of a displaced people. He dialed Bud's number.

EXAMPLE 8. The unrevised TOC for the Sanchez-Collingwood and Dominguez manuscript. The chapter titles read like article titles in a special issue of a scholarly journal. Note the different levels of abstraction and semantic patterns; the result lacks cohesion.

*Between Amnesties: Mexican Journeys toward U.S. Citizenship*

Introduction: Work, Family, and the System

I.  Legitimacy through Work

Chapter 1.   Car Wash: Mexican Attitudes toward Work
Chapter 2.   *"Fruta del Diablo"*: The Thorny Issue of Special Agriculture Workers in the Artichoke Fields of Watsonville
Chapter 3.   "Degrees in Spanglish and Broken Hearts": Housekeepers' Stories on Pacific Heights
Chapter 4.   Clinica de Salud: The Ironies of Health Care among Mexican Migrants
Chapter 5.   God and Glamour: Special Immigration Status for Priests and *Telenovela* Stars
Chapter 6.   The Mexican Millionaires' Club: Citizenship via Alien Investment
Chapter 7.   *"Mi no Arrimados"*: Why the Guest Worker Plan Won't Work

II.  Legitimacy through Family

Chapter 8.   *"Parentelas, Compadrazgo, y Cuatismo"*: Mexican Attitudes toward Family
Chapter 9.   Bloodlines and Amnesty Lines: A Brief History of Laws Governing U.S. Citizenship
Chapter 10.  The Transborder Economy: Sending Home Money and Middle-Class Values
Chapter 11.  Gold-Digging for Green Cards: Mexican Women, American Men
Chapter 12.  *La Casa Chica,* American Style
Chapter 13.  The Altar as Border Crossing: Mexican Men, American Women

III.  Playing the System

Chapter 14.  The Narrowing Gap of Political Asylum
Chapter 15.  *Palomillas* and the Virgin of Guadalupe
Chapter 16.  Between Amnesties: The Winds of Political Change

Conclusion: The Spirit of César Chávez

## Cull Theses from Topics

The first key ingredient of a sharp thesis statement is a clear and compelling *point of view*. This quality is the author's special take on the material, the same animating spirit we found behind a book concept at proposal stage. Now, the DE must identify the most compelling and useful thesis statement from a range of options contained by the book's concept. To do this, the DE forages among the newly defined subject's many subcategories, or "topics," to see which provokes the author's strongest convictions.

Defining a thesis can be more difficult for a narrative (see chapter 4) than an expository work (see chapter 5). Some publishers and authors may question whether a biography of a famous person, for example, requires a thesis at all. But as any modern historian or journalist will attest, all narrative—however closely it cleaves to unadorned fact—puts an interpretive spin on reality. By defining a thesis, authors acknowledge their point of view up front; in so doing, they both enlist the trust of the reader and impose structural coherence on their discourse.

Expository and even polemical works can have thesis problems, too, but theirs are usually problems of excess. They rarely lack a point of view. A journalist who has spent years dogging a corrupt politician, say, will marshal every bit of evidence against a foe until the main line of argument bristles with tangents. Selecting a main thesis gives the reader a rope to hold on to while scaling the summit of a complex argument.

REVIEW NOTES FOR TOPICS. The DE's job is to help authors sift through the many topics contained within their main subject and determine which are possible main theses. The first step is to copy over onto a clean sheet, from the list you created in chapter 2, all SUBJ items, and only those items, pertaining to the main concept.

LOOK FOR A CLEAR POINT OF VIEW. Next, the DE can contemplate each SUBJ item and, if it has a clear and explicit point of view, relabel it "THES" as a potential thesis. The DE should be sure to avoid putting thesis statements into the author's mouth; if the author has no discernible point of view on a topic, it should be labeled "TOP" for "topic" and disqualified from consideration. However, if a TOP note conveys a piquant attitude that remains understated, the DE may draft a more explicit restatement to serve as a thesis.

CREATE A LIST OF CANDIDATES. In my experience, authors tend to balk when offered only one choice for main thesis. The DE's goal at this time is to identify as many workable theses as possible. Later, the DE will winnow the field to a short list of prime candidates from which the author may choose.

By the time Bud completed his first pass through *Between Amnesties,* his legal pad contained eleven pages of notes on structural and stylistic issues, sprinkled with perhaps two dozen recurring notations labeled "SUBJ" for "possible main subject." This proliferation enveloped his brain in fog, so he took a walk to the corner store. When he returned, his head cleared by a swallow of Red Bull, he reminded himself that there was really only one main subject, namely, the role of Mexican cultural values in "keeping down" the U.S. community of undocumented workers. Less clear was whether a single pattern could be found underlying discrete attitudes toward masculinity, femininity, money, religion, family, community, government, and other important topics.

Bud copied the SUBJ notations onto a clean sheet (example 9). This time, instead of subcategorizing each notation by content, he considered whether it was a mere topic or a bona fide *thesis*. Those with thesis potential he labeled "THES," the remainder "TOP."

Often, Bud's first impression was that a notation had thesis potential, but closer inspection revealed that the authors had failed to take a clear stand on the matter. For instance, on page 39, the authors recorded an intriguing contradiction: Mexican workers at an urban car wash told interviewers they had no desire to buy into the value system of American materialism, yet they daydreamed aloud about owning the luxury vehicles that passed under their red washrags. The authors noted this ambivalence, but they fell short of offering an interpretation of it.

Just as often, however, Bud found himself underestimating the authors, thinking they'd failed to make their point of view clear on a topic and then realizing, on further scrutiny, that their position was at least implied. For example, on page 151, several paragraphs discussed the phenomenon of the *arrimado*, the permanent houseguest. Interviewees remembered guests in their childhood households with a mixture of respect for their parents' patient hospitality and disdain for the guests' freeloading. The authors did not explicitly compare the uneasy position of the *arrimado* (literally, "parasite") to the status of "guest worker" assigned the interviewees themselves by the American government, but the implication was ripe for the picking.

As Bud assessed the thesis potential of each topic, he crossed out his original note and rewrote it as an explicit statement of the authors' seeming point of view. He ended up with twelve theses that were not only workable but truly intriguing—it would be tough to narrow the field. Before he did that, however, he needed to assess their originality.

## Beware of the Rehash

The second key ingredient of a sharp thesis statement is its *originality*. In works of a conceptual nature, with theories flying left and right, the DE must take care to distinguish the established theories of others from the author's own original theses. Authors who like "complicating" their subjects sometimes do so out of intellectual laziness, invoking whole theoretical frameworks that have been erected by others without advancing a single thought of their own.

DISQUALIFY BORROWED THESES. The DE should make a separate pass through the list of THES and TOP items and cross out those that are recognizable as derivative thinking. If uncertain about whether a particularly compelling thesis is original, the DE may need to do a little research or ask the publisher to provide an expert for consultation. Such questions of provenance should be resolved now to avoid basing a developmental plan on a thesis that turns out to be borrowed.

DETERMINE THE AUTHOR'S MOTIVES. If this review results in a paucity of workable theses, then the DE needs to consider the author's motives. Authors who resort to derivative thinking usually don't realize they're doing so. They tend to fall into one of two categories: converts and preachers.

The convert is one for whom an existing framework is a recently discovered window into reality. In this regard, there's little difference between a newly born-again Christian and the mohawk-wearing, tongue-pierced slam poet whose dissertation applies Barthe's concept of the camera-as-eye to, say, security cameras in a Silicon Valley mall. Converts can often be prompted to come up with a truly fresh thesis.

Preachers have hitched their careers—or even their identities—to a particular theoretical wagon and so can't afford to reevaluate the assumptions of which it is constructed. Proponents of twelve-step programs, new diets, and get-rich-quick schemes are as prone to this error as are academic theorists. Preachers are harder to rehabilitate than converts because of their degree of personal investment in what they regard as their own intellectual projects, but they can sometimes be prompted to freshen their ideas as well.

Most of the draft thesis statements on Bud's list (example 10)—which he labeled A through N for convenience—withstood the scrutiny of an eye looking for derivative thinking. In virtually all cases, the authors had taken existing theoretical frameworks and applied them to their subject in ways that created new insights. A few statements, however, gave pause.

For instance, the thesis about Mexicans' aboriginal health practices (thesis C) flirted with the danger of exoticizing the immigrants as "primitives." In Mexican culture, where the vast majority of the population is *mestizo,* people of mixed Spanish and Indian ancestry celebrate the cultures of their indigenous forebears even as they prize the light skin, blond hair, and blue eyes of their European heritage. The modern Mexican state had long ago made education in native folkways compulsory, and most of the immigrants had learned Indian dances in elementary school, worn Indian costumes on holidays, and suffered folk remedies administered by their grandmothers—like shooting syringefuls of castor oil into constipated children's buttock muscles. The fact that the immigrants thought of their native medical tradition as healthier did not make it so.

Another thesis statement that raised concern equated the mistress of *la casa chica* with the postmodern Other (thesis K). The authors found that many of the undocumented workers surveyed grew up with fathers who had more than one nuclear family. In Mexican society, it was commonplace for a man to marry, have children, and then further demonstrate his masculinity by taking a mistress, installing her in her own house (*la casa chica,* meaning "the little house"), and fathering a second brood. In some cases, wives and mistresses eventually became friends, with both families gathering around the table at *la casa grande* on holidays. The authors saw dysfunction in both "legitimate" and "bastard" families: children watched their mothers suffer, competed for their fathers' affection and resources, and internalized these traits, often repeating the same marriage pattern as adults.

What rang untrue to Bud was the imposition of the concept of Otherness. Hardly a sociological or anthropological text had been written in the previous two decades that did not capitalize this word, yet defining it precisely was impossible. Nor did these two authors define their use of the term; when Bud queried them via email for clarification, they seemed mainly attracted by the pun on the phrase "the other woman." So he decided to recommend suppressing the Otherness thesis altogether. The health practices theme could stay, but it would not be a candidate for main thesis because it lacked the breadth and originality of some of the other choices. To choose a main thesis, Bud would need to play a game with nesting logic.

EXAMPLE 10. Making thesis statements explicit for the Sanchez-Collingwood and Dominguez manuscript. Here the editor has coaxed out the explicit messages implied by his notations.

~~TOP   39 car wash employees want cars, TVs, say no need to be "rich"~~

A. THES   Materialism: Undocs are suspicious of American materialism as a force of spiritual impoverishment, but they are tempted by its comforts and emblems of social status.

~~TOP   57 girl says "we Catholics are fatalistic, like Frida Kahlo"~~

B. THES   Fatalism: Undocs consider fatalism a part of their Catholic heritage.

~~THES   96 intuitive knowledge of the body until hypochondria learned from us~~

C. THES   Health Practices: American medicine undermines the undocs' spiritual connection with ancient Indian health practices, yet they turn to so-called Western medicine in times of crisis.

~~TOP   151 arrimado (perm guest) in one family stayed 32 years~~

D. THES   Houseguests: The mixture of duty and resentment evoked by *arrimados* disposes undocs to reject the American government's characterization of them as "guest workers."

~~TOP   189 Watsonville workers send most of paycheck to parents~~

E. THES   Parents: The transborder economy is less an expression of ambition than of loyalty to family, especially devotion to parents.

~~THES   191 respondents say family more important than church, state~~

F. THES   Family Loyalty: Undocs consider family bonds the most important in their culture.

~~TOP   215 godparents' influence can be sinister, Italian style~~

G. THES   Godparents: The pervasive network of godparenting fills in gaps in family networks and extends family influence into business and government.

~~THES   231 cuates (buddies) give men extra support beyond family~~

H. THES   Buddies: The buddy system (*cuatismo*) extends the social support network beyond bloodlines while affirming the primacy of men's position in society.

~~THES   262 laws are like the weather, inarguable, neither good nor bad~~

I. THES   Fatalism in Politics: Undocs' fatalism extends to their attitudes toward dramatic changes in American immigration policy.

~~THES   326 la casa chica, the ultimate ambivalence: man wants to have cake and eat it too~~

J. THES   *La Casa Chica*: A shadow version of family loyalty binds men to their mistresses and "illegitimate" children.

~~THES   334 mistress is the Other woman—get it?~~

K. THES   Otherness: The mistress of *la casa chica* is the ever-present Other in Mexican society, just as undocs are the Other in American society.

~~THES   352 machismo is the attitude "problem" most Mexicans name first~~

L. THES   *Machismo*: *Machismo* is the straw man for a complex set of Mexican attitudes toward both genders that hampers equality and empowerment.

~~THES   387 all mothers treated as saints; assertion of patriarchy~~

M. THES   Female Virtue: Praising women's virtue is a chivalrous means of keeping them down.

~~TOP   435 César Chávez revered as a saint, not as a peer, social worker thinks~~

N. THES   *Machismo* in Politics: Undocs' fatalism seems passive but remains shot through with *machismo*, undermining efforts to achieve civil rights through peaceful resistance.

## Choose the Main Thesis

The third key ingredient of a sharp thesis statement is *relevance*. Even the most original thesis, suffused with the most colorful point of view, will fail if it seems beside the point. The DE must identify a statement that is central to all the material discussed substantively in the book without reverting to broad generalization.

DISCARD MARGINAL CANDIDATES. To whittle the list down, the DE can first throw out all theses—however appealing—that do not pertain to at least 75 percent of the text's content. If an author must write more than 25 percent of the text from scratch, then she or he is writing a different book.

APPLY NESTING LOGIC. The DE can then winnow the list further by applying a kind of nesting logic: thesis B is more specific than thesis A because it depends on thesis A to make sense; therefore, thesis A is the larger thesis. I often picture thesis statements as nesting Russian dolls of varying sizes and ask myself, which fits inside which?

NOMINATE A WORKING THESIS. The resulting short list may contain an obvious choice for main thesis—a concept capacious enough to include the other five. More often, the DE will need to craft a thesis that serves as an umbrella for all six. The DE should take care to avoid (a) generalizing the main thesis into a bland truism and (b) grafting the shortlisted theses into a many-tentacled monstrosity. The main thesis must serve as the publisher's marketing hook, but there must also be enough bait on the hook to earn the reader's trust—otherwise, the thesis will be perceived as a mere sound byte.

The DE should be careful not to press this thesis too vigorously on the author. I prefer to identify a short list of candidates from which the author may select. This approach sometimes yields a better choice than I would have made and always results in a greater degree of author buy-in. Even when leaving this choice to the author, however, the DE must nominate a single thesis as a "working thesis" to draft a full developmental plan.

So far, from his list of thesis statements, Bud had eliminated two candidates from consideration as potential main thesis: health practices (thesis C), which would remain in play as a subordinate thesis, and Otherness (thesis K), which would be removed completely. Next, he needed to cut his options further, and to evaluate how they related to one another.

But first, were there any candidates Bud could eliminate on the basis of lack of substantive weight? That is, were there any theses that, if chosen as main thesis, would require massive amounts of new writing? Well, the observation about materialism (thesis A) was intriguing, but the authors dealt with it only briefly, in the car wash chapter. Likewise, the fatalism of Mexican cultural heritage (thesis B) was an assumption that threaded through the text but did not receive explicit treatment. So these themes could safely be excluded from Bud's deliberations.

The remaining theses were somewhat interrelated and often contradictory. Thesis I applied the generic theme of fatalism to politics by explaining how immigrants were disinclined to protest new American restrictions on immigrants, instead accepting them as "God's will." Yet thesis N undermined this portrait of Mexican passivity by asserting that it was violence-loving *machismo* that kept immigrants from sustaining César Chávez's peaceful resistance movement. Thesis L, in turn, challenged this notion of univalent *machismo,* asserting instead that the term was shorthand for a whole complex of attitudes toward both genders. Theses D, E, G, H, and J all dealt with ways in which the bonds of family loyalty—arguably the foundation of Mexican culture—were extended beyond the boundaries of the nuclear family. Sheesh, thought Bud, what an intricate web!

Of all the thesis choices, Bud found himself gravitating toward two: *machismo* and *la casa chica.* These phenomena were complementary, and each term served as a kind of shorthand for a whole constellation of gender-inflected societal relationships. If there were any way to unite thematically the authors' findings, and sell books, what better hook than sex?

Bud started tucking "smaller" theses inside "larger" ones, bundling them into groups. First, he tried making thesis L, about the complexity of the notion of *machismo,* the main thesis (example 11a). Theses F, J, M, and N fit neatly inside L as expressions of *machismo*, but it was not clear how the others related. The prevalence of permanent houseguests in Mexican society (thesis D) did not seem particularly fueled by macho motivations, nor did other traditional values such as fatalism, materialism, or health practices. Houseguests, however, fell in neatly with theses E, G, and H under the rubric of "family loyalty." And Bud grouped materialism (thesis A) and health practices (thesis C) under a new topic called spirituality (thesis O).

This shuffling process left Bud with three main thesis candidates: *machismo,* fatalism, and spirituality. Next, he attempted to come up with an "umbrella" thesis statement that would cover those three components (example 11b):

Thesis P: Traditional values undermine efforts by Mexican undocumented workers to fight for civil rights in the United States.

Too vague. This generalization was boring and also came dangerously close to impugning an entire society's way of life. He took another stab at representing the complexity of the authors' arguments:

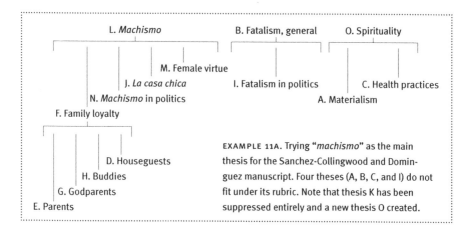

EXAMPLE 11A. Trying "*machismo*" as the main thesis for the Sanchez-Collingwood and Dominguez manuscript. Four theses (A, B, C, and I) do not fit under its rubric. Note that thesis K has been suppressed entirely and a new thesis O created.

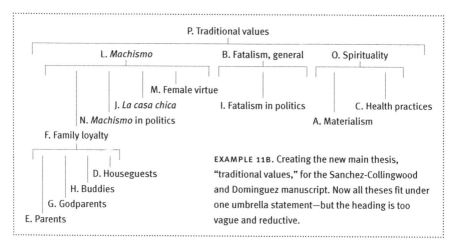

EXAMPLE 11B. Creating the new main thesis, "traditional values," for the Sanchez-Collingwood and Dominguez manuscript. Now all theses fit under one umbrella statement—but the heading is too vague and reductive.

Thesis P: Traditional Mexican values such as *machismo,* fatalism, and distrust of materialism and modern medicine complicate efforts to promote the civil rights of undocumented workers in the United States.

Better, but still less than thrilling. Several of the authors' main ideas were now represented, but the thesis did not demonstrate how those ideas related. He tried again:

Thesis P: Traditional Mexican values such as *machismo,* fatalism, and distrust of materialism and modern medicine—which find expression financially in the transborder economy, socially in *la casa chica* arrangements, and politically in ambivalence toward "guest worker" status—complicate efforts to promote the civil rights of undocumented workers in the United States.

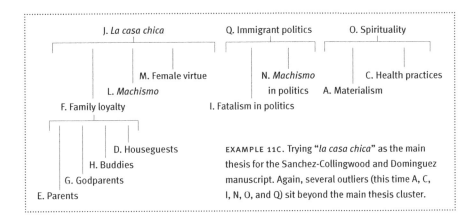

EXAMPLE 11C. Trying "*la casa chica*" as the main thesis for the Sanchez-Collingwood and Dominguez manuscript. Again, several outliers (this time A, C, I, N, O, and Q) sit beyond the main thesis cluster.

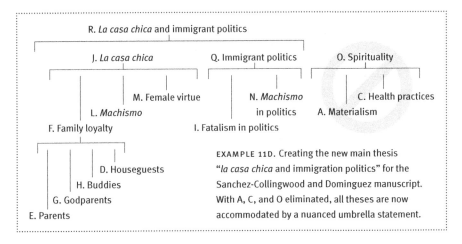

EXAMPLE 11D. Creating the new main thesis "*la casa chica* and immigration politics" for the Sanchez-Collingwood and Dominguez manuscript. With A, C, and O eliminated, all theses are now accommodated by a nuanced umbrella statement.

This thesis had a case of TMI—too much information—with too many independent themes flailing about like tentacles.

Since Bud wasn't having much luck with *machismo* writ large, or "traditional values," he tried starting over with *la casa chica* as his candidate for main thesis (example 11c). Could he successfully bundle all the other thesis statements within that notion? Immediately, the pieces of the puzzle started falling into place. Whereas *machismo* dealt explicitly with men's role in Mexican society and only implied women's, children's, and other household members' roles, the phenomenon of *la casa chica* referred to a highly complex set of relationships between man and wife, man and mistress, mistress and wife, man and children, and legitimate and illegitimate children. Other kinds of close social bonds only added richness to this tapestry, as both houses—*casas chica y grande*—could have permanent guests, both sets of children could have godparents, and the man's buddies could visit both homes freely.

Several themes were still not fitting inside the shell of *la casa chica*. Most tangential were materialism and health practices: rather than retain them and force the main thesis to become vague or gangly, Bud decided to cut them. This left him with just two straggling themes: the roles of fatalism (thesis I) and *machismo* in politics (thesis N). Because the unrevised manuscript devoted an entire third part to immigrant politics under the heading "Playing the System" (example 8), it seemed unwise to cut these theses from the book. Bud would need to find a bridge between the complex social dynamics represented by *la casa chica* and the urgent political situation of Mexican immigrants in the United States. He penciled in a new thesis Q, "immigrant politics."

Bud now had one of his patented "Eureka!" moments. If the web of social relationships stretching between the big house and the little house was rich with complexity, how much more byzantine must it become when this web was stretched across the Mexican-U.S. border? He went back to his notes from his interview with Maria, the anthropologist half of the author duo. At some point during their conversation, she'd said something about *la casa chica* being "the emblem of all the dysfunction in Mexican society." The stressful conditions of migrant life only "intensified this unhealthy dynamic," she'd said. Bud went prospecting for similar statements in the manuscript and there, on page 326, right under his nose, was the perfect main thesis:

Thesis R: The tradition of *la casa chica*, which gives "illegitimate" families a prescribed role in Mexican society even as it affirms their second-class citizenship, predisposes undocumented workers to accept uncomplainingly their role as "illegal" workers in American society.

This thesis had it all: a sharp hook, an original observation, and the breadth to embrace subsidiary themes (example 11d). How had Bud missed it? Well, the potential of *la casa chica* hadn't been obvious during his first pass through the manuscript; it was the experiments with nesting logic that had clarified its usefulness. The sentence now stood out as if printed in gold leaf.

### Create a Working Title

The Perfect Title can be an elusive animal. At the University of California Press, we've been known to hold brainstorming sessions after hours at the local brewery in the hope that lubricating our minds will help us crack a particularly hard case. Once, I remember, the Perfect Title declined to present itself to the author until her book was at the printer—too late for us to make the change. At this early stage, however, all that is needed is a working

TABLE 1. Strategies for creating a working title

| STRATEGY | DEFINITION | EXAMPLES |
|---|---|---|
| Personal Name | For a biography or character-driven novel, the subject's name—surname only, if famous enough—with or without a subtitle signaling the author's point of view | *Walt Whitman: The Song of Himself*<br>*Ulysses S. Grant: The Unlikely Hero*<br>*Borges: A Life*<br>*Zappa* |
| Place Name | A place central to the text, or the site of its climactic action, perhaps with a descriptor to distinguish the present work | *Gorky Park*<br>*Animal Farm*<br>*The Stones of Florence*<br>*Imperial San Francisco* |
| Reportage | Common nouns that name the central subject or conceit | *Guns, Germs, and Steel*<br>*Illness as Metaphor* |
| Emblem | A well-chosen detail from the text, often a concrete noun with symbolic resonance | *The Moviegoer*<br>*The Bell Jar* |
| Paired Emblems | Contrasting emblems that evoke a paradox central to the text | *The Diving Bell and the Butterfly* |
| Explicit Metaphor | A metaphor that recurs explicitly in the text | *The Grapes of Wrath*<br>*House of Sand and Fog* |
| Implicit Metaphor | A metaphor that does not recur explicitly in the text but that conveys the author's point of view | *Running with Scissors*<br>*The Horseman on the Roof* |
| Double-Edged Colloquialism | An informal phrase used in the text that takes on deeper meaning when elevated to the status of a title | *The Night in Question*<br>*The Big Sleep*[a] |
| Pun | A play on words that aptly crystallizes the author's thesis | *The Power of Babel* |
| High Concept | A surprising combination of descriptor and noun that conveys the text's main concept | *Unforgivable Blackness*<br>*Gravity's Rainbow*<br>*Pale Fire* |
| Irony | A title that states the opposite of what the book is actually about | *The Age of Innocence*<br>*Prague*[b] |
| Humor | A joke that conveys the author's point of view | *Yoga for People Who Can't Be Bothered to Do It* |
| Quotation | A phrase from the Bible or other foundational text, implying a comparison, often ironically, with the text at hand | *At Play in the Fields of the Lord*<br>*Tender Is the Night* |

*(continued)*

TABLE 1 (*continued*)

| STRATEGY | DEFINITION | EXAMPLES |
|---|---|---|
| Full Sentence | A title containing a main verb, usually in present tense, that describes the main action of a narrative | *The Mambo Kings Play Songs of Love*<br>*Cotton Comes to Harlem* |
| Sentence Fragment | A phrase or clause cut short, as if the author were interrupted in mid-thought, that obliquely summons the emotional tenor of the text | *To the Lighthouse*<br>*Into Thin Air*<br>*All the Pretty Horses* |
| Oratorial Flourish | A phrase with the dramatic flair of formal speech that serves, in essence, as the text's opening phrase | *Speak, Memory*<br>*I Know This Much Is True* |
| Stock Formula | An oft-used title formula applied to an unlikely subject | *A Natural History of the Senses*<br>*A Brief History of Time* |
| Genre Formula | A stock formula taken from a different genre than the text's own | *Kitchen Confidential* |

[a] *The Big Sleep* uses a droll (and now extinct) colloquial synonym for death to signal the narrator's fearless and ironic stance toward murder.

[b] *Prague* follows a season in the lives of American expatriates who hang out in early-post-Communist Budapest, never getting around to the Czech city, which they imagine to be more "authentic" than their Hungarian outpost.

title—one that reflects the recently selected main thesis accurately enough to guide DE and author during the revision process.

CONSIDER TITLING STRATEGIES. Table 1 demonstrates eighteen strategies for titling a book (or chapter, for that matter). This list is not exhaustive, but it does run the gamut from common nouns to proper names, from emblems to metaphors, from lowbrow puns to higher-brow humor and irony, from fragments to full sentences, and from colloquialisms to oratorial flourishes. A DE struggling to hit upon the Perfect Title can try brainstorming for at least one example of each of these eighteen strategies.

CREATE A SHORT LIST OF CANDIDATES. Suppose the DE has come up with twenty title ideas. The next step is to reduce that list to a half dozen or fewer to make the final selection manageable for the author and publisher. Before tossing an idea, however, the DE should see if it would work better if it were strategized differently. Imagine if *The Mambo Kings Play Songs of Love* had been christened *Love Songs of the Mambo Kings*, or if *Cotton Comes to Harlem* were simply *Cotton in Harlem*—the active verbs are what make these titles memorable.

NOMINATE A WORKING TITLE. When presenting a half dozen title choices to the author and publisher, the DE should not be bashful about promoting a favorite. By writing the developmental plan under this choice, the DE will demonstrate how a working title operates as a guide to the developmental process.

The existing title, *Between Amnesties,* had the virtues of accuracy, brevity, and a certain dramatic tension, but it emphasized the politics of the border, which was of secondary concern to both the authors and their subjects. The subtitle, *Mexican Journeys toward U.S. Citizenship,* nicely conveyed the text's strategy of interweaving multiple narratives, so it could probably stay.

Bud started his brainstorming (example 12) with the metaphor central to the new thesis, namely, *la casa chica.* Surely it would yield some compelling title options. But the very complexity of *la casa chica* as a social phenomenon, and as a metaphor for U.S.-Mexican relations, made it difficult to translate into a working title. References to "The Little House" would only evoke ". . . on the Prairie" for most Americans.

So Bud turned to the text for inspiration, beginning with the table of contents. The title of chapter 13, "The Altar as Border Crossing," had a nice ring: it alluded to the dimension of family dynamics complicated by transborder politics, but it hardly touched the central theme of fatalistic acceptance by undocumented workers of their "illegitimacy" in American society. Chapter 2's title, "*Fruta del Diablo,*" the immigrant pickers' name for the prickly artichoke, tipped the scales of melodrama once translated as "Fruit of the Devil." The conclusion's "The Spirit of Chávez" had some potential, but the famous martyr's name was evocative only of the general subject matter, not the main thesis.

In the body of the text, a number of piquant phrases resonated with the book's main theme. A tool shed in an artichoke field that served as a refuge for workers during sudden storms was sardonically dubbed the Watsonville Country Club. When several dozen *jornaleros*—waiting on a curb for gringos to hire them as day laborers—spoke of Mexico, tears filled their eyes: "Machos Don't Cry." A housekeeper who sent money back to Oaxaca each month, where her sons and daughters were being raised by their grandmother, lamented, "My Children They Have Forgotten Me." A man who had married a gringa and established a successful used-car business in Los Angeles worried about the effects of urban gang culture on his children, saying, "I'm Raising Cholos." Finally, Bud came across this quotation in the manuscript: "When they call me 'illegal,' I feel it in my heart." Perfect! With this quote as the opening epigraph, the title could read *My Illegal Heart.*

✳

Once Bud had a main thesis and working title in hand, the trick was to rearrange the manuscript's content around them without forcing square pegs into round holes or sacrificing richness.

Under the title "Mexican Values, American Dreams," the introduction would outline the book's argument (example 13). Then the chapters would be arranged to follow suit: three chapters on family loyalty, then two on gender roles, two on transborder *la casa chica* arrangements, one on personal honor, two on ambition, and one on fatalism. The last three chapters would make concrete recommendations to activists in the immigrants' rights movement: to take greater advantage of an existing network of established informal mutual-aid societies called *palomillas;* to resist Bush's guest worker plan; and to become educated about the other immigration reform bills being debated by Congress.

Bud wrote up the developmental plan and sent it to Hayden Foster, who was enthusiastic. The authors, however, were divided in their responses: the anthropologist, Maria, was taken with the idea of using *la casa chica* as a prism through which to view their subject, but the sociologist, Jaime, felt that doing so misrepresented the emphasis of their empirical work, which had not focused particularly on *la casa chica.* After rounds of email haggling, Maria and Bud convinced Jaime that the "little house" phenomenon could be presented as the confluence of the broader familial dynamics that the questionnaire had explored so thoroughly.

When the book finally entered the national debate, some reviewers questioned the validity of the authors' thesis in light of growing immigrant activism. But Mexican activists themselves embraced the trope of *la casa chica* as a rationale for why it had taken them so long to fight for their civil rights. Soon, the term was appropriated by the media as shorthand for all the cultural barriers inhibiting the self-empowerment of Mexican illegal aliens. Meanwhile, the authors resumed their field work in preparation for their next book. The last Bud heard, they were studying Mexican soldiers who fought in Saudi Arabia in order to gain U.S. citizenship, Latino gangs who protected their black markets by intimidating activists, and families whose sons and daughters had died on long desert treks around the new border wall.

On National Public Radio, Maria was asked, "When the *madre* of *la casa chica* has finally been welcomed into the big house, will there be peace?" She answered, "Oh yes, she'll take her place quietly at the table. But she and her children will never forget."

Experience is knowledge. The roots of our words "narrative" (Latin *gnarus*) and "story" (Greek *istor*) both mean "knowing." In this era of videogame plotlines, those words have come to denote a random sequence of events stripped of meaning. Indeed, some brain experts consider memory an evolutionary adaptation that assigns meaning arbitrarily to enable the storage and retrieval of data. But the idea that experiences are inherently meaningless strikes me as being about as dogmatic as any religious belief. Experience is knowledge, quite simply, because we are constrained to move through time. The outcome of event A always limits our options as we approach event B. Over time, we look back at our experiences and see them stretch behind us in a line, a path, a pattern of meaning.

Templates for storytelling are embedded in our brains. Whether a particular template serves a narrative well depends largely on how well it allows for thematic links among the events narrated. In our case study, the DE helps an author to decide which of four competing storylines to privilege and provides strategies for subordinating the other three while braiding all four strands into a coherent whole.

### Author Profile: The Historian

In recent decades, it has become widely accepted that all history is colored by the biases of those who record it. This new awareness has caused some historians to take a forensic turn, looking for clues in archeology and material culture, while others have gone theoretical, embracing the interpretive tools of sociology, psychology, or culture theory. These new perspectives have added richness and depth to our understanding of the past even as they have made us painfully aware of its incompleteness. Today, many historians wrestle with the bias in their own work—some opt for denial, others for exaggeration, still others for a kind of false modesty that drowns their point of view in details.

In a sense, all storytellers are historians—memoirists are historians of their own lives, journalists of the public moment, novelists of imagined places and times—and DEs find the historian's bias dilemma in a wide variety of manuscripts. Whether working with a family genealogist or a classicist reinterpreting an ancient battle, the DE is called upon to curb excesses, cull extraneous detail, and encourage a clear and convincing point of view.

Rabi'a el Saadawi was born in Yazoo, Mississippi, in 1955 and christened Aisha Yates. A year before she was born, her father, Alfonzo "Yazoo" Yates, became one of the first bluesmen to record under a genuine royalty contract in the post–"race record" period. Her mother was a soloist in a Baptist choir who spurned the "devil's music" her husband played, although not the money he earned by it. Aisha couldn't sing a note, but she found a surrogate passion in books on African American folk culture by Zora Neale Hurston. At Howard University in the 1970s, Aisha decided to follow in her heroine's footsteps by documenting the rise of African American music out of slave and post-slavery culture; she was convinced that her father's alleged devilry and her mother's divine gift shared common roots.

Then came graduate study in Berkeley, where she met members of the Sufi Mosque and converted. She renamed herself after Rabi'a bint Esmail al-Adawiya, an eighth-century saint who was sold into slavery and is credited with introducing the theme of Divine Love into Islamic mysticism; her surname she took from the Egyptian writer Nawal el Saadawi, a current pioneer for women's rights in the Muslim world. The poems of Rumi confirmed her belief that sensuality and spirituality could peacefully coexist: his songs about drinking and lust could have been improvised by her father over a stinging guitar, while his hymns to Divine Love evoked her mother's Negro spirituals.

The new Rabi'a wrote seminal studies of women converts to Islam in black America, and her memoir of making hajj to Mecca in 1994 was widely acclaimed for its vivid and evenhanded treatment of Muslim sectarianism. As a member of the liberal intelligentsia, she created a stir in 1990 by taking the veil, for reasons she had yet to fully explain. Now Rabi'a was working on her most important subject to date: a legendary figure named Mezzy Walker, who could prove to be the "missing link" between early Moorish slaves and the blues. She'd never before attempted a narrative of such historical sweep. To complicate matters further, the imam of her mosque was possessor of the Mezzy Walker archives and had stipulated right of final approval as a condition of granting her access. She appealed for help to Vanna Smythe, her editor at Brazier Books, for the moment leaving her imam unapprised.

## Client Profile: The Copublisher

Copublishers can be a lucrative source of work for DEs. However, not all copublishers are equal in this regard. The most common type of copublishing arrangement is between two houses who divvy up global distribution rights: a British house might sell off North American rights to a U.S. house, for instance, while retaining rights to the rest of the English-speaking world. This relationship usually has little bearing on the project's editorial development.

The more creative and challenging copublishing arrangements are those between a publisher and a cultural institution. Museums, schools, churches, government agencies, grassroots organizations, and many other kinds of entities establish publishing programs as a means of raising funds and extending their community outreach. Some of these groups have no production resources whatsoever; others have a small editing and design staff to produce brochures, posters, and programs but are unprepared to take on bookmaking. Still others retain complete control of the book's production and partner with the publishing house for distribution purposes only. Because these organizations are not primarily bookmakers, they tend to rely on DEs as consultants.

The DE who accepts a copublishing assignment should be sure to understand the nature of the contractual relationship among the collaborating entities. The DE will usually be hired by a publishing house but must not assume that this client calls the shots. Knowing who is really boss can save the DE weeks or months of frustration.

Farid Ibrahim al-Khadir had been imam at the Sufi Mosque in Berkeley, California, for more than a decade when Aisha Yates joined. She was a bright junior professor, but Farid hadn't paid her special attention—after all, his community had included famous actors, musicians, dancers, scientists, and philosophers since its founding by his predecessor in 1962. Unlike the American Sufi Fellowship, its Zen-influenced counterpart in San Francisco, the mosque had retained many of the traditions of mainstream Islam, including the daily call to prayer. But their progressive *shariah*—or set of rules to live by—also reflected the roots of Sufism by recognizing women as equals and eschewing outmoded laws of diet and attire. No one had been more surprised than Farid when Aisha, now Rabi'a, donned the veil.

Another surprise awaited when Rabi'a—who had volunteered to organize the papers of Farid's great teacher from Chicago, Hanbal ibn Muhammad Ali, after his death in 1997—discovered the Mezzy Walker archives. Farid had never heard of the mythical blues singer, but he quickly grasped the importance of the discovery: a *muezzin* and Sufi captured in Gambia and enslaved in the Mississippi Delta just prior to Emancipation could easily have had a formative influence on the blues. Farid himself had always heard the stylized keening of the *muezzin* in the moans of the bluesmen. To establish this link could do much to open up dialogue between peace-loving Sufism and militant Black Islam.

The articles Rabi'a had produced thus far were wise and illuminating, but somehow they didn't add up to a coherent story. She promised him an opportunity to review the final manuscript, which was being published under the joint imprint of the mosque and Brazier Books. An earlier, popularized version of Hanbal's teachings had sold 100,000 copies in a similar arrangement with Brazier. The Mezzy Walker story had the potential to reach a much larger audience of music lovers with the message of Sufism, but only if Rabi'a kept her spiritual gaze focused. Farid would ensure that she did.

## Assignment: The Sprawling Saga

When Vanna Smythe contacted her about the Rabi'a el Saadawi assignment, Hedda Miller hesitated. Her empirical cast of mind had little patience with mysticism, and she wasn't sure she could relate to a so-called liberal woman thinker who wore a head scarf. But she loved the blues—she and her cats listened to them at two in the morning, when she did her best freelance work. Her old farmhouse seemed to creak in sympathy with the twang of Sonny Boy Williamson's mouth harp. And the thought that some mythical folk hero, like Paul Bunyan or John Henry, could turn out to be a real historical figure—that was tantalizing.

Mezzy Walker's story spanned two continents, eight decades, and most of the key events in the transition from slave society to the post-Reconstruction period. But if the outline of Walker's biography was meaty enough to support a book-length work, the historical documentation was not. Mezzy had left little trace: he never cut a record, considering them the audio equivalent of the false image-making forbidden by the Koran. The only proofs of his existence were accounts in a cache of personal letters collected by Hanbal Ali and a lengthy interview conducted, but never published, by the *Chicago Defender* in 1908. These finds were archival gold, but they couldn't fill a book.

The author wisely chose to flesh out Mezzy's tale with larger societal narratives charting the presence of Islam among American slaves and the development of the blues. She had many insights into her material, but her chapters were discrete essays that veered between broad historical survey and closely

EXAMPLE 14. The unrevised TOC for the el Saadawi manuscript. The chapter titles do not build on each other—they read like the titles of articles published in different venues, which is what most of them are.

*Smashin' Seabirds: The Life and Legacy of Mezzy Walker*

Introduction: American Sufism Then and Now

1. Smashin' Seabirds: An Iconoclast's Legacy
2. The Missing *Chicago Defender* Interview
3. On the Veracity of Folk Legends
4. African Origins of the Song of Complaint
5. A Gallery of Muslims Enslaved in the New World
6. Sufi among the Seminoles
7. African Origins of the Pastoral Ballad
8. America as False Mecca
9. Levee Hollers, *Muezzin* Calls, and the Birth of the Blues
10. The Lynching of Mezzy Walker and the Rise of Black Islam

Conclusion: A New *Shariah* for the Twenty-First Century

argued exegeses of the Walker texts (example 14). Hedda's first task would be to decide whether the material would be better served by narrative or expository treatment.

## Untangle Timelines from Arguments

All discourse is storytelling. In a narrative, the story follows a subject (usually, but not always, a human character) through a series of events over time. In exposition, the story follows an idea through a series of arguments, also over time. In both cases, the forward motion of time is a key organizing feature. Most manuscripts have both timelines and lines of argument—the DE's task at this juncture is to decide which will dominate the book's structure. In this chapter, we'll follow the ramifications of choosing timeline over line of argument; in the next chapter, we'll do the reverse.

The pivotal question is whether the book's main subject is a concrete subject or an abstract idea. This distinction is not always crystal clear: most human characters interest us because they represent (or run counter to) a broader historical or cultural trend; and most ideas intrigue because they have some real-world application. To get a handle on whether narrative or exposition should dominate, the DE can make these assessments.

ASSESS SHARPNESS OF FOCUS. If the book's main subject is a single person, place, thing, or event, then narrative mode is probably indicated. If the subject is a cultural, societal, or global phenomenon, then expository mode may be more apt.

ASSESS ORIGINALITY. If the author's take on the subject is more a point of view than a full-blown interpretation of events, then narrative mode may be best. If the author's interpretation is so original that it requires marshaling evidence from diverse sources and disciplines, then exposition may be indicated.

ASSESS RELATIVE WEIGHT. The first two considerations aside, if the author's text contains 300 pages of story and only 100 pages of interpretation, or vice versa, then the dominant mode must obtain.

In Hedda's experience, most manuscripts with developmental problems clearly favored narrative or expository treatment, but this one by el Saadawi truly sat on the fence. She dug out notes from her class with Dr. Worth and was reminded to perform three assessments.

The first test was for sharpness of focus, and it yielded mixed results. On the one hand, Mezzy Walker was a colorful character whom readers would want to follow on his odyssey through life. Full of ingenious escapes, humorous adventures, brave battles, artistic achievement, and eventual tragedy, Mezzy's life was a movie option waiting to be picked up. On the other hand, the varied events in his life were emblematic of experiences of whole generations of Africans forcibly transplanted to America, and el Saadawi drew many insights from those connections. Hedda could see the text going either way.

How original were the author's insights? The second test had Hedda leaning toward expository mode. El Saadawi had done some impressive analysis of the historical import of early Islam and Sufism among American slaves and about the shared musical roots of Islamic culture and blues culture. The several key conclusions were as follows:

- Conclusion 1: That the ancient "song of complaint" still heard in the Sahel of Africa is the shared antecedent of both the *muezzin*'s call and the keening "holler" of the blues singer.
- Conclusion 2: That Mezzy's recognized influence on early blues masters represents the expression of Sufi values through this most American of musical traditions.
- Conclusion 3: That Sufism influenced early African American culture to embrace the flesh as a vessel for the spirit rather than its prison.
- Conclusion 4: That acknowledgment of the Sufi origins of the blues could help all American Muslims achieve a new *shariah* that looks for commonality and peace among America's diverse religious traditions.

Hedda found these arguments provocative and fascinating, but not entirely convincing. Mezzy's influence on the blues was pretty solidly documented, but the broader influence of Sufi slaves on black Christianity was much more tenuously established.

Still torn, Hedda turned to the third test, which assessed relative weight. She counted the pages of narrative versus argument—which was easy to do because el Saadawi had written the chapters as individual essays, and each was dominated by one mode or the other. Along with the introduction and conclusion, chapters 3, 8, and 9 were solidly expository, while the remaining chapters were narrative, although they told their stories in service of the author's arguments. So there she had it: the scales tipped in favor of narrative.

## Find the Main Timelines

Having decided to favor story over argument, the DE must now devise a strategy for managing the manuscript's narrative content. In some cases, the removal of expository material may leave a clear-cut, straightforward narrative—in which case, the DE can skip directly to finetuning the timeline (see below). In many projects with developmental needs, however, the DE will find an overabundance of competing narratives, some fully told, others only alluded to. To evaluate these diverse materials, the DE must identify the main timelines.

CREATE A MASTER TIMELINE. First, the DE creates a master timeline containing all significant events that occur in the manuscript, from earliest to most recent. In a text with a scrambled timeline, this can be quite challenging, unless the author has been scrupulous about managing tense changes and providing dates and times.

If the text is in relatively good shape, the events in this "kitchen sink" timeline will fall into a pattern of regular intervals (hours, days, years). Usually, however, a project with developmental needs will result in a draft timeline in which time speeds up, slows down, and jumps across stretches without comment. For now, the DE doesn't worry about these rough spots but simply focuses on getting the temporal sequence in correct order.

UNTANGLE TIMELINES. With the master timeline laid out, the DE can now lift out individual storylines and separate them for comparison. Most master timelines will contain the narratives of multiple characters and communities, some overlapping, others contiguous, still others separated by a gap of weeks or years. Here, the DE's function resembles untangling a rope—after the convoluted mess has been laid out flat on the dock, the knots and snags can be seen more easily and individual strands liberated.

It wasn't until she'd created a master timeline that Hedda saw clearly the shape of Mezzy Walker's story (example 15). And what a rollicking saga it was: Mezzy was a kind of Zelig of American slavery.

Among the last captives to make the Atlantic passage, Mezzy served briefly as a butler in a southern plantation and then blazed an itinerant trail that touched

EXAMPLE 15. Master timeline and component timelines in the el Saadawi manuscript. In the right-hand column, the manuscript's narrative events remain a jumble, but ordering the events by date allows the DE to lift out four different storylines.

| | | |
|---|---|---|
| **1800** | 1775 | Peeter Salem (Saleem) fights in Battle of Bunker Hill |
| | 1803 | Two Muslim Gullah communities founded |
| | 1833 | Maroon leader Abraham signs relocation treaty |
| | 1845 | Mezzy born in Gambia |
| | 1856 | Hajj Ali ("Hi Jolly") joins U.S. cavalry as cameleer |
| | 1859 | Mezzy goes on hajj |
| | 1860 | Mezzy captured and enslaved |
| | 1863 | Mezzy escapes and lives among Seminoles |
| | 1863 | Muslims fight for Union in Civil War |
| | 1870 | Delta reclamation begins |
| | 1872 | Mezzy sets up as cattle rancher |
| | 1875 | Mezzy joins Hi Jolly in Arizona |
| | 1884 | Mezzy works on levees as muleskinner |
| | 1890 | Folk blues prevalent in rural areas |
| | 1892 | Mezzy hops boxcar to Chicago |
| **1900** | 1903 | W. C. Handy first hears blues played at Crossroads |
| | 1908 | Mezzy interviewed by *Chicago Defender* |
| | 1910 | Inayat Khan brings universal Sufism from India to U.S. |
| | 1912 | Mezzy lynched |
| | 1912 | Handy publishes "Memphis Blues" |
| | 1914 | Black migration north begins |
| | 1917 | First jazz recording, "Livery Stable Blues" |
| | 1920 | Mamie Smith's "Crazy Blues" ushers in Jazz Age |
| | 1926 | Blind Lemon Jefferson makes first race record |
| | 1927 | Sufi International Order takes up headquarters in NYC |
| | 1929 | W. D. Fard founds Lost-Found Nation of Islam |
| | 1935 | Lomaxes and Zora Neale Hurston document blues |
| | 1954 | Author's father makes blues recording |
| | 1957 | Eisenhower speaks at opening of Islamic Center in D.C. |
| | 1957 | Race record period ends with real contracts |
| | 1965 | Malcolm X assassinated |
| | 1966 | Author's junior high school desegregated |
| | 1975 | Author first hears Sufi teachings |
| | 1975 | Warith Deen Mohammed mainstreams Nation of Islam |
| | 1990 | Author takes veil |
| | 1994 | Author goes on hajj |
| | 1996 | Clinton White House celebrates end of Ramadan |
| | 1997 | Author appointed professor of history |
| **2000** | | |

Left-column storyline brackets: Mezzy's story · History of Islam in U.S. · History of the blues · Author's story on many aspects of black Reconstruction experience. He was said to have fought with the Maroons in the Dismal Swamp and the Seminoles of the Florida panhandle; he cosigned the treaty that resettled the Indians in Oklahoma and became a prosperous cattle rancher; he lost his business to Jim Crow, moved west to raise camels for the U.S. cavalry with the legendary Hajj Ali (a.k.a. "Hi Jolly"), and was eventually indentured as a muleskinner on the Delta levee system. While there, he was said to have perfected the art of the "holler," influencing a score of country bluesmen before moving north to Chicago. He stayed there for a decade, never consenting to be recorded, although most of the bluesmen and -women of that era cited him as a mentor. For reasons that remain a mystery, he returned to the Delta in 1912 and was lynched for allegedly making a pass at a white woman.

This itinerant biography overlapped with the two larger cultural narratives that el Saadawi wished to relate, namely, the history of Islam in America and the development of the blues. Historically speaking, Mezzy's life sat smack-dab in the middle of the Islam narrative and barely overlapped with the beginnings of the more recent blues narrative. Therefore, if Hedda chose to use the events of Mezzy's life to frame both of these larger stories, she'd have to employ some clever timeline tricks.

Finally, there was the problem of the author's own timeline, which cropped up anecdotally at various points in the manuscript. Of the generation of self-reflexive ethnographers schooled in the 1970s and 1980s, el Saadawi felt obliged to disclose her bias by telling how the events of the larger narrative affected her personally. But, in historical terms, el Saadawi was a latecomer to the central narratives, and her relationship with Islam in particular was complicated and unclear. So Hedda decided to put the author's story on the back burner and focus on getting the three main timelines in sync.

## Brainstorm Timeline Strategies

Up to this point, the DE has focused on getting the temporal order straight. For most books, a straight timeline is the best way to keep a storyline simple and clear. This timeline is the structure of the fairy tales we hear from infancy, and because of these early experiences we tend to assume it is the most accurate narrative form. We all start out breathlessly recounting our schoolyard adventures with relentless fidelity to time: first this happened, and then this happened, and then so-and-so said this . . .

But as we grow older we learn to leave out irrelevant details and skip over spells of inactivity, so that even the straight timeline departs from the absolute reality of time. As our understanding of time grows more complex, we begin to realize that many, many stories are taking place simultaneously.

And we experience other twists and turns in the flow of time via our dreams and memories, our readings of history and prophecy. By adolescence, our storytelling mode incorporates a full complement of sophisticated narrative tricks for playing with time.

Before composing a new timeline for a manuscript, the DE does well to brainstorm whether any templates other than the straight timeline might be apt. These patterns for "juggling time" can be difficult to orchestrate across the length of a book—they are more often used at the chapter or passage level to vary a narrative's pace. These other templates include the reverse timeline, alternate viewpoints, parallel timelines, rotating narratives, and alternate outcomes. (An infinite number of variations on these templates can be achieved by delaying, refracting, or omitting key events in the timeline—see sidebar, "The Art of Suspense.")

The result of this brainstorming session may well be a strengthened resolve on the part of the DE to stick to a straight timeline. But by considering the more complicated templates and devices now, the DE can eliminate those that are infeasible and keep ready those that may come in handy as the new timeline takes shape.

The descriptions that follow cite examples from fiction because the templates can be seen more clearly in prose over which the author has complete control. But these templates are just as useful in works of nonfiction.

REVERSE TIMELINE. As the name implies, this is the straight timeline run backward. A classic device of science fiction writing, this strategy is most familiar to us from film and television, where it has become standard idiom for a kind of epiphany: in a reverse montage, a character suddenly realizes the causal relationships between events that until then seemed unrelated. As a narrative device, the reverse timeline is usually an approximation: it moves the story backward at regular intervals but, between intervals, tells each episode in forward temporal motion.

A spectacular exception is *Time's Arrow* (1991), in which Martin Amis reverses his protagonist's life story moment by moment. For the reader, it's like watching a movie rewind: characters walk backward, speak backward, experience their bodily functions in reverse, and experience their emotions in an inverted order that is surprisingly affecting. The novel is a profound, ironic meditation on the nature of human love, cruelty, and guilt.

ALTERNATE VIEWPOINTS. In this version of the straight timeline, the point of view is passed among several central characters. Because no two people experience the same event in exactly the same way, this device resonates with readers as authentic. The principal challenge in deploying this device is to avoid repetition: the reader should hear about an event more than once only when the narrators have distinctive perspectives to offer.

## The Art of Suspense

In a fundamental sense, all books are mystery stories. Readers are attracted by an intriguing premise—an unsolved mystery—and keep reading until the author has answered all their questions. If the central mystery is solved too early or late in the book, the reader will put the book aside in boredom or frustration. But if the author feeds the reader clues bit by bit, a growing sense of anticipation lures the reader onward.

The basic timeline options explored in this chapter are all equally useful in building suspense. That's because suspense relies not on the manipulation of temporal sequence but rather on the sequence in which readers come to know crucial facts. True, authors often divulge or withhold information by jumping back and forth in time, but it is the steady disbursal of clues that keeps the reader engaged. This effect can be achieved quite vividly without temporal shifts: our earliest mythmakers held their audiences spellbound with stories adhering strictly to the straight timeline.

CREATE TENSION. The first step in building suspense is to establish a central conflict: two kings are at war; a prostitute has been murdered; a young artist suffers angst; a new economic theory has come under fire. By withholding information about how this conflict will be resolved (or not), the author creates a sense of mystery.

ARRANGE EPIPHANIES. Next, the author disburses clues to help the reader solve the central mystery: the kings are brothers whose father banished the elder; the prostitute was known to consort with drug lords; the young artist is mistreated by his classmates; the proponent of the new economic theory is an oil baron. The clues should be spaced out in the narrative or argument so that each one catches the reader by surprise.

PLACE THE CLIMAX. The central clue—the solution to the mystery—should be withheld until late in the book: the elder brother kills the younger and usurps his throne; the prostitute was mistaken for an informant; the young artist's angst inspires revelatory works of art; the economic theory is shown to serve the short-term political goals of the oil lobby. In most books, the climax occurs in the penultimate chapter, leaving one chapter to tie up the loose ends.

TIE UP THE LOOSE ENDS. Once the climax has passed, the author must tie up any unresolved loose ends quickly: the fratricidal king dies of remorse; the informant's true identity remains a mystery; the young artist's satisfaction with his art assuages his angst; the discredited theory is formally rejected by the nation's leading schools of economics. The French term for this process, *dénouement*, means to untie the last knot.

As the examples above suggest, the art of suspense may be employed in the service of either narrative or exposition. In deductive arguments, in which the main conclusion is stated up front, the mystery is not the conclusion itself but rather how the author will arrive at it (see chapter 5).

In his masterly short story *In a Bamboo Grove* (1922), Ryūnosuke Akutagawa tells the story of a rape and murder through the testimony of a series of witnesses. Each sworn statement adds details to the central story: a woodcutter finds the first, scant evidence; a priest impugns an unidentified passerby; a policeman links a particular bandit to the evidence. Then the three star witnesses each, in turn, confess to the murder: the bandit out of pride, the wife out of guilt, and the dead husband (speaking through a medium) out of shame. Although readers are left wondering who actually thrust the knife, they realize that, on a moral level, all three confessions are true.

PARALLEL TIMELINES. These are multiple straight timelines, often with each narrated from a different point of view, and usually with some point of intersection late in the book. This device is the stock-in-trade of disaster films, which introduce the audience to a handful of (thinly drawn) characters before placing them all aboard a sinking ship. A celebrated example is Thornton Wilder's *The Bridge of San Luis Rey* (1927), in which five characters' lives lead inexorably toward a fatal crossing on an ancient Peruvian footbridge. Here, the challenge is to ensure that all timelines pay off at the end—the reader should not be left wondering about any of the narrative strands.

ROTATING NARRATIVES. These multiple straight timelines do not intersect directly but resonate with each other thematically. In the virtuosic *Cloud Atlas* (2004), David Mitchell rolls out six narratives that progress from an 1850 expedition among remote Pacific islands, through Depression-era Belgium and 1970s Los Angeles, to contemporary Britain, before launching into a near future in which Korea gains world dominance by clone power and, finally, a distant future in postapocalyptic Hawaii. Mitchell interrupts each of the first five narratives at a climactic moment, then resumes them in reverse order to gradually tie up the loose ends. Connections between the stories are oblique, with each story playing a minor role in the next until, at the center of the Hawaiian story, a Huck Finn character verbalizes the thematic links as a "cloud atlas" guiding the course of human history.

ALTERNATE OUTCOMES. This is a single straight timeline repeated several times, with each version yielding a different outcome. This strategy is a favorite of mystery writers: the events leading up to a crime are narrated several times, each with a different suspect featured. The technique is so common that Agatha Christie famously inverted it. In *Murder on the Orient Express* (1934), she narrated plausible versions of the crime with a dozen different suspects, then revealed that all the versions were true—that each suspect had literally had a hand in the victim's death from twelve stab wounds.

This device is difficult to use in narrative without resorting to gimmickry and losing the reader's sympathy. Its expository counterpart, however (see chapter 5), is very useful in exploring the different possible outcomes of a single line of reasoning.

Hedda was pretty sure she'd be sticking with a straight timeline for this book. Its multiple storylines had enough twists and turns in them that adding temporal shifts would be gilding the lily. Even so, she liked to go through the exercise of reviewing the various timeline templates and tricks that Dr. Worth had taught.

She knew right away that the most exotic option, the reverse timeline, could be eliminated from consideration. Of course, technically, this timeline could be executed, beginning with el Saadawi's own narrative and tunneling backward through history to the origins of first the blues and then the early Muslim slaves. But el Saadawi's story did not warrant this banner treatment, and the historical developments were novel assertions that challenged conventional wisdom enough without the further complication of a reverse narrative.

The use of alternate viewpoints would also be tough to execute. Neither of the two broader narratives, religious and musical, featured a singular point of view; even Mezzy's point of view was hard to pin down, his correspondence written with stoic reserve. Parallel timelines could be discounted because the three main storylines were not parallel: as a Muslim slave, Mezzy came late to the historical narrative; as a blues singer, he was mostly a forerunner.

The alternate outcomes option had a bit more potential, but not much. If the book were framed by Mezzy's biography, then el Saadawi could provide multiple speculations as to why Mezzy returned to the Delta to die. If the book were framed by the larger narrative of Islam in America, the author could trace narrative arcs leading to a number of possible outcomes ranging from increased sectarian strife to Muslim assimilation into American society. But again, these pyrotechnics seemed unnecessary in a narrative already replete with surprises.

Finally, Hedda considered the rotating narratives option. If she were to select Mezzy's story as the framing narrative, then she'd have to somehow stuff the larger histories into that narrower frame—and for that purpose, rotating narratives could be quite effective. Each chapter could begin with a period in Mezzy's life, then segue into parallels in American Muslim history, and wind up with relevance to the future development of the blues. Hedda was beginning to see the silhouette of a plan.

## Compose the New Timeline

By now, brainstorming should have given the DE a clear sense of the advantages and challenges associated with using each of the component timelines as a narrative framework. To finalize this decision, DEs may review their options in light of two crucial factors.

CONSIDER THE AUTHOR'S STRENGTHS. First, the DE should choose timeline strategies in light of a candid assessment of the author's narrative abilities. The DE may devise an ingenious plan for weaving a dozen narrative strands into a densely textured fabric, but if the author doesn't have a knack for transition, the DE will end up ghostwriting. The text's subject may cry out for novelistic treatment, but if the author isn't proficient with the tools of a novelist—character, setting, and plot—then the DE's plan will fail.

CONSIDER THE READER'S NEEDS. Second, the DE should verify that the composite timeline will meet the needs of the audience. A timeline with many twists and turns may suit laypersons reading the book primarily for entertainment, but a specialist who needs direct access to data will be impatient with such techniques. Conversely, a straight timeline may prove mind-numbing to the average reader whose curiosity about a subject isn't sated until page 295.

Brainstorming had led Hedda to favor a rotating narrative. For this plan, Mezzy's biography was the most natural choice of framing timeline. After all, el Saadawi was arguing that Mezzy personally influenced the development of the blues. And if his role in the growth of Islam in America was less pivotal, as a Sufi he nevertheless represented that strain of Islam which the author considered to have the brightest future for integration with democratic society.

But was the author capable of executing a strategy as complex as the rotating narrative? And did that structure really suit the needs of the book's audience?

The publisher's brief stated that the book would necessarily have a specialist market in the fields of Islamic studies and music history because of the original archival research it contained. This audience, already familiar with the details of the broader narratives, might well be frustrated by the scattering of Mezzy anecdotes like breadcrumbs along the discursive trail. But Brazier saw potential for "crossover appeal" to a trade audience, and surely the average reader would benefit from having the relevance of key events in Mezzy's life "spelled out" in their historical contexts. By drafting the material as a series of essays, the author had already signaled a commitment to highlighting these comparisons, and the form of the rotating narrative would make her job easier.

Hedda now had the outline worked out to her satisfaction (example 16). Time to gussy it up a bit.

## Finetune the Timeline

So, the grand narrative has been established, with events from multiple narratives corralled into single file. Now the DE must impose logical breaks on this uninterrupted stream of story. Some of the breaks will be obvious, as

The el Saadawi timelines recombined. Note how each chapter is a single rotation of three narratives: first Mezzy's biography, then the history of Muslim slaves, and finally the story of the blues.

1. Humble Origins
   Mezzy born in Gambia
   Other Moorish slaves high born
   Low birth of blues as Delta reclamation
      begins
2. Early Hardship
   Mezzy goes on hajj
   Muslim Gullah communities founded
   Folk blues arise out of hardscrabble
      Delta life
3. Capture at the Crossroads
   Mezzy's Atlantic passage
   Muslim slaves in increasing numbers
   Handy first hears blues played at
      Crossroads
4. Slaves of Privilege
   Mezzy serves as butler
   Muslim slaves as crew leaders, overseers
   Handy publishes "Memphis Blues"
5. Escape and the Fugitive Life
   Mezzy's escape
   Rewards posted for Muslim slaves
   Blues nurtured in prison chain gangs
6. Life among the Indians
   Mezzy's time with the Seminoles
   Other Muslim guerrilla leaders in the
      swamps
   The New Orleans jazz tradition of "Mardi
      Gras Indians"
7. A Life of Free Enterprise
   Mezzy sets up as cattle rancher
   Muslim merchants prosper in D.C.

First jazz recordings offer hope of
   prosperity
8. Romantic Love
   Mezzy falls in love in Arizona
   Polygamy of Hajj Ali ("Hi Jolly") tolerated
   Race records usher in licentious Jazz Age
9. Indentured Servitude
   Mezzy forced into labor as muleskinner
   The Muslim contribution to the levee
      system
   Race record labels cut artists out of
      profits
10. Migration and Immigration
   Mezzy hops boxcar to Chicago
   Sufism arrives on the shores of the
      United States
   Black northward migration at its zenith
11. On and Off the Record
   Mezzy interviewed by *Chicago
      Defender*
   Sufi International Order publishes tracts
   Lomaxes and Hurston document the blues
12. Freedom at Last
   Mezzy achieves freedom through death
   Islam gains acceptance as protected
      religious faith
   Race contract period ends
13. Legacy
   Mezzy inspires Seabird smashers
   Islam experiences backlash after 9/11
   Blues influence rock'n'roll and rap
      music

when the perspective shifts from one character to another. Other breaks may be harder to place; in those cases, there may be no "right answer." For instance, in an autobiography, a wedding might serve equally well as the ending of a chapter about childhood or as the opening for a chapter about adult life.

OBSERVE RULES OF BALANCE. There are no hard-and-fast laws about how to balance a table of contents, but several rules of thumb are widely observed by authors and editors:

- Most books of average length (say, 275 printed pages) should have a minimum of six chapters; a good chapter length is between 20 and 40 double-spaced manuscript pages.
- A book should not be divided into parts if any of those parts will contain only one chapter. Similarly, chapters should not be divided into subsections if any of the chapters will contain only one subsection.
- Except in special circumstances, if one chapter contains subsections, all chapters should contain subsections.
- Some variation in length of parts, chapters, and subsections is permissible, even desirable—but chapters of five pages or fewer should be avoided, as should single-paragraph subsections.

Enough "shoulds" already. These rules reflect the expectations today's reader brings to a nonfiction book, but authors and DEs can deviate from these conventions so long as the reader will be able to infer a good reason for the departure. Thus, for instance, if a baroness will serve as the prism through which an author views medieval society, the reader will forgive a first chapter summarizing the noblewoman's biography that is shorter or longer than the other chapters in the book. Alternatively, the author and DE might decide to cut up the biography into unnumbered interludes—each one or two pages long—that return the reader to the baroness-as-prism at regular intervals.

DRAFT WORKING CHAPTER TITLES. Once pacing and balance are established, the DE should draft working titles for all chapters. The table of contents should tell enough of a story to capture the bookstore browser's attention without giving away too much of the plot. The table of contents is like a cinematic trailer: a good one causes the filmgoer to say, "I wanna see that movie," while a bad one gives away a drama's climax or a comedy's funniest moment. Again, I offer rules of thumb with the clichéd proviso that rules are made to be broken:

- Short, pithy chapter titles are generally better than long.
- Chapter titles should mostly be grammatically parallel (i.e., all fragments, all full sentences, all prepositional phrases, or all adjectival or nominative phrases).
- A chapter subtitle should be used only if at least one other chapter has a subtitle.
- Quotations in chapter titles should be avoided unless the book is an oral history.
- Concrete chapter titles are preferred over abstract ones.

Each chapter in this book begins with a "bad" table of contents and ends with a "good" one; compare the pairs to pick up pointers for drafting tables of contents that sell.

---

Hedda had been assuming that she would structure the manuscript one narrative rotation per chapter, with each opening on an episode in Mezzy's life. But now that she looked at her current outline, she was having second thoughts. The main narrative spanned two continents and two centuries, and the reader might appreciate a larger organizational framework. Should she consider aggregating the chapters? Or grouping them in parts?

To answer the first question, Hedda looked at which chapters had mutual affinities and decided that the chapters could logically be combined in pairs: chapters 1 and 2 could become a single chapter about African origins; chapters 3 and 4 about slavery days; chapters 5 and 6 about runaway life; chapters 7 and 8 about Emancipation; chapters 9 and 10 about the Reconstruction era; chapters 11 and 12 about the northward migration; and chapter 13 about the legacy of all of these historical developments. Hedda then did some quick "casting off," or counting of pages. Because the unrevised manuscript blended the three main narratives so thoroughly, she could only come up with rough numbers, but her best guess was that the seven-chapter plan would result in a shortest chapter of 21 pages and a longest chapter of 86 pages. This disparity was much too ungainly to allow for a balanced outline.

Next, Hedda considered what logical part breaks might reasonably be imposed on her outline. A table of contents with seven parts containing two chapters apiece was out of the question; what larger units of time could she distinguish? The first scheme that came to mind was this: part I about slavery days (chapters 1 through 6), part II about Emancipation and Reconstruction (chapters 7 through 10), and part III about the post-Reconstruction era (chapters 11 through 13). Another option would be to divide the text into just two parts, "Slavery and Emancipation" and "Reconstruction and After," with the break between chapters 6 and 7. But both schemes seemed artificial, and neither added much in the way of clarity.

So Hedda decided to stick to her original plan of one narrative rotation per chapter, but with the final rotation treated as a conclusion rather than an ominously numbered chapter 13. If Hedda could get the author to point up the themes in a new introduction focused on the main thesis, then the thematic links would function effectively and subtly.

Having settled her qualms, Hedda could now go about drafting chapter titles. Happily, the text was a treasure trove of evocative song titles from Mezzy Walker's repertoire. "Studyin' Sunrise" was the most contemplative of the blues numbers, evoking the serenity of the *muezzin*'s wait for dawn, and it aptly set the tone for Mezzy's early, spiritually rich life in Africa. "Yassuh Whiskey" was a subversive pun on Yazoo, the name of the town in which Mezzy was owned (and the author, coincidentally, born). Some song titles, like "The Bloodhounds on My Trace" and "What the Mob Don't Know (Gonna Hurt Me)" had obvious relevance, while others were more poetically evocative. The African American expression "Nose Wide Open" managed to express both the intoxication of romantic love and the feelings of tenderness and sympathy of animal handlers for their charges. And "Hungry Cuz I Can Be" was Mezzy's brave assertion that hunger imposed by poverty was no less holy and cleansing than volitional fasting at Ramadan.

The only title not drawn from Mezzy's songbook was "Smashin' Seabirds." "Seabird" was black slang for the Seeburg Company's jukebox, which would become the chief outlet of entertainment and cultural pride during the "race records" period. Mezzy never lived to see the jukebox, but some of his followers in Chicago noted the adverse effect of the recording industry on the art of improvisation—audiences clamored for performers to "sing it like you did on the record"—so for a brief period in 1928 they took to vandalizing the machines throughout the downtown area "in the name of Mezzy." The phrase "Smashin' Seabirds" had been misleading and anachronistic as a title for the book, but here, as a title about Mezzy Walker's musical legacy, it seemed apt.

## Restore Bits of Argument

We noted above that most nonfiction books have both a timeline and a line of argument. Our purpose in choosing timeline over argument was to lend the manuscript structural coherence—to give the reader a main storyline to follow. With that main line firmly established, we can break it up a bit and allow a digression now and then, like a movie voiceover, to help interpret events for the reader.

LOCATE CHOICE BITS. Return to your trusty legal pad of notes and look for the most interesting and important of the discarded bits of argument. Then review your revised table of contents for chapters in which those bits might fit well. When leavening a narrative with bits of argument, be sure to space out those expository digressions: you don't want them all in the first half of the book, for instance. The reader should develop a sense of rhythm between the dominant and subordinate lines.

ARRANGE THE BITS. Do your best to arrange the subordinate bits of argument so that they build their own momentum. In a manuscript narrating the life of Einstein, the reader will expect a parallel line that follows the conceptual development of theoretical physics.

KEEP DIGRESSIONS SHORT. Finally, take care to avoid interrupting the main line with overlong digressions. Most subordinate bits are best kept to a couple of paragraphs, though you might allow an occasional detour of three to five pages. The longer the digression, the more important it should be to the main line of discourse. In that Einstein biography, you might allow a long digression to explain the theory of relativity in layperson's terms, but you wouldn't give that much space to any of Einstein's more obscure discoveries.

With her narrative plan firmly in place, Hedda now looked for ways to reintegrate the four conclusions she'd identified when she was untangling timelines from arguments. She went back to her notepad to see how many times, and in which chapters, the four arguments cropped up. In each case, she found a whole section of argument ten to twenty pages in length—these were too long to be dropped into the narrative whole. So she decided on a strategy of breaking down each argument into paragraph-length points to be integrated with the narrative, then allowing a longer digression of several pages at the argument's summative moment.

For now, at the planning stage, she was mostly concerned with where, and in which order, these "digressive" conclusions would fall. Conclusion 1, about the grounding of both *muezzin* and blues musical forms in the African song of complaint, could fall in any of the first three chapters, which shared a theme of commiseration. Now that she thought about it, conclusion 2, concerning Sufi influence on the blues, should occur later than conclusion 3—which postulated Sufi influence on the African American version of Christian belief—because the religious dynamic was evident long before the blues were born. Conclusion 4, proffering a new *shariah* of peace, was easy to place: the author's final word on the relevance of her narrative, it belonged near the end of the book.

With the order of the author's line of argument established, Hedda considered exactly where to place the summative bits (example 17). Her impulse was to place them at the ends of chapters rather than interrupting the "Mezzy, Muslims, blues" rotations.

Conclusion 1 could cap off any of the first five chapters, but she decided to place it at the end of chapter 3 for two reasons: first, it would speak eloquently to the theme of the title, "Lonesome Lawd"; and second, it would flow naturally from the moment that music historians consider the "birth of the blues"—the day in 1903 when W. C. Handy first heard the blues played at "the Crossroads" of the Southern and Yazoo railroad lines.

Conclusion 3 (now in second position) was harder to place. Its claim could speak to any of the events narrated from chapter 4 onward, but positioning it after the blues narrative in any of those rotations could make for an awkward transition. After several days of feeling stymied, Hedda had a realization: the

EXAMPLE 17. The same el Saadawi timeline, but with chapter titles drafted and conclusions placed. This plan avoids bunching up the conclusions; it situates them in the discussions to which they most pertain and arranges them in roughly ascending order of speculative originality.

1. Studyin' Sunrise: Humble Origins
   Mezzy born in Gambia
   Other Moorish slaves high born
   Low birth of blues as Delta reclamation
     begins
2. Travelin' Man: Early Hardship
   Mezzy goes on hajj
   Muslim Gullah communities founded
   Folk blues arise out of hardscrabble
     Delta life
3. Lonesome Lawd: Capture at the Crossroads
   Mezzy's Atlantic passage
   Muslim slaves in increasing numbers
   Handy first hears blues played at
     Crossroads
   **Conclusion 1: The song of complaint**
4. Yassuh Whiskey: Slaves of Privilege
   Mezzy serves as butler
   Muslim slaves as crew leaders, overseers
   Handy publishes "Memphis Blues"
5. The Bloodhounds on My Trace: Escape and
     the Fugitive Life
   Mezzy's escape
   Rewards posted for Muslim slaves
   Blues nurtured in prison chain gangs
6. Angel Left a Feather: Life among the Indians
   Mezzy's time with the Seminoles
   Other Muslim guerrilla leaders in the
     swamps
   The New Orleans jazz tradition of "Mardi
     Gras Indians"
   **Conclusion 3: Sufi influence on slave
     Christianity**
7. The Whole Damn Jinte: A Life of Free
     Enterprise

Mezzy sets up as cattle rancher
Muslim merchants prosper in D.C.
First jazz recordings offer hope of
  prosperity
8. Nose Wide Open: Romantic Love
   Mezzy falls in love in Arizona
   Polygamy of Hajj Ali ("Hi Jolly") tolerated
   Race records usher in licentious Jazz Age
9. Beautemous Hollers: Indentured Servitude
   Mezzy forced into labor as muleskinner
   The Muslim contribution to the levee
     system
   Race record labels cut artists out of profits
10. The Roustabout's Dream: Migration and
     Immigration
   Mezzy hops boxcar to Chicago
   Sufism arrives on the shores of the United
     States
   Black northward migration at its zenith
   **Conclusion 2: Sufi influence on the blues**
11. Hungry Cuz I Can Be: On and Off the Record
   Mezzy interviewed by *Chicago Defender*
   Sufi International Order publishes tracts
   Lomaxes and Hurston document the blues
12. What the Mob Don't Know (Gonna Hurt
     Me): Freedom at Last
   Mezzy achieves freedom through death
   Islam gains acceptance as protected
     religious faith
   Race contract period ends
Smashin' Seabirds: Legacy
   Mezzy inspires Seabird smashers
   Islam experiences backlash after 9/11
   Blues influence rock'n'roll and rap music
   **Conclusion 4: A new *shariah* of peace**

fusion of flesh and spirit in religious belief was also a characteristic of American Indian culture. The narrative detailed how both Muslim and Christian slaves had fought with the Indians in the swamp wars against white encroachment on native land; in gratitude, the Indians sheltered runaway slaves. African American respect for Indians eventually inspired the New Orleans tradition of the Mardi

Gras Indians with which chapter 6 ended. So conclusion 3 could be slotted in there.

Conclusion 2 (now third) was easier to place, as it dealt directly with the blues and would afford an easy transition from the blues passage at the end of either chapter 10 or 11. Although either position would work, Hedda chose to place the argument at the end of chapter 10 because she wanted to signal that the hypothetical influence of Sufism on the blues would have occurred informally in the musical style's early years, prior to the establishment of the Sufi International Order in New York City.

Finally, conclusion 4 would stay where it was in the author's original draft, at the close of the book, where it provided a perhaps unduly hopeful view of the future for Islam in America. Hedda suspected that the Muslim situation would get worse before it got better, but her job was to organize the author's thoughts, not interject her own.

✳

With a fully developed outline now in hand, Hedda could write up a plan for the client. (For the plan in its entirety, see chapter 6.) In it, she detailed the logic by which she arrived at her choices of narrative mode over exposition, of Mezzy's biography as the framing timeline, and of the placement of el Saadawi's four main arguments. The author and publisher were pleased with the results, but Imam al-Khadir was a tougher sell. Unsurprisingly, the Berkeley imam worried that the book focused too heavily on the blues and not enough on Sufism.

Vanna Smythe asked Hedda to join her in a four-way telephone conference with the author and the imam. In years of solitary life as a freelance editor, Hedda had grown uncomfortable with business meetings, but she recognized that face-to-face, or voice-to-voice, communication could sometimes achieve goals that letters and emails could not.

When the conference began, Vanna attempted to persuade the imam that focusing on the blues theme, and Mezzy as a colorful American character, would help the book reach a larger audience.

"Those readers will hear all about Sufism once they start reading," she said, "but if we hit them with Sufism up front, we'll reach a smaller demographic of people already sympathetic toward mysticism."

"I understand," Imam al-Khadir said. "But just reading this table of contents, you wouldn't know that Sufism is a part of the story at all."

"How about," Hedda interrupted. "Ms. el Saadawi, you've already written quite a bit about Sufism generally. Somewhere—I can't remember where, ex-actly—you said that Mezzy had two legacies, one musical and the other spiri-

Muezzin *on the Levee: The Life and Legacies of Bluesman Mezzy Walker*

Introduction: America's First Sufi? The Spiritual Legacy

1. Studyin' Sunrise: The Call to Prayer
2. Travelin' Man: The Road to Mecca
3. Lonesome Lawd: The Atlantic Passage
4. Yassuh Whiskey: Butler in the Big House
5. The Bloodhounds on My Trace: Life in Hiding
6. Angel Left a Feather: War and Peace among the Seminoles
7. The Whole Damn Jinte: A Season of Prosperity
8. Nose Wide Open: Loving Women, Kissing Camels
9. Beautemous Hollers: Life as a Muleskinner
10. The Roustabout's Dream: North at Last
11. Hungry Cuz I Can Be: Making the Chicago Scene
12. What the Mob Don't Know (Gonna Hurt Me): Death by Lynching

Conclusion: Smashin' Seabirds: The Musical Legacy
Afterword: A View from Behind the Veil
Appendix: A Brief History of Muslims in the New World

tual. What if we decided to add an introduction on Mezzy's spiritual legacy to complement the conclusion about his musical legacy?"

"Yes!" said the imam. "That is where Sufism belongs, up front." After a dramatic pause, the author weighed in: "I agree; that seems to be a good solution."

The group worked out some other details, including the addition of an appendix that would succinctly outline the history of Muslims in the New World. Hedda revised the working table of contents accordingly (example 18) and updated the plan to reflect these decisions. In the months that followed, Hedda and Rabi'a spoke often over the phone, brainstorming for transition material, which Rabi'a would draft and Hedda would edit into effective form. Eventually, Hedda felt comfortable enough with Rabi'a to ask about her veil.

"You're such a powerful—I hate to use the phrase—role model to young women," Hedda said. "Why put on this symbol of subjugation, especially when your own congregation doesn't require it?"

"I don't know," admitted Rabi'a. "Maybe it's because I want to reach out to other Muslims here in the United States. You know, the word *islam* means 'to submit,' and this veil is a sign of my submission to God. Maybe that's why Mezzy went back to the Delta. He knew it was dangerous, just like I know it can be dangerous to walk these streets in a head scarf. But he was submitting to the will of God. Sometimes you just know that, if you want the world's perceptions to change, you have to be the one to change them."

Author and editor fell silent. Both knew they had witnessed the birth of a key insight. They agreed to add an afterword in which the author reinstated—albeit in much briefer form—her personal narrative, which had been excised from the main body of the text. It was this personal insight that gave the book's story contemporary relevance—it found its way into the book's flap copy and press releases and was often the point of embarkation for interviews. Hedda heard from Rabi'a a couple of times after the book was published, then no more. She thought of her whenever she started an evening's work by clicking her iPod to shuffle through her playlist of Delta blues.

# 5 ✳ EXPOSITION ✳ *Deploying the Argument*

Theorists may resist the assertion that exposition is another form of storytelling. For more than two thousand years, rhetoric has been distinguished from storytelling as a skill relying on abstract processes of logic and persuasion; since Hellenistic times, Platonic ideals have hovered on a geometric plane just above our heads, turning our real experiences into examples of universal types. This disconnection of concepts from narrative particulars allows a philosopher to notice broad patterns in human affairs, a biochemist to see the math behind a bodily function, a civic leader to extrapolate universal rights from the suffering of individuals. It also allows us to understand our experiences as examples of larger trends. But the kernel of any theory, however grand, is a human story: in our culture, $E = mc^2$ is shorthand for our foundational story, the birth of the universe. When we argue for rights or values or theories that we hold dear, we must not forget the real experiences at their core.

This chapter focuses on manuscripts for which a clear main thesis has already been developed. (If yours does not have one, please return to chapter 3.) There are many ways to argue any given thesis. This chapter helps DE and author to beat a path from main thesis to main conclusion through the dense underbrush of supporting arguments.

In our case study, a scientist with important neurological discoveries to his credit has extended his studies into the realms of psychotherapy and international politics. The arguments he uses to support his main thesis vary in strength and relevance, and the publisher is concerned that his forays outside his own discipline will draw fire from critics in all three areas. The DE is engaged to help the author prioritize his supporting arguments, weed out those that detract from his discourse, and deploy the keepers effectively.

## Author Profile: The Theorist

In the late twentieth century, a mania for theory accompanied revolutions in social change, cultural awareness, and scientific understanding. Now that the theory boom is bust, it is hard to say whether all that postmodern thinking was cause, effect, or coincidence. It seems reasonable to surmise that the theorists' dismantling of old notions of gender, race, class, age, and sexuality played a decisive role in accelerating a process of social enlightenment. But the theory rush left us with more questions than answers, and the real work of theorists today is to build new understandings out of the deconstructed ruins. Today, many theorists have conflicted feelings about their role as "assimilationists," as members of the "post-avant"—some desperately insist that the revolution remains alive, while others have become acolytes of the masters, mechanically applying their techniques to increasingly narrow areas of study.

Nor are these struggles limited to the intellectual elite. Postmodern awareness of the constructed nature of the self has "trickled down" to nourish the self-help industry, with its roots in modern psychotherapy. How we think about our families and friends, our spouses and careers, our neighborhoods and nations, has been greatly influenced by this trend. Whether working with a self help guru or a social activist, the DE must help find a balance between assimilation and originality, to scour derivative thinking and burnish the new.

Magnus Gaines understood that he would be held a laughingstock in some circles, but it was a risk he was willing to take. The importance of his key discovery, the so-called Limbic Bridge in the human brain, commanded the respect of the entire scientific community, so he was in a unique position to pioneer neurological exploration into realms previously reserved for psychotherapy and metaphysics.

Haphazard House had published Magnus's two previous books with enthusiasm but dithered about this one, worrying that it jeopardized the author's public image as a trustworthy voice from the scientific community. So Magnus turned to Dungeness University Press, rationalizing to himself that his most groundbreaking work would benefit from the imprimatur of the academic world. Three anonymous scholars had read his manuscript respectfully and supported its publication, but only on the condition that he remove what one called his "naïve prescription for world peace," which of course was the point of the book. These colleagues praised his neurological discoveries and then wholly discounted his insights into their relevance.

Fortunately, the Dungeness editor was sympathetic to his thesis. She seemed to understand that his discovery of "mutual gaze" as a conduit of spiritual connectivity between humans was no less earthshaking than that of the Limbic Bridge. The real question, she said, was how to rework the text so it passed scholarly muster without dulling its cutting edge. To achieve that goal, some sort of consulting editor was having a look at the manuscript.

Sitting in half-lotus position on his back porch, his limbs wet from sun salutations, Magnus thought, "So much for mental focus!" He brought his mind back to a state of emptiness by training his gaze on his third, inner eye, *broomadyha drishti*.

### Client Profile: The University Press

When the university presses lost the lion's share of their library market in the mid-1980s, they survived by reinventing themselves as "scholarly trade" publishers. The smaller presses became the regional publishers of their states, while the larger ones entered the fray with the major trade houses. Serendipitously, the takeovers of the New York houses by media conglomerates in the 1990s created a window of opportunity for the university presses: as the trade houses' new finance-minded executives weeded out books with projected sales under 20,000 copies, the presses picked up these same titles as frontlist features. In the new millennium, the tide has turned again and the trade houses are starting to steal away the university presses' bestsellers with larger advances. Now more than ever, the presses compete by offering "boutique" treatment: nicer book design, higher production values, and more rigorous vetting and attentive editing.

If you are a DE considering an assignment from a university press, be sure you understand where the money is coming from. Most presses have limited funds budgeted for developmental editing, so many projects are underwritten by generous grants from foundations, whose larger social or political agendas must be kept in mind. Also, be sure you know the profile of your client: some presses still answer to a faculty board and must therefore justify all publishing plans as "scholarship of merit," while others have been cut loose by their parent universities and are now freer to publish nonscholarly fare like cookbooks and travel guides. Finally, keep in mind that these authors are scholars whose livelihoods rest on their reputations. Tenured professors are usually more open to reworking their text for trade audiences; those seeking tenure will likely insist on retaining their judicious tone, specialist jargon, ubiquitous qualifying phrases, and extensive documentation.

As managing editor at Dungeness, Tessa Argent had the dubious privilege of advising acquisitions editors about manuscripts with developmental needs. Although she often told them she had no "fairy dust" to sprinkle over manuscripts, whenever a project came to her with market potential and serious problems, she couldn't resist the challenge. Now the Gaines manuscript sat on her desk, waiting for her to ship it off to a DE.

Usually, Tessa was asked to turn scholarly monographs into trade books, with mixed success. But this author already had a strong track record. His first two books, both published by Haphazard House, had been praised for their lucid treatment of broad subjects: first human emotions, then long-term memory. Reviewers had said he combined a premier neurologist's knowledge with the gifts of a storyteller. The new project, however, had just been severely criticized by three peer reviewers as, in the words of one, "an alarming amalgam of sound neuroscience and psychobabble." Which was how the project had come to Tessa.

Since his previous successes, the author had taken up with Yogiraj Gandhi, a wealthy Indian religious leader, who was funding Gaines's efforts to study the neurological underpinnings of yoga and promote world peace, and the text showed the influence of this unorthodox mentorship. The press's savvy young acquiring editor in religion studies, Naomi Malcolm, had assured the author that he could keep his spiritual theme. She had selected reviewers friendly to the mingling of religion and science: a neuroscientist with an interest in Kabbalah, a religion professor, and an Indian anthropologist. But each had rejected the author's overarching claim, namely, that the spiritual practice of "mutual gaze" would resolve all human conflicts, both interpersonal and international.

The press had given Gaines an unprecedented advance on royalties of $25,000—small potatoes to a trade house like Haphazard, but big bucks to Dungeness. Earning back that advance would be impossible if the book got jeers in the media. Tessa wasn't sure that outcome could be avoided, but she did have in mind the perfect DE—Bud Zallis, a fellow who possessed both formidable diplomatic skills and a high tolerance for New Age thinking.

## Assignment: The Theory with Too Many Tangents

From Bud's perspective, the main argument of *Mutual Gaze* was pretty fascinating. Simply put, Gaines believed that humans could resolve most of their conflicts by bringing heightened consciousness to their *oculesics*—that is, the intense, emotional communication that passes between individuals through their eyes. Gaines provided a robust grammar of this ocular language, which Western science had long reduced to a half-dozen rudimentary eye movements. Building on precepts drawn from Islam, Hinduism, and Buddhism, with particular emphasis on the nine yogic gaze positions called *drishti,* he demonstrated that verbal exchange was often contradicted by subconscious ocular messages. In his Seattle clinic, he worked with psychotherapists to harness these messages to resolve conflicts between spouses, parents and children, business partners, and others with intimate relationships.

The way Gaines explained it, human eyes were once hardwired to the faculties of attention and focus. To this day, the brains of many vertebrates direct visual gaze and mental attention from a shared neural center—thus, lizards, for instance, cannot turn their attention toward a subject without pointing their gaze at it. Somewhere along the evolutionary line, the human brain developed different neural centers for attention and gaze—we can look straight at a friend while paying attention to a stranger at the far end of a bar. Eastern religions had long understood that cultivating control of attention via the gaze was a powerful tool of communication. They'd also known what Gaines's EEG brain scans now proved, that the Limbic Bridge between emotions and long-term memory poured out directly through the eyes.

Where Bud, along with the three scholarly reviewers, lost sympathy with the author was in the fourth part of his manuscript (example 19), in which Gaines speculated how the technique of mutual gaze might resolve deeply entrenched enmities like those between Hutu and Tutsi or 9/11 survivor and al-Qaeda operative. These chapters lacked grounding in fact and were ridden with stereotypes and clichés. The author would be roasted alive if they saw print in their present form, but Bud would need to find some way to retain their essence because the author had switched publishers in order to keep them.

The manuscript had other problems, too. The author had taken a historical rather than pedagogical approach, waiting to discuss the physiology of oculesics until halfway through the manuscript. As befitted the work of a scientist, the text was organized very logically, but it was an idiosyncratic logic that the average reader would have trouble following. Bud's job was to disassemble the author's baroque edifice and rebuild it with simpler, straighter lines.

## Untangle Arguments from Timelines

As we discovered in the last chapter, both exposition and narrative are forms of storytelling. In exposition, the "protagonist" is an idea and the "plot" a series of supporting arguments through which that idea must pass, like a classic hero whose journey is marked by tests of strength and wit. Because most manuscripts have both timelines and lines of argument, the DE's task is to decide which will dominate the book's structure. In the last chapter, we privileged timeline; in this chapter, we'll follow the ramifications of choosing a line of argument.

Whereas the storyline of a narrative is an element that any child can

*Mutual Gaze: The Neuroscience of World Peace*

Introduction: What Is Oculesics?

Part I.  Oculesic Relativity
  1.  The Poverty of Western Ocular Vocabulary
  2.  The Richness of Eastern Traditions of Spiritual Gaze
  3.  The Oculesics of Oppressed Classes

Part II.  Linguistic Relativity
  4.  At a Loss for Words: The Inadequacy of Language to Resolve Conflict
  5.  The Sapir-Whorf Hypothesis of Linguistic Relativity

Part III.  Mutual Gaze in the Clinical Setting
  6.  Gaze Speech in Other Vertebrates

  7.  The Biology of Oculesics in Humans
  8.  The Evolution of Gaze Speech
  9.  Conflict Resolution: Methodology
  10. Conflict Resolution: Case Studies

Part IV. Mutual Gaze in the Public Arena
  11. Israel versus Palestine
  12. Hutu versus Tutsi
  13. Tamil versus Sinhalese
  14. White Supremacist versus African American
  15. 9/11 Survivor versus al-Qaeda Operative

Concluding Remarks

grasp, the storyline of an argument can be harder to perceive. This is because the *structure* of an argument is often confused with *modes* of exposition such as empirical analysis, qualitative analysis, poetic association, and various logical and rhetorical techniques. Just as a narrative storyline is a skeletal structure that must be fleshed out with characters, dialogue, and settings, so an expository "storyline" must be clothed in one or more of these modes. DE and author need not be intimidated by this panoply of modes, nor must they master the rules of debate. The simple nesting logic employed in chapter 3 to select a main thesis can be used again here to determine the flow of argument.

But first the DE must verify that exposition should dominate the revised manuscript. To do this, the DE can perform the same three assessments made in the previous chapter.

ASSESS SHARPNESS OF FOCUS. If the book's main subject is a single person, place, thing, or event, then narrative mode is probably indicated. If the subject is a cultural, societal, or global phenomenon, then expository mode may be more apt.

ASSESS ORIGINALITY. If the author's take on the subject is more a point of view than a full-blown interpretation of events, then narrative mode may be best. If the author's interpretation is so original that it requires marshaling evidence from diverse sources and disciplines, then exposition may be indicated.

ASSESS RELATIVE WEIGHT. The first two considerations aside, if the author's text contains 300 pages of story and only 100 pages of interpretation, or vice versa, then the dominant mode must obtain.

Before he could start reorganizing the text, Bud needed to verify that it should remain in expository mode. He did this by making the three basic assessments that Dr. Worth had drummed into his students' heads: sharpness of focus, originality, and relative weight.

The first criterion was easily dispatched. In the current version, the author and the yogiraj showed up frequently as characters in the narrative, but the concept of mutual gaze was the true "hero" of the story, the recurring character that was featured in almost every chapter. This broader conceptual focus indicated exposition.

So did the second criterion: the author's argument reached conclusions that could hardly be more original. Bud went back to the notes he had taken during his first pass through the manuscript and listed no fewer than nine strong conclusions:

- Conclusion 1: That the ocular vocabulary of the West is impoverished in comparison with that of the East.
- Conclusion 2: That a rich tradition of spiritual gaze spans all of Asia with roots common to Islam, Hinduism, and Buddhism.
- Conclusion 3: That spiritual-gaze adepts can achieve results considered magical such as thought transference and mind reading.
- Conclusion 4: That self-taught "creoles" of ocular language surface in the cultures of oppressed peoples such as slaves, untouchable castes, and subjugated women.
- Conclusion 5: That verbal language alone is unequal to the tasks of resolving word-based ideological conflicts and fostering world peace.
- Conclusion 6: That the venerable Sapir-Whorf hypothesis of linguistic relativity—which posits that humans' thoughts and perceptions reflect the grammatical structures and vocabularies of the spoken languages they are born into—is equally true of ocular language.
- Conclusion 7: That oculesics has deep roots in the evolution of all vertebrates and especially humans.
- Conclusion 8: That the visceral empathy of mutual gaze helps resolve conflicts in interpersonal relationships between spouses, family members, friends, and other close associates.
- Conclusion 9: That mutual gaze holds the key to resolving entrenched ethnic conflicts.

Just listing these conclusions in the order in which they appeared in the manuscript gave Bud a sense of how they'd need to be reordered—there was no way, for instance, that conclusion 5 should appear before conclusion 8, since the latter was a less "global" application of the same concept of conflict resolution through mutual gaze. But he was getting ahead of himself.

It was the third criterion, relative weight, that gave Bud pause. Although the unrevised manuscript was dominated by argument, when Bud totted up the pages devoted to telling anecdotes and full-fledged stories, they were about 30 percent of the whole. These narrative bits and chunks fell into two categories: case studies drawn from the author's work in a clinical setting, and hypothetical scenarios applying his theory to prominent ethnic conflicts in the international sphere. Bud briefly considered whether a narrative framework might be suitable for a book that was largely expository, but he decided that the flow of argument was too complex. Better to have the stories hang from an explicitly expository framework. Later, he'd figure out which anecdotes to foreground and where to place them. For now, he needed to get a better handle on the flow of the main arguments.

### Find the Main Arguments

Most of the arguments in our lives are circular. Whether we're fighting over a prized heirloom or the television remote, these disagreements are essentially static—each party remains entrenched in his or her own point of view. The ensuing carousel of bickering can be funny or suspenseful in a narrative, but in exposition it bores and frustrates a reader. A *line of argument* begins in a thicket of evidence and uses a series of supporting arguments to move toward a main conclusion.

CREATE A MASTER LINE OF ARGUMENT. The DE now creates a master argument containing all significant supporting arguments that occur in the manuscript. In narrative, we constructed a basic timeline simply by ordering material by date and time, but in exposition, the outline of a basic argument can be harder to discern. Here, the DE may find it helpful to create a flow chart like those used in mathematical logic. This chart can flow in one of two directions.

In *inductive reasoning,* an argument moves from evidence to conclusion via a series of logical tests. Particulars give rise to generalities, smaller ideas fit inside larger ones; the DE's long evidentiary list narrows toward a single conclusion. When a detective examines the scene of a murder, looking for clues to the killer's identity, she is employing her inductive faculties— though most English speakers incorrectly use the word "deduction" to refer to all forms of detective work. Induction is the gold standard among lines of argument because it begins free of preconception or bias.

In *deductive reasoning,* an argument moves from conclusion to evidence via a series of logical tests. In deductive reasoning, generalities give rise to particulars, larger ideas to smaller ones; the DE's conclusion widens to embrace a long evidentiary list. When the same detective suspects a killer's identity from the outset and focuses on finding clues to disprove the mafioso's alibi, she is employing her deductive faculties. Deduction is a popular line of argument because it conveniently states its conclusion up front. But deduction can give rise to logical fallacies—arguers may be tempted to cherry-pick only that evidence which supports their claim.

KEEP DIRECTIONAL FLOW FREE. The DE may build the logical flow chart using inductive or deductive mode without committing the developmental plan to either of those lines of reasoning. Suppose the DE maps out the flow chart inductively, with the list of evidence on the left side of the page and the conclusion on the right. Once drafted, the chart can be read in both directions—deductively from right to left, inductively from left to right—leaving the DE free to reorder the text either way. At this stage, the DE should keep an open mind to either directional flow.

Although Gaines's main thesis was pretty clear from the get-go, Bud always leaned toward inductive thinking, so he listed the evidence on the left side of his page and worked rightward (example 20).

In most cases, several pieces of evidence contributed to each of the nine conclusions. For instance, before asserting the relevance of Sapir and Whorf's theory of linguistic relativity to oculesics, the author reviewed the idea's scholarly history, beginning with Edward Sapir's "linguistic determinism" and charting its elaboration by Benjamin Whorf into full-blown "linguistic relativity." Bud was charmed by Whorf's famous example of the Hopi language. Where Indo-European languages imposed a distinction between nouns and verbs, often creating awkward and arbitrary constructions ("it rains" but "lightning strikes"), Whorf's Hopi saw only processes ("it lightnings," "it mountains," "it rivers"); their view accorded with what Einstein and others were discovering about the physical universe. Gaines sided with the majority of linguists by rejecting Sapir's assertion that language restricts thought, and he reviewed the subsequent studies that disproved Whorf's view of Hopi as romantic primitivism. But, like those linguists, Gaines embraced a looser formulation of the hypothesis that accepts a noncausal link between language structure and patterns of thought.

Similarly, each of the other eight conclusions resolved from a complex body

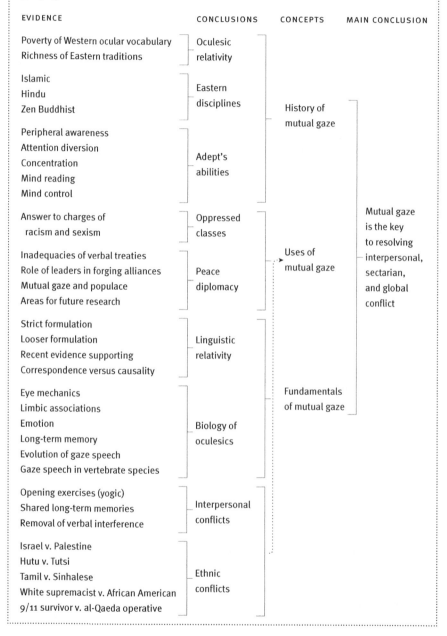

EXAMPLE 20. Master argument and supporting arguments in the Gaines manuscript. The flow chart as a whole constitutes the master argument; the trail from each point of evidence to the main conclusion is a supporting argument. The chart can be read inductively from the left and deductively from the right. The dotted arrow shows the DE rearranging his evidence to fit into broad concept groupings.

EVIDENCE / CONCLUSIONS / CONCEPTS / MAIN CONCLUSION

Poverty of Western ocular vocabulary
Richness of Eastern traditions
— Oculesic relativity

Islamic
Hindu
Zen Buddhist
— Eastern disciplines

Peripheral awareness
Attention diversion
Concentration
Mind reading
Mind control
— Adept's abilities

— History of mutual gaze

Answer to charges of racism and sexism
— Oppressed classes

Inadequacies of verbal treaties
Role of leaders in forging alliances
Mutual gaze and populace
Areas for future research
— Peace diplomacy

— Uses of mutual gaze

Mutual gaze is the key to resolving interpersonal, sectarian, and global conflict

Strict formulation
Looser formulation
Recent evidence supporting
Correspondence versus causality
— Linguistic relativity

Eye mechanics
Limbic associations
Emotion
Long-term memory
Evolution of gaze speech
Gaze speech in vertebrate species
— Biology of oculesics

— Fundamentals of mutual gaze

Opening exercises (yogic)
Shared long-term memories
Removal of verbal interference
— Interpersonal conflicts

Israel v. Palestine
Hutu v. Tutsi
Tamil v. Sinhalese
White supremacist v. African American
9/11 survivor v. al-Qaeda operative
— Ethnic conflicts

of evidence. Once Bud had made these connections, he attempted to group the nine conclusions into larger conceptual units. After trying several schemes, he settled on three conceptual categories: the history, uses, and fundamentals of mutual gaze. These in turn flowed into the main conclusion, which Bud drafted as "Mutual gaze is the key to resolving interpersonal, sectarian, and global conflict."

The completed flow chart both clarified Gaines's supporting arguments and illustrated some of the flaws in the present structure. The author's concluding world-peace scenarios (in the original chapters 11 through 15) needed to be linked to the discussion of uses above. And surely a discussion of fundamentals should precede uses, and perhaps even history. Now that he'd untangled the fishing lines, Bud could consider various ways to braid them into a single strong rope.

## Brainstorm Argument Strategies

With the basic line of argument identified, the DE considers options for reordering the text. As we have seen, a line of argument is actually a complex flow chart, with supporting arguments coming together like columns of ants converging on a dropped ice cream cone. In the flow chart all supporting arguments can be viewed at once, but in the manuscript the DE and author will need to decide which supporting argument to put forth first, second, third, and so on. In other words, the multiple branches of the flow chart must be collapsed into a truly linear argument.

Let's return to our metaphor of the abstract idea as protagonist. In exposition, the classic hero of the story is the main argument's conclusion. In a deductive argument, the identity of the conclusion-as-hero is clear from the outset; the reader simply goes along for the ride as he defeats, dodges, or befriends each argument thrown in his path by the gods. In an inductive argument, the conclusion-as-hero starts out hidden in a crowd; his face comes into focus gradually as each supporting argument adds clues to his identity. When choosing between induction and deduction, the author and DE must weigh the relative merits of clarity and mystery.

Following are brief descriptions of argument templates that can be useful in fleshing out an expository outline. Alternate viewpoints, parallel arguments, rotating arguments, and alternate outcomes can be employed in either inductive or deductive mode. If these templates look suspiciously like those available to a narrator, remember that a line of argument and a timeline are both storylines. Whereas the timeline strategies discussed in chapter 4 are used mostly to spice up a text, these argument strategies can serve as core organizing mechanisms.

ALTERNATE VIEWPOINTS. This line of argument advances a single claim by employing a round-robin of perspectives. In this mode, the reader becomes accustomed to a sequence of voices that take turns speaking. This structure is the expository equivalent of a Ken Burns history documentary in which a series of "talking heads" provides commentary that is stitched together with an omniscient voiceover. The rotation among the alternating viewpoints—which represent different supporting arguments—need not be in lockstep order, but the reader should sense a rhythm to the progression. Because different viewpoints bring with them different assumptions, this approach can be tricky to manage.

PARALLEL ARGUMENTS. Here, multiple lines of argument contribute to an overarching claim made late in the book. In a book intended to prove the economic motives of human rights abuses in South America, for instance, separate arguments about Chile, Paraguay, Argentina, and Peru might culminate in the claim that people are "disappeared" in those countries whenever they threaten the hegemony of the wealthy. In this strategy, supporting arguments are advanced separately and integrated only at the very end of the book. This expository structure is particularly useful in marshalling large bodies of data toward a single, strong conclusion.

ROTATING ARGUMENTS. In this arrangement, multiple lines of argument have no point of intersection but resonate with each other thematically. This device is often used when an area of inquiry is a matter of ongoing public debate: a book on stem-cell research may present a variety of perspectives so that readers can make up their own minds. Not all such debates are new: take, for example, age-old disputes over the historicity of certain events in the life of Jesus Christ. In this strategy, the main thesis must be novel enough to get attention yet accommodating enough to embrace the other perspectives in the rotation.

ALTERNATE OUTCOMES. Multiple rehearsals of the same line of argument that result in different conclusions, this structure is particularly useful in revealing hidden assumptions or illuminating different facets of a complex reality. Consider the large and contentious subject of offshore outsourcing of blue-collar jobs: Does this phenomenon hurt the American economy by taking jobs away from citizens? Or does it help by lowering costs of goods and services? Does it exploit workers in foreign countries, or give them access to the bottom rung of the ladder of upward mobility? An author writing a book on this subject might effectively review the same string of evidence from different perspectives, thus laying bare the complexities of a topic often polemicized.

Bud looked back at the unrevised table of contents. At first blush, the author had been rigorously logical in ordering his discussion: he began by establishing the parallels between oculesic relativity (part I) and linguistic relativity (part II), then demonstrated the power of mutual gaze in the clinic (part III) before broadening its significance as a tool in resolving larger conflicts (part IV). But scrutinized more closely, this TOC revealed an author doing a kind of backward two-step: he placed culture before biology and oculesics before linguistics, leading with the unfamiliar rather than the familiar, the conjectural before the proven.

Bud knew he would have to invert this order, but he wasn't sure how. For starters, he put aside the interpersonal case studies (chapter 10) and the ethnic conflict scenarios (chapters 11 through 15); those elements were essentially anecdotal and could be used to illustrate bits of the core argument, but they did not help *make* the argument.

Next, Bud went back to his notebook from Worth's class to review his options for lines of argument and quickly eliminated three out of the four templates. Gaines's single-minded dedication to his thesis would brook no discussion of multiple rotating arguments, much less alternate outcomes. And the author's use of parallel arguments was limited to the case studies, in which he demonstrated how the same methodology could address different kinds of interpersonal crises.

Bud was thinking he'd stick with a straight inductive line of argument when he revisited the first template, alternate viewpoints. It occurred to him that the manuscript already contained an implicit oscillation between two broad points of view, of the spiritual-minded East and the scientific-minded West. With adjustments here and there, he could probably bolster this East, West, East, West pattern, giving the discourse an underlying rhythm and imparting a sense of cultural balance.

## Compose the New Argument

The process of charting the main argument's flow has already identified the supporting arguments; the DE's task now is to determine the order of those subarguments. The time has come to commit to an inductive or deductive approach. As when composing a new timeline, DEs should keep in mind two crucial factors.

CONSIDER THE AUTHOR'S STRENGTHS. First, the DE should make a candid assessment of the author's expository instincts. Authors who write expository works tend to be more deductive or inductive by nature—they're either bird dogs or magpies. The bird dogs sight their conclusion early on, from a great distance, and drive relentlessly forward through thick underbrush until they reach it. The magpies see their thesis glinting in every detail they come across—they are frequently distracted, take many detours (often interesting ones), and reach their conclusion by a process that feels almost accidental. Both strategies can be engaging and persuasive—the trick for the DE is to avoid working against the author's essential nature.

CONSIDER THE READER'S NEEDS. Second, the DE should verify that the line of argument chosen will meet the needs of the audience. Here, demographics come into play. In a book about financial planning, if the target audience is baby boomers, then the author will need to address the challenges facing people who have lost the solid financial footing enjoyed by their parents' generation. If that same book is pitched to Generation X, then the author will need to explore the perils of saving for retirement over the course of several career transitions.

Bud's brainstorming up to this point had already laid the groundwork for the main line of argument. He knew that he would place biology before culture and facts before conjecture; he also knew that he would attempt to alternate between chapters providing non-Western and Western points of view. But he still hadn't decided on whether to build the argument deductively or inductively, and he had yet to determine an order for the parts and chapters.

Bud strongly favored induction in his own editorial process, but he realized that Gaines favored deduction and decided that he'd better play to the author's strength rather than his own. This decision would mean stating the main conclusion forcefully in the introduction and then reviewing the pieces of evidence in rigorous order from most compelling to least. An inductive line would be more forgiving, because the reader would be accompanying the author on his exploratory journey through his subject. But that psychological stance would ring false if Bud projected it onto Gaines.

Bud's flow chart suggested eight chapters in three parts. (The ninth argument, Ethnic Conflicts, was really an extension of the fifth argument, Peace Diplomacy.) Now that he was thinking deductively, he saw clearly that he should start with the fundamentals of mutual gaze, move on to its historical significance, and wind up with its current and future uses. Within those parts, he would maintain an East-West dialogue but start with the Western perspective, because the book's English-speaking audience would find it more accessible and persuasive.

A few of the chapters could arguably be considered either Western or Eastern. The chapter on linguistic relativity, for instance, applied a Western discipline, linguistics, to the study of non-Western languages and therefore could be assigned to either category. The same went for the chapter on ethnic conflicts: in those scenarios, either Westerners battled non-Westerners or they served as diplomats mediating conflicts between non-Western factions. To maintain his West-East pattern, Bud decided to push both of these fence-straddling chapters onto the non-Western side of the argument.

When Bud finished his draft outline, one pair of chapters remained out of order. The author had discussed non-Western gaze adepts—practitioners of ancient disciplines like yoga who were alleged to have achieved mind control and telepathy—in the latter half of old chapter 2, before going into the oculesics of oppressed classes in chapter 3. Bud liked this order because Gaines's evidence showing that oppressed groups developed their own "ocular creoles" was pretty flimsy, but the order wrecked his West-East pattern.

Let's see, mulled Bud. The author theorizes that groups like African slaves in colonial America developed, out of necessity, a rich vocabulary of stares and glances that allowed them to communicate openly in the presence of their oppressors. The same thing happened with pariahs in India, slaves in China, and women in harems, according to Gaines, but in those societies the ruling classes were more attuned to gaze speech and could keep it in check. In the West, the hubris of the rulers led them to ignore the constant "chatter" of eyes around them and the creoles developed richer, fuller vocabularies. So it makes sense, Bud concluded, to count this chapter as a Western one and place it before the chapter on Eastern adepts.

At last Bud had an outline that worked (example 21). Like a freshly washed car, all it needed now was some detailing.

## Finetune the Argument

So, the complete argument has been composed, with pieces of evidence shepherded into multiple supporting arguments, which in turn have been corralled into single file. Now the DE must impose logical breaks on this uninterrupted stream of argument. Some of the breaks will be obvious, as when the argument shifts from one major supporting argument to another. Other breaks may be harder to place; in those cases, there may be no right answer. For instance, in an argument against subliminal advertising, the role of product placement in Hollywood films may provide the ending for a chapter on corporate ingenuity or the opening for a subsequent chapter on public gullibility.

OBSERVE RULES OF BALANCE. As was previously noted, there are no hard-and-fast laws about how to balance a table of contents, but several rules of thumb are widely observed by authors and editors. See chapter 4, "Finetune the Timeline," for guidelines on how to draft a balanced TOC.

DRAFT WORKING CHAPTER TITLES. Once pacing and balance are established, the DE should draft working titles for all chapters. The table of

EXAMPLE 21. The Gaines manuscript's new line of argument. This structure places fundamentals before real-world applications, and historical events before future experiments.

Part I. The Fundamentals of Mutual Gaze
1. The Biology of Oculesics
   Eye Mechanics
   Limbic Associations
   The Evolution of Gaze Speech
   Gaze Speech in Other Vertebrate
     Species
2. Linguistic Relativity
   Sapir-Whorf, Strictly Speaking
   Looser Formulations
   Correspondence versus Causality
   Recent Evidence

Part II. The History of Mutual Gaze
3. Western Ocular Vocabulary
   Degree of Contact
   Eye Movements
   Eye Gestures
   Facial Expressions
4. Eastern Traditions
   Hindu
   Islamic
   Zen Buddhist

5. Oppressed Classes
   Gaze Speech among Women
   Mutual Gaze in Slave Cultures
   The Riches of Taciturnity
6. Adepts' Abilities
   Peripheral Awareness
   Attention Diversion
   Concentration
   Mind Reading
   Mind Control

Part III. The Uses of Mutual Gaze
7. Resolving Interpersonal Conflicts
   Opening Exercises
   The Importance of Shared Long-Term
     Memories
   Removing Verbal Interference
8. Resolving Ethnic Conflicts
   Early Treaties Made and Broken
   The Role of Gaze in Forging Alliances
   Mutual Gaze and the Masses

contents should let bookstore browsers "overhear" enough of the argument to draw them in but not give away too much of the argument's substance. In a book about governmental erosion of environmental protections, chapter titles might refer to the loosening of restrictions on commercial fishing, offshore oil drilling, and land development, but they would fall short of disclosing crucial evidence against regulatory agencies. For guidelines on writing effective chapter titles, see chapter 4, "Finetune the Timeline."

Once he stepped back from his outline, Bud realized he was unhappy with its three part breaks. Parts I and III contained only two chapters apiece; they didn't break the rule against parts containing only one chapter, but they came close. More important, the fact that part II contained as many chapters as parts I and III combined might give browsers the impression that the book was mostly about the history of mutual gaze, whereas the author was primarily concerned with the phenomenon's relevance in today's society. The part breaks had been helpful in guiding Bud's reordering of the chapters, but he saw now that he could yank them and the structure would stand on its own.

Next, Bud mined the text for piquant phrases that could serve as chapter titles. The author's passages on Eastern spiritual disciplines were a rich source of imagery: the phrase "Lords of Light" would be apropos for chapter 6's discussion of Eastern adepts, and "Featherbeds of Evil" would aptly describe chapter 8's regions of ethnic conflict. Chapter 1, about the biology of oculesics, could be aptly entitled "Gates of the Fiery World." But these overtly spiritual and exotic phrases would undermine the scientific authority of the author's voice and consign the book to the New Age shelves. So Bud restricted himself to a single yogic metaphor, "The Third Eye," and used it as the title of chapter 4, which was devoted to the subject of Eastern spirituality.

The text was also rife with vivid biological terms. Bud toyed with phrases like "Thinking with Your Amygdala," "Peripheral Seers," and "Apertures of Understanding" as ways of melding the scientific and metaphysical messages of the text. But Gaines's own table of contents had been extremely factual and unadorned, and Bud doubted the author would go for such poeticizing of eye and brain mechanics. So instead he turned for inspiration to the case studies. "I Know What You're Thinking," a common expression acknowledging the oculesic communication that most of us take for granted, became poignant when a mother mused that she'd never be able to say it to her autistic child. A man losing his best friend and business partner in a battle over assets cried out in desperation: "See into Me!"

This left Bud with five chapters still untitled. He rounded out the table of contents with double entendres like "Tongue-Bound," "Insolent Looks," and "Disarming Glances"; ironically rehabilitated the expression "Navel Gazing" by yoking it with "and Enlightenment"; and gave concrete form to theory with the question, "Does Language Mold or Cloak Our Thoughts?" The result, he decided, achieved the right balance between authority and approachability.

## Restore Bits of Timeline

We noted above that most books have both a timeline and a line of argument. Our purpose in choosing argument over timeline was to lend the manuscript structural coherence—to give the reader a main line of thought to follow. With that line firmly established, we can now lighten up a bit, allowing a digression now and then, like a teacher who departs from her lesson plan to tell a joke or give an example.

LOCATE CHOICE BITS. Return to your legal pad of notes and look for the most interesting and important of the discarded bits of narrative. Then review your revised table of contents for chapters in which those bits might fit well. When leavening an argument with bits of story, be sure to space out those anecdotal digressions: you don't want them all in the second half of the book, for instance. The reader should find a sense of rhythm between the expository and narrative lines.

ARRANGE THE BITS. Do your best to arrange the bits of timeline so that they build their own momentum. In a book about theoretical physics, Einstein anecdotes might pop up regularly, set-pieces in which he stars as the wild-haired genius making the earthshaking discovery du jour and dispensing unconventional wisdom.

KEEP DIGRESSIONS SHORT. Finally, take care to avoid interrupting the main line with overlong digressions. Most subordinate bits are best kept to a couple of paragraphs, though you might allow an occasional detour of three to five pages. The longer the digression, the more important it should be to the main line of discourse. In that expository book about theoretical physics, a story recounting Einstein's discovery of the theory of relativity might go on for several pages, but the story of his wedding day would get no more than a few sentences, if any.

Now that Bud had gotten the argument ironed out, he was ready to deal with the narrative material he'd earlier set aside. As he'd noted back then, these anecdotes fell in two categories: actual stories of interpersonal conflicts mediated by mutual gaze therapy in Gaines's clinical setting, and hypothetical scenarios in which that therapy might be applied to some of the world's most entrenched ethnic conflicts.

Bud decided straight off that the clinical stories would be effective chapter openers because they'd provide emotional context for the supporting arguments. To place them, however, he'd need to figure out which story suited which chapter (example 22). Chapter 1, for instance, went naturally with the story of the autistic child, since the little boy's inability to communicate through mutual gaze demonstrated the physiological nature of the mechanism.

But other pairings were less obvious. The story of a bilingual marriage between an Austrian woman and a *mestizo* Mexican man attempting to "see past" their cultural differences could serve equally well as entrée into chapter 3's discussion of Western neglect of gaze speech, chapter 5's survey of oppressed peoples, or chapter 8's exploration of ethnic conflict. But Bud found anecdotes that were more apt for each of those cases, and the bilingual marriage ended up fronting chapter 2's presentation of the theory of linguistic relativity. This pairing was more than a little apt because the Austrian woman's unconscious romanticizing of her husband's "aboriginal roots" resonated with Whorf's idealization of the Hopi.

With the case studies placed, Bud turned to the problem of the author's imagined diplomatic scenarios. These could not be foregrounded in the same way as the case studies, but neither could they be omitted entirely—their reten-

EXAMPLE 22. The same Gaines line of argument, but with part breaks removed, chapter titles finessed, and anecdotes placed. Case studies are in boldface, hypothetical scenarios in italic.

1. I Know What You're Thinking: The Biology of Oculesics
   **Case 1: The Autistic Child**
   Eye Mechanics
   Limbic Associations
   The Evolution of Gaze Speech
   Gaze Speech in Other Vertebrate Species
2. Does Language Mold or Cloak Our Thoughts? The Hypothesis of Linguistic Relativity
   **Case 2: A Bilingual Marriage**
   Sapir-Whorf, Strictly Speaking
   Looser Formulations
   Correspondence versus Causality
   *[Scenario: Tamil v. Sinhalese]*
   Recent Evidence
3. Tongue-Bound: The Poverty of Western Ocular Vocabulary
   **Case 3: A Marriage in Middle-Aged Crisis**
   Degree of Contact
   Eye Movements
   Eye Gestures
   Facial Expressions
4. The Third Eye: Eastern Traditions of Spiritual Gaze
   **Case 4: Taking Care of a Senile Elder**
   Hindu
   Islamic
   *[Scenario: Israel v. Palestine]*
   Zen Buddhist

5. Insolent Looks: The Oculesics of Oppression
   **Case 7: A Runaway Teenager**
   Gaze Speech among Women
   Mutual Gaze in Slave Cultures
   *[Scenario: White Supremacists v. African Americans]*
   The Riches of Taciturnity
6. Navel Gazing and Enlightenment: The Gifts of the Adepts
   **Case 5: Sharing Custody**
   Peripheral Awareness
   Attention Diversion
   Concentration
   Mind Reading
   Mind Control
7. See into Me: Resolving Conflict in the Clinical Setting
   **Case 6: An Intimate Business Partnership**
   Opening Exercises
   The Importance of Shared Long-Term Memories
   *[Scenario: Hutus v. Tutsis]*
   Removing Verbal Interference
8. Disarming Glances: Mutual Gaze in the Theater of Conflict
   **Case 8: An Interfaith Marriage**
   Early Treaties Made and Broken
   The Role of Gaze in Forging Alliances
   *[Scenario: 9/11 Survivors v. al-Qaeda Operatives]*
   Mutual Gaze and the Masses

tion was a condition of the author's agreement to publish with Dungeness. Bud knew he would have to boil down a chapter's worth of material to render each scenario in a few pages. And he decided to place them at strategic points in the middles of chapters, where they would illustrate concepts without seeming to be meant as literal prescriptions for political change.

Thus, Bud found a home for the Israel-Palestine conflict in chapter 4, where the fundamentalism of the embattled sects of Jews and Muslims would serve as counterpoint to the mystical traditions of both religions. The war between Tutsis and Hutus fit well with chapter 7's section "The Importance of Shared Long-Term Memories" because the two African peoples had coexisted peacefully for many

centuries under the shared hardship of colonial rule. The same could be said of
the Tamil-Sinhalese feud, but that scenario was more illustrative of chapter 2's
linguistic relativity, since Indo-Aryan lineage was at the heart of that conflict.

Bud thought it wise to embed the two most inflammatory scenarios in the
latter half of the book, by which point he hoped the author would have earned
the reader's trust. The clash of white supremacists and African Americans went
naturally with chapter 5's discussion of mutual gaze in slave culture; and the en-
mity between 9/11 survivors and al-Qaeda operatives would lend topical fresh-
ness to chapter 8's discussion of the potential for mutual gaze to resolve ethnic
conflict.

Bud was house-sitting for friends south of the city, in a condo overlooking a bay-
side lagoon, when he wrote up the developmental plan for the Gaines project.
It was spring, the mergansers and buffleheads wore their breeding plumage,
and the bat rays glided in the shallows like another species of water bird. His
friends had left him a pair of opera glasses to watch the progress of two hum-
mingbird chicks in a nest outside their window. He dreaded reporting what he'd
witnessed—the healthier chick had crushed the weaker one and now sat on the
corpse while the mother zoomed in less and less frequently to hover and feed.

This ultimate expression of sibling rivalry brought back Bud's own history of
interpersonal conflicts, from childhood through a succession of disastrous romances. He'd even been attacked and beaten on the streets by a group of wan-

nabe gangsters. How could he find the author's theme of "world peace through mutual gaze" so convincing when the violent laws of nature were constantly in evidence around him? Bud decided to open his written assessment with that question—it would be his way of letting Gaines know that he sympathized with the thesis but still had reservations.

The developmental plan, with its svelte new table of contents (example 23), passed muster with Tessa Argent and the Dungeness publishing committee, and the author agreed to cooperate. For a man on the verge of marginalization as a New Age kook, Gaines was surprisingly businesslike—almost brusque—in his one-line emails: he responded to each batch of editing with a succinct verdict.

The publication of *Mutual Gaze* coincided with a fresh outbreak of suicide bombings in Saudi Arabia. Despite Bud's efforts to bury the author's zanier claims deep in the text, reviewers lashed out at the book, calling its author's position irresponsible at a time when the nation was at war. But Gaines remained unflustered; in radio and television interviews, he dryly maintained that human nature was equally capable of conflict and resolution. The yogiraj had chosen well when he made Gaines his figurehead in the Western scientific community. Bud sincerely hoped that their views would ultimately prevail.

# 6 * PLAN * *Drafting a Blueprint*

Now that the DE has thoroughly cogitated and mused, it's time to present those ideas to the publisher and author. Some experienced DEs reading this handbook may be surprised that we've waited so long to draft the blueprint for revision. They may be accustomed to writing plans that focus only on concept, content, and thesis, leaving open the logistics of narrative or expository restructuring. Indeed, some publishers expressly require that a plan be no more than two to three pages long; they want a quick synopsis before deciding whether to make the financial commitment. But I have found that authors and publishers remain skeptical of plans for extensive revision unless they can see how those goals will be accomplished.

Before starting to compose a plan, the DE should ask whether the publisher has a preferred format for such plans, and whether the plan is being written for the publisher's eyes only or will be shared with the author. In the latter case, the DE will want to take extra care to phrase criticisms constructively and tactfully, saving any rougher language for a cover memo to the publisher. Over the past decade, while writing more than fifty of these documents, I've gravitated toward a format that balances empathy with the author's intentions against candid evaluation of the manuscript's shortcomings.

For our case study, we revisit the project featured in chapter 4 to see how the evaluation process translates into a written presentation. We also consider whether to include a full list of chapter theses in the plan. Some authors will be energized by this level of concrete detail; others may feel their control of the text is being usurped. If chapter thesis statements are not included in the plan, they become the first item of business once the plan has been approved.

Finally, we take a few minutes to consider how a detailed developmental plan can be used to make limited strategic interventions in manuscripts when the publisher cannot afford to subsidize a full developmental edit.

## Write Up the Plan

The developmental plan contains up to a dozen components, depending on whether the DE is reviewing a proposal or a completed draft, and whether the DE is recommending for or against development.

WARM OPENING. The DE must demonstrate that he or she has approached the project with an open mind and has some kind of understanding of, if not personal experience with, the subject. If the book is about the decline of monastic orders in Catholicism, I might begin by evoking regular childhood visits to my Trappist uncle's abbey; if the book is about a financial investment scheme, I may confess to my own feeble efforts at real estate mogulhood. Some DEs may prefer to work this statement into the middle of the plan, or to conclude with it. Wherever the statement appears, its purpose is to express empathy with the author's discursive project and, at the same time, identify the DE as a member of the author's prospective audience.

To: Brazier Books
From: Hedda Miller
Re: Rabi'a el Saadawi, *Smashin' Seabirds: The Life and Legacy of Mezzy Walker*

Years ago, while backpacking through what was then Yugoslavia, I had
my only direct contact with Islamic culture. In the central mountains of
Bosnia-Herzegovina, in the medieval walled town of Jajce, my companion and
I encountered Muslim women in colorful head scarves and silk pantaloons
treading carefully through the muddy streets. After that, references to the call
of the *muezzin* in literature and film always evoked for me, not the blinding
white of the desert, but the green, wet mountains, the rivers and creaking wa-
terwheels, of that verdant region.

CONTENT SUMMARY. Next, the DE gives a boiled-down version of the content summary (see chapter 2). In this section, it is important to acknowledge the manuscript's accomplishments before zeroing in on its flaws.

Now, when I turn on my favorite blues recordings, I hear the penetrating call
of the *muezzin* in their voices, thanks to this fascinating manuscript by Rabi'a el
Saadawi. This text tells how a Gambian *muezzin* enslaved in America became a

seminal influence on that most American of musical forms, the blues. It offers in-controvertible archival evidence of the existence of this legendary figure, Mezzy Walker, and it situates him in the context of two larger historical narratives: the arrival of Islam on the shores of the New World, and the birth of the blues. Finally, it offers insights into the nexus of Islam and the blues via the author's own story as an African American daughter of the bluesman Yazoo Yates. Now a Sufi convert, el Saadawi is perfectly situated to illuminate her groundbreaking subject.

PROBLEM SUMMARY. This paragraph characterizes the manuscript's main developmental problems candidly but fairly. Rather than give a litany of issues (see "Itemized Structural Issues" and "Itemized Stylistic Issues" below), it attempts to get at the core of the author's discursive dilemma. Does the author bludgeon the reader with inconsequential details? Does the author assume the reader knows too much about an arcane topic? Get sidetracked by tangential topics? Express opinions too contentiously? Fail to convey a point of view? This summary should encapsulate the gist of the manuscript's problems in a few choice phrases.

Unfortunately, these insights are somewhat buried in the current draft. The reader encounters a series of essays—some more autobiographical, others less so—and must piece together Mezzy Walker's picaresque and ultimately tragic story from discrete, sometimes repetitive passages. A detailed review of the lives of other Muslim slaves, many of whom arrived long before Walker, adds little to the main narrative, since Mezzy seems to have been the only *muezzin*—and the only Sufi—among them. In general, the author foregrounds the Islam narrative at the expense of the blues narrative; as a result the reader has few clues to the book's most important and original thesis. And the author's habit of injecting herself into the larger story adds to the confusion.

VISION STATEMENT. Having dashed the author's hopes, the DE can now resurrect them with a vision statement that gives new direction to the author's project. As noted in chapter 1, the DE should not offer a vision state-ment unless he or she truly believes that successful revision is feasible.

This manuscript has a story to tell, and it is Mezzy Walker's. His relevance to history as a Muslim American and a progenitor of the blues is key, but it is his own adventurous life that will compel readers to turn the pages. In the span of his sixty-seven years, Walker lived through many of the formative experiences of African American history: capture, the loss of a rich African heritage, the Atlantic passage, enslavement and escape, collaboration with Indian rebels, a season of prosperity in the early Reconstruction period, loss of possessions and civil rights to Jim Crow, indentured servitude on the levees, a hand in creating the Delta blues, migration northward, and, finally, lynching. With extensive rearrangement and limited new writing, the author could tell this story effectively, allowing its momentum to build and its relevance to develop gradually.

READERSHIP PROFILE. Usually incorporated into the vision statement, this profile outlines all of the kinds of readers to which the book might realistically be made to appeal. The vision statement should explain how the revised manuscript will reach these various constituencies.

Who will want to read this book? Anyone interested in the blues, for starters. Blues aficionados are ardent collectors of books, recordings, and memorabilia; I suspect this volume will become a must have in that community. More broadly, anyone engaged with the question of America's relationship with Islam will be drawn to this book. Since 9/11, the presence of Muslims in American society has been a topic of intense discussion. This project will lend historical depth to those conversations as well as provide insight into the contributions of Muslims to American culture.

WORKING THESIS. Next, the DE rehearses the process by which he or she arrived at the working thesis. I prefer not to strong-arm the author into accepting a particular thesis; instead, I say, "Here are a half-dozen candidates that could work; and here's the one I think will work best, and why." The DE ends by inviting the author to come up with a better thesis, so long as the new one meets the criteria established by the DE's choice.

*Working Thesis.* I've identified a handful of main arguments in the current draft. Any of these could serve as the main thesis of the book.

1. Musical: That the ancient "song of complaint" still heard in the Sahel of Africa is the shared antecedent of both the call of the *muezzin* and the keening holler of the blues singer.
2. Spiritual: That Sufism influenced early African American culture to embrace the flesh as a vessel for the spirit rather than its prison.
3. Spiritual/Musical: That Mezzy's recognized influence on early blues masters represents the expression of Sufi values through this most American of musical traditions.
4. Sociocultural: That acknowledgment of the Sufi origins of the blues could

help all American Muslims achieve a new *shariah*—a set of rules to live by—that looks for commonality and peace among America's diverse religious traditions.

It is my sense that the book would best be served by the third option. Option 1 would limit the scope of the narrative to the blues story only. Option 2 would bury the blues focus in the author's larger discussion of spiritual qualities that—while fascinating—come across as relatively vague. And option 4 seems most appropriate for a conclusion or afterword; as a main thesis, it would undermine the reader's confidence in the author's reliability as a historian, since she'd be telling each episode of Mezzy's life with an emphasis on the moral of the story. Option 3 has the virtue of balancing the musical and spiritual themes equally and focusing on the point at which those two intersect, namely, Mezzy Walker's seminal influence.

WORKING TITLE. If the plan calls for a new title, the DE proposes an apt choice here. The DE may review a number of options and explain why the title chosen best reflects the working thesis just identified. The author may be very attached to the old title, so the DE should explain why that title is not suitable. For some projects, finding a good working title may be difficult. It can be tempting to defer this discussion until later, but the DE should resist this impulse; a wimpy title can reinforce a wimpy discursive approach.

*Working Title.* The author's original title is viscerally appealing, but it misrepresents the book in two respects. First, it's anachronistic: the smashing of Seabird jukeboxes was done by Mezzy's acolytes years after he died and so relates only to the legacy portion of his "life and legacy." Second, it places the emphasis on his iconoclasm, which, while an important theme, risks casting him as more of a rebel than he actually was. If the purpose of this book is to demonstrate the commonality of Islam and African American culture via the blues, then an act of vandalism—however meaningful—hardly seems like the first impression we want the reader to get.

In searching for a new title, I considered many of the song titles that have ultimately found their places at the heads of chapters but decided they would be too restrictive because they refer to specific phases of Mezzy's life rather than his life as a whole. That said, I'd still consider using "Beautemous Hollers" because it speaks directly to the key phase in Mezzy's life—the years when he served as a muleskinner on the Delta levee and influenced some of the canonized progenitors of the blues. My own suggestion for working title, Muezzin *on the Levee: The Life and Legacies of Bluesman Mezzy Walker,* has several advantages. Like "Beautemous Hollers," it refers to that pivotal season in Mezzy's life, but more concretely. And it emphasizes the incongruity of a Muslim singer atop an icon of the Reconstruction period, the Mississippi Levee.

REVISED CONTENTS. With thesis and working title established, the DE provides a revised table of contents that will convey the thrust of the revision plan. In a few concise paragraphs, the DE explains the revision strategy underlying the new contents page. (The new TOC itself may go at the end of the document as an attachment.) Again, the DE invites the author to come up with a better alternative.

*Revised Contents.* The expanded table of contents at the end of this plan [see example 17] assumes that we have selected option 3 as our main thesis. Note that each chapter begins with an episode from Mezzy's life, then segues to a development in the Islam story, and ends with a passage in the blues story. The Mezzy sections move forward in time, as do the Islam sections and the blues sections. But the three sections are not always strictly contemporaneous. In chapter 1, for instance, we first hear about Mezzy's birth and childhood circa 1845, then the early lives of other Muslims enslaved in America between the 1770s and 1860, and finally the beginnings of the blues with the reclamation of the Delta around the 1870s. The transitions among these sections will be thematic, leaping forward or backward in time as the case may be.

Each chapter, then, is a single rotation among the three main narratives. The author will note that I have not included her own story. My attempts to do so failed. The author's story did not have material suitable for several of the chapters, and where material was available, the thematic connections seemed more labored. If the author has ideas about how to integrate her story more thoroughly with the main narrative, I am open to hearing them. Otherwise, I strongly encourage her to reserve that material for a future book; it is one I'd very much like to read.

ITEMIZED STRUCTURAL ISSUES. Here's where those dozen pages of notes taken during content summary come in handy. The DE itemizes the manuscript's main structural problems, noting examples by page number and offering concrete solutions. Common structural issues include poor transitions, repetition, digressions, and flaws in chronology and logic—the very items for which the DE coined abbreviations.

*Other Structural Issues.* The unrevised draft contains quite a bit of material that has no obvious place in the new outline. However, I will conserve whatever material I can by integrating it with the new narrative flow. Of particular note:

- Old chapter 4, a long discourse on the African origins of the "song of complaint," will be recast more succinctly as the argument at the end of new chapter 3.
- Key portions of old chapter 7 (e.g., mspp. 226, 233–41), another long discourse on the African origins of the pastoral ballad, will be distributed through new chapters 7 and 8, which cover the relatively stable and pastoral phase of Mezzy's life.
- Relevant bits of old chapter 3 (e.g., mspp. 61–63, 69), on the veracity of folk legends, will appear in new chapter 11, which focuses on folklore documentation.
- The story of the rise of Black Islam, which dominates the latter two thirds of old chapter 10 (mspp. 334ff), seems less relevant to this volume than the material about the rise of the Sufi orders. This story is told elsewhere, and Mezzy's connection to it is indirect. Therefore, I recommend omitting it altogether.

Once this plan has been discussed, amended, and approved, I will create a full tabular chart showing where each passage from the unrevised manuscript will appear in the revised work.

ITEMIZED STYLISTIC ISSUES. Again, the DE disgorges from the notepad, this time coughing up problems of style. These include poor diction, lapses in tone, awkward syntax, lack of detail, and poor use of quotations, to name a few. If a dozen occurrences of a problem have been noted, all twelve should be listed, lest the author doubt the problem's severity.

*Stylistic Issues.* The author's prose is clean and compelling, so there are just a couple of stylistic problems to monitor.

Islamic Terms: The author sometimes uses religious language to discuss musical or sociocultural material. Sometimes this diction results in fresh metaphors that effectively compare Muslim and American culture: "the sheriff spun around quick as a dervish" (msp. 79); "the mob's murderous *jihad*" (msp. 316). Other times, the technique overreaches: "when Divine Love crossed the county line" (msp. 26); "the five pillars of southern hospitality were erected with the sweat of slaves" (msp. 103). Still other times, the results are gnomic: "When he paid the camp store, Mezzy felt he was paying the *zakat* to Mister Charlie" (msp. 145). As we restructure the text, I will flag such phrases for revision.

Excessive Modesty: Although it can be admirable in face-to-face communication, too much modesty in writing can come across as distant, even false. The author has a tendency to use indefinite articles to subvert her own voice: "Father's frustration had a constricting effect on the heart," when she means "my heart" (msp. 261); "the example of Leili and Hagar, the runaway slaves, inspires" when she means "inspires me" (msp. 122). Again, I'll flag such occurrences as we rework the text.

UPBEAT SUMMATION. The final paragraph reiterates the DE's belief in the project's worth, finds pleasure in the prospect of helping to bring it to the light of publication, and invites the author to participate in finetuning the plan before editing commences.

*In Sum.* Please keep in mind that all the groundwork laid by this plan is alterable. My goal is not to preempt the author's choice in matters of focus and organization; instead, I've tried to show how the manuscript might look if revised according to a vision that I see clearly. But I am open to working with the author and publisher to modify that vision and the plan that flows from it.

Thank you for the opportunity to read this manuscript. It tells a fascinating story. I look forward to hearing from you at your earliest convenience.

AMENDMENTS. The final section lists changes made to the plan after its review by the author and client. A few of these will usually be added shortly after the plan is presented, but others may accrue throughout the process of developmental editing. In this way, the plan serves as a kind of evolving contract between the parties involved.

*Legacy Amendments.* In a telephone conference on March 3 involving Imam al-Khadir, Vanna Smythe, the author, and the DE, it was agreed that an introduction would summarize Mezzy Walker's spiritual legacy and a conclusion his musical legacy. Accordingly, the word "legacy" has become pluralized in the book's title.

*New Appendix.* It was also agreed that old chapter 5, "A Gallery of Muslims Enslaved in the New World," would appear as a backmatter appendix.

*New Afterword.* In a phone conversation on May 7, the author and DE have agreed to add an afterword to the book that will speak to the author's identification with Mezzy Walker. The author sees Walker as having submitted to the will of God when he returned to the Delta, despite the harrowing outcome of his decision; she will recount her own taking of the veil as a similarly dangerous act of faith.

## Compose Chapter Theses

Now the DE should fashion a working thesis for each chapter (and substantive frontmatter and backmatter element) to ensure that each builds on the last, to address gaps in the discursive flow, and to rout repetition and circularity. If this list is not submitted with the developmental plan, it should be the first order of business once revising begins.

To create these statements, the DE can use the same method by which the main thesis was forged, repeating the process chapter by chapter. A main thesis can be somewhat lengthy, but a chapter thesis must be simple and sleek. Read together, a book's chapter theses should make the storyline plain, as in these examples for the chapter 4 case study. If, in the judgment of DE or publisher, the author is likely to be spooked by a fully formulated list of chapter theses, the author may take the first crack at preparing the list and the DE can poke, prod, and trim it into shape.

Introduction: America's First Sufi? The Spiritual Legacy
Thesis: The influence of Mezzy and other early Muslims on American culture—especially African American culture—was a uniquely Islamic blend of commiseration, incarnation, and iconoclasm.

1. Studyin' Sunrise: The Call to Prayer
   Thesis: Unlike many early Muslim slaves, who were born in high places in African society, Mezzy was of humble origins—a fact that would allow him to identify deeply with the blues.

2. Travelin' Man: The Road to Mecca
   Thesis: To wrest spiritual meaning from hardship: this was the goal of Mezzy's pilgrimage to Mecca, and it resonated with the early experiences of the Muslim Gullahs and the Christian Delta pioneers of the blues.

3. Lonesome Lawd: The Atlantic Passage
   Thesis: When W. C. Handy famously "discovered" the blues, he recognized it as the expression of centuries of sorrow epitomized by the Atlantic passage and shared by Mezzy and other slaves of Muslim faith.

4. Yassuh Whiskey: Butler in the Big House
   Thesis: The legitimization of the blues by Handy's publication of the first blues song was analogous to the relative privilege that some Muslim slaves, including Mezzy, enjoyed by virtue of their literacy.

5. The Bloodhounds on My Trace: Life in Hiding
   Thesis: Escape from bondage was a central theme of the blues, invented by men and women, Muslim and Christian alike, who knew firsthand the fear of being hunted.

6. Angel Left a Feather: War and Peace among the Seminoles
   Thesis: In the New Orleans tradition of "Mardi Gras Indians," descendants of slaves pay tribute to the Indians who harbored their runaway forebears, but the Indians also benefited from the relationship—witness the guerrilla leadership of several Muslim escapees, including Mezzy.

7. The Whole Damn Jinte: A Season of Prosperity

Thesis: The optimism of the jazz era for African Americans in the 1920s was foreshadowed by a brief season of unmolested freedom and prosperity in the late 1860s.

8. Nose Wide Open: Loving Women, Kissing Camels

Thesis: During that same brief season, African Americans rediscovered the joys and heartaches of volitional love after centuries of having their spouses and children routinely sold away from them, again presaging the "free love" spirit of the jazz era.

9. Beautemous Hollers: Life as a Muleskinner

Thesis: The usurious contracts offered artists during the "race records" period harked back to harsher economic injustices perpetrated on former slaves by the white majority during the Reconstruction of the South.

10. The Roustabout's Dream: North at Last

Thesis: Mezzy was among the first of thousands of southern blacks to migrate north toward the hope of a better life, just as the first formal emissaries of Sufism were arriving on U.S. shores.

11. Hungry Cuz I Can Be: Making the Chicago Scene

Thesis: Mezzy's refusal to record thwarted his financial success and his canonization, but his reluctant interview with the *Chicago Defender*—in a climate of awareness increased by the Sufi International Order's publications and the work of blues folklorists—provides crucial evidence of the link between Islam and the blues.

12. What the Mob Don't Know (Gonna Hurt Me): Death by Lynching

Thesis: Dying in 1912, Mezzy did not live to see the full emancipation of blues artists nor the full recognition of Muslim contributions to American society, but he served as an example of hope in submission to the will of God.

Conclusion: Smashin' Seabirds: The Musical Legacy

Thesis: Mezzy's influence on American music corresponds to his spiritual influence: his *muezzin* call gave the blues their keening voice of commiseration; his Sufi sensuality harmonized with the earthy blues; and his iconoclasm helped stoke the fires of improvisation.

Afterword: A View from Behind the Veil

Thesis: The author's decision to take on the veil was an act of submission to the will of God, and witness of her faith to those around her, that she relates to Mezzy's possible motive for returning to the Delta despite its manifest dangers.

## Intervene Strategically

Sometimes a publisher can afford to pay a DE for twenty or thirty hours of time to develop a revision plan but cannot underwrite the two hundred to three hundred hours required to execute the plan. In these cases, the publisher might try commissioning a plan and then charging the author with its implementation. Because authors are ensconced in the mindset that produced the unrevised draft, this approach can have mixed results: usually, the final draft shows obvious improvement but falls short of the full, glorious reincarnation that the DE prescribed.

The author-as-DE plan works best if it targets specific interventions that will make a difference in the book's ability to reach its audience. For instance, the plan might focus on reworking the subheadings throughout the book while leaving the general text relatively untouched. The plan might give the author small writing assignments to enliven dry stretches of exposition with anecdotes, or to expand captions so the relevance of the art program is clearer. It might even provide some examples of line editing to guide a shift in the author's style away from specific flaws and tics. In these cases, the publisher and DE should ask themselves, what about this book are reviewers most likely to complain about?

High-powered copyeditors are sometimes asked to perform key developmental tasks within the scope of their copyediting budgets. These so-called triage assignments are not good publishing practice: developmental work takes time, and freelancers should be paid for their time. Hungry editors who accept such assignments establish a precedent that their clients will likely exploit more routinely in the future. When responding to a request for developmental triage, a freelancer should define the developmental task clearly, estimate the time it will take, and specify a developmental rate higher than the normal copyediting rate by 25 to 50 percent. This approach manages client expectations, keeps the enterprise on an honest footing, and redounds to the benefit of the book and all parties involved.

# 7 * R H Y T H M * *Setting the Pace*

When I was growing up, each spring and fall my mother would announce, "It's time to move the furniture." Her husband and three sons would fall into line, moving the sofa to the opposite wall of the living room, each bed to a new window view. For the first few days afterward, we barked our shins against night tables and tripped over hassocks. But then we settled into the new arrangement, and our movements through the house became as routine and unconscious as before. I was in college before I realized that this semiannual ritual was not observed in most households.

After six chapters of planning, we have now arrived at the stage at which the real work of developmental editing begins: we must rearrange the text's furniture. The results will be disorienting at first, but once we've got the main pieces in their new positions, we can adapt the pace of the narrative or exposition to the altered arrangement and smooth out the changed rhythm. In the process, we'll find that we apprehend freshly passages previously taken for granted, seeing them in a new light.

In our case study, the author knows how to tell a story—his wild fabrications are renowned locally—but his mastery of oral delivery on the *Five O'Clock News* has not prepared him for the challenges of writing a book-length account. His pride as a storyteller, his control of access to his material, and the "small world" dynamic of regional publishing combine to make a particularly challenging DE assignment.

## Author Profile: The Sole Authority

Among all the books waiting to be written, most could be tackled profitably by any number of authors. For those subjects, the publisher's challenge is to find the most suitable author: a person with access to the book's material, a balanced yet sharp perspective, a proven track record of meeting deadlines, and the narrative or expository skills to pull off a book-length treatment.

But for some projects the choice of author is nonnegotiable because the putative author controls access to the book's material. This author may be a literary executor guarding the collected papers of a famous subject; the owner of a famous property, such as a building or sculpture; or a celebrity who wants to write an autobiography. Or, this author may have become the Expert on the book's subject by dint of long years of obsessive study: she or he alone may have logged the hours that would yield a full accounting of the obscure archeological record of a hill in Turkey, the confidential memos of an embroiled corporation's personnel department, or the complex social relationships of meerkats in the Kalahari. Often these "sole authorities" are lacking in the other qualifications for authorship: they may have little or no experience in book writing, and their point of view can be far from unbiased.

Freelance DEs are likely to deal with an Expert at some time in their careers. These authors are often the ones who can benefit most from developmental editing. In the more successful of these collaborations, the authors have an almost missionary zeal for the propagation of their hard-won knowledge and are willing to defer to the DE's expertise in the sphere of book development.

As was his habit each morning, Harvey Rhodes climbed to the jutting platform near the top of his crooked lighthouse, drank his coffee, and scoured the horizon for a glimpse of Isla Querida. No sign of the wayward island, just Jeb Michener's party boat heading out for the day.

Harvey waved and headed back down the circular stairs, determined to open his tiny museum promptly at nine. Currently, visitorship was still pretty sparse — usually fewer than a dozen folks a day. But once the book came out, he expected traffic to increase at least tenfold, so he spent a couple of hours every day chiseling pumice specimens into smaller pieces for eventual sale as souvenir chunks of the fabled Isla Querida. He worried a bit about running out; last year's winter storms had blown in a paltry crop.

That is, *if* the dad-blamed book ever came out. Perry Groenig had kept his manuscript for months already, and now he was supposedly consulting another editor. The story of Querida's emergence from the mists of legend had been Harvey's own life story, and it had been a challenge to set down all the facts. Now Perry, who was basically a good guy and certainly a valuable contact in Bay Area publishing, was dragging his heels for reasons unknown.

Harvey put on his goggles and took up his jeweler's chisel and hammer. The trick, he knew, was to make the break look natural.

## Client Profile: The Regional House

Regional publishers have the characteristics of other small trade publishers (see chapter 3), but instead of focusing on a few subject strengths they cover a broad array of subject areas for their geographical regions. In essence, the region *is* their subject. Staples of regional publishing include guides to hotels, restaurants, museums, parks, and sites of historical interest; cookbooks; field guides to flora and fauna; and compilations of oral history, arts and crafts, and folklore. Most publishers with nationwide distribution will publish only for broad regions like the Southwest or New England; regional publishers can produce books that contain much more information on a single state or metropolitan area, with the bonus of providing an "insider's view."

Sooner or later, anyone involved in Bay Area publishing learned to recognize Perry Groenig. Founder of the nearly eponymous Peregrine Press, he could be seen dining any day of the week with prospective authors, his warm raconteur's voice carrying above the restaurant din, his Einsteinian hair ablaze with light. The publishing community had considered him an upstart at first, but his string of regional bestsellers soon earned respect: from *East Bay Wine Tasting* to *Murals of the Mission District* to *Willie Brown's Hats,* he knew what his neighbors wanted to read.

And now Perry was pitching Bud a DE job at a favorite Mexican restaurant. For most of Perry's twenty-two years operating out of his converted garage in Potrero Gulch, his wish list had included a book that he'd despaired of ever getting: the myth of Querida, an island said to float off the coast of California. The First People had incorporated the huge pumice raft into their legends and had charted the positions of its distinctive eyelet shape in their cave paintings, as far south as Baja and as far north as Mendocino. When the Europeans came, they took up the legend as their own, projecting onto this local Atlantis the obsessions and anxieties of each subsequent era, transforming the isle by turns into an elusive bonanza for seal hunters, a hideaway for William Randolph Hearst, a high-security prison that made Alcatraz look like a day spa, a gulag for Asian detainees during World War II, and fertile soil for primo marijuana in the hippie era. Since the early 1960s, the self-appointed keeper of the Querida myth had been Harvey Rhodes.

"Harvey and I go way back," Perry said, laying into his *carne asada.* "Harvey has promised me this book since forever. And of course, I've tried to push him gently in a certain direction, away from his own story. He has too many personal axes to grind. The establishment has done him wrong, to be sure, but all that ranting puts a bad taste in the reader's mouth. But he can't stop himself."

He thumped the tall stack of manuscript pages, the title page now flecked with salsa.

Ordinarily, Perry explained, he did not have the budget to hire a developmental editor. He did most of the "macro-level editing" himself, and his trusted assistant handled the copyediting and the rest of production. But in this case he needed an impartial third party. If Bud's assessment seconded the opinions Perry had been giving Harvey for the past fifteen years, then maybe, just maybe, the irascible author would listen.

## Assignment: The Local History Turned Personal

Bud concurred with Perry's assessment: the main problem with the Rhodes manuscript, though not apparent from its TOC (example 24), was its odor of resentment. Rhodes had completed his Ph.D. in biology at UC Davis and was teaching at Cal State, Fort Bragg, when the news of his discovery of Isla Querida had broken in the local media and forever lost him his chance at tenure. Ever since, he'd been consigned to the fringes of academia. No matter how much evidence he amassed, no matter how many tests authenticated his geological and archeological specimens, he remained an "independent scholar" with whom no respectable institution would affiliate. Understandably, his manuscript bore the marks of his frustration: he rehearsed these injustices at great length, reviewing copious memoranda and board hearings.

For years, Perry had been trying to get him to leach the bitterness from his prose on grounds of self-preservation—"you're just digging yourself a deeper grave, Harve." But there were also editorial grounds for removing most of this material: the reader's confidence in Rhodes's authority would be undermined by such obvious settling of old scores. What Rhodes intended as an exposé of deeply ingrained institutional problems only exposed his own contrary nature.

What Bud found most fascinating was the physical evidence: chunks of pumice embedded with fossilized pollens and the bones of extinct species; a hunk of concrete and gold-leaf mosaic from Hearst's swimming pool; driftwood carved with the poems of Asian detainees; remnants of plank canoes, called *tomols,* used by the First People. If these relics were forgeries, they were clever ones, because teams of scientists using carbon dating and art-historical expertise had been unable to expose them as fakes.

But Perry had warned Bud against pursuing the question of veracity. "Let the scholars parse the evidence," he said. "Stories can be important to a community whether or not they're true. What I want to publish is the story of Querida, in all its magical glory." That, and he wanted the manuscript length reduced by half so he could hold a price point of $24.95 in paperback. Bud had his work cut out for him.

EXAMPLE 24. The unrevised TOC for the Rhodes manuscript. The outline of the island's story is muddled, with major subjects like the giant penguins, the man-eating lichen, and Hearst showing up in more than one part.

*Finding Isla Querida: The Archeology of Desire*

## Rearrange the Furniture

DEs, now it's time for you to get your hands dirty, to begin the hard work of cutting, pasting, and rearranging. Don't worry about pacing at this point—you'll smooth out the rhythm of the discourse once you can see how the big pieces have fallen.

COPY THE UNEDITED MANUSCRIPT. Before starting, make a copy of the unedited manuscript for reference—once you've dismembered the "live" manuscript, you'll have a hard time remembering how the pieces originally fit together. This goes for both paper and electronic manuscripts.

ASSIGN PASSAGES TO NEW POSITIONS. Some DEs prefer to jump right into the text, moving around passages; such editors feel their way through the conceptual linkages as they go. Others flesh out their tables of contents even further, noting topics and page spans before they begin actually rearranging the furniture. Some DEs use a Microsoft Word table that records each passage in its old and new positions. This extra work can go a long way toward assuaging the author's fears that an important passage might get left out.

TRACK EACH PASSAGE'S NEW AND OLD POSITIONS. Whichever method you choose, be sure to keep track of where each passage is coming from and where it's going. If you're editing electronically using the Track Changes feature in Word, distinguish between passages you're eliminating and those you're moving—both look like they're being deleted, but the latter are actually being cut and then pasted elsewhere. It helps to add comment flags that link the points of deletion and insertion: "I've moved this passage to the end of new chapter 3," and later, "I've moved this passage from the middle of old chapter 1." To make these links even more useful, note the page spans from the original, unedited manuscript. If you try using the page numbers of the live text, you'll drive yourself crazy, as the pagination keeps shifting during the course of reorganization.

Harvey Rhodes's preferred mode of communicating was the fax machine. He possessed a telephone number and an email address, but whenever Bud left a voicemail or sent a message, Rhodes responded with a lengthy facsimile memo. The faxes themselves were cordial and enthusiastic about the proposed developmental plan, but something about their formality made Bud nervous.

The planning stage was relatively straightforward. Once Rhodes agreed, in principle, to a drastic reduction of the space devoted to his personal war with the scientific establishment, the island's tale would be easy to tell. In the unrevised manuscript, the island's story was told using three overlapping timelines. Part I covered the island's geological birth and its eventual colonization first by plants, then by animals, and finally by indigenous people. Part II described Harvey's encounters with the island's rocks, plants, and animals and then took the human story beyond the First People to the days of magnate Hearst. Part III went back to square one again by reviewing the physical evidence from each of the island's distinctive eras, though it garbled the temporal sequence somewhat by discussing the artifacts in the order in which they were discovered. This last part brought the story from Hearst's era to the present. Bud created a single timeline that conflated these three parts.

Next, Bud constructed a simple Word table and assigned passages to slots in the timeline (example 25). For instance, a single chapter 3 would comprise the text's botanical subjects: evidence that the island has a vast "rudder" of kelp regularizing its course along the California Current (old chapter 2), the evolution of the island's narrowly endemic plant species (half of old chapter 3), Rhodes's personal encounter with a gruesome flesh-eating species of Querida

EXAMPLE 25. A Word table for keeping track of reordered passages in the Rhodes manuscript. The left-hand column is a straight timeline with the dates omitted. The third column, "Edited Pages," indicates how many pages will remain after editing.

| Chapter | Existing Pages | Edited Pages | New Pages | Total Pages |
|---|---|---|---|---|
| Foreword by local celebrity | — | — | 10 | 10 |
| 1. Rhodes as "keeper" (157–202, 203–14, 215–75) | 119 | 20 | 2 | 22 |
| 2. Geology (3–36, 363–85) | 57 | 23 | 2 | 25 |
| 3. Flora (37–71, 72–84, 291–319, 402–16) | 92 | 23 | 2 | 25 |
| 4. Fauna (85–95, 96–111, 320–39, 417–34) | 65 | 23 | 2 | 25 |
| 5. First People (119–44, 386–401) | 42 | 23 | 2 | 25 |
| 6. Arrival of whites (112–18, 145–54) | 17 | 17 | 2 | 19 |
| 7. Hearst myth (340–60, 435–49) | 36 | 21 | 2 | 23 |
| 8. Prison myth (450–69) | 20 | 20 | 0 | 20 |
| 9. Detention center myth (470–77) | 8 | 8 | 8 | 16 |
| 10. Marijuana myth (478–92) | 15 | 15 | 0 | 15 |
| 11. Lighthouse (493–514) | 22 | 22 | 0 | 22 |
| 12. Sea rescues (276–90) | 15 | 15 | 0 | 15 |
| Final thoughts (515–20) | 6 | 5 | 0 | 5 |
| [Deleted part titles] | 6 | 0 | 0 | 0 |
| Total pages | 520 | 235 | 32 | 267 |

lichen (old chapter 10), and the fossil evidence of the island's earliest species of lichens, kelps, and pollen-bearing plants (half of old chapter 15). Similarly, the new chapter 4 conflated stories of the island's animal life, including zoological endemism (the other half of old chapter 3), the arrival of a now-extinct species of human-sized penguins (most of old chapter 4), Rhodes's discovery of an ankle bone unique to penguins establishing the giants' existence on Querida (old chapter 11), and his confounding of skeptics when the fossil was proven authentic (the other half of old chapter 15).

Although Bud's plan boiled down Rhodes's own story to a fraction of its current length, it did give him pride of place. A vivid account of his discovery of Querida (old chapter 6), the creation of his early research camp on the Lost Coast (old chapter 7), and his heroic battle against scientific narrow-mindedness (old chapter 8) would open the book as new chapter 1. And the book would climax with the Sisyphean construction of his lighthouse (old appendix) and the undeniable derring-do of his seven sea rescues (old chapter 9) involving dozens of survivors, a cast of characters ranging from a lone surfer to commercial fishermen, marine biologists, and ecotourists. This use of his own material to frame the larger argument seemed to satisfy the author, at least at first. There were choppier waters ahead.

## Draft New Passages

Once all existing text has been either cut or repositioned, the author and DE must work together to fill in gaps. This is the most sensitive moment in the collaboration. Until now, all material in the revised manuscript has originated with the author, but here the DE will contribute new ideas that may threaten the author's sense of ownership of the text. From the DE's perspective, an author making objections at this stage can seem petty or naïve about the craft of book writing. From the author's perspective, the DE can seem like an interloper who seeks the thrill of authorship without the responsibility that accompanies it.

These feelings are natural and should be acknowledged openly with good humor and tact. A DE should offer new passages respectfully, saying, "If this draft doesn't feel right, please edit it freely, or substitute a similar passage in your own voice." Authors, for their part, should acknowledge a DE's intentions and invite further input: "I agree that this chapter could open more colorfully, but I'd prefer a jungle scene to a beach scene. Here's my attempt; let me know what you think."

CONSIDER THREE DRAFTING OPTIONS. Suppose the plan calls for ten new, dramatic chapter openings of two to three pages apiece. Option 1 is for the DE simply to prompt the author to write the new passages. At the first dramatic opening, the DE appends a query that gives the author a writing assignment, specifying goals for content, style, and length. This option works best if the author has a flair for storytelling and concrete language— even talented writers sometimes need prompting to focus their attention on what they should be writing about.

Option 2 involves the DE interviewing the author via phone or email and then massaging those notes into a coherent passage, which the author can tweak so that the language fits his or her own voice. This option is appropriate when an author is having trouble envisioning the new passage. Once the passage is drafted, the author will usually become inspired to either tinker with the DE's prose or write a whole new passage using the DE's draft as a model.

Option 3 has the DE drafting all new passages without prior author involvement. If the percentage of new material required by the plan is high, this approach may be the only feasible way to get the book revised on an aggressive publishing schedule. In this case, the author must be empowered to revise the draft material—though without preparatory discussion, there's a danger of the author undoing the DE's more important contributions.

DO A TRIAL RUN. All three approaches can be used in the course of a single collaboration, if the author is open to them. Most DEs favor options 2 and 3 but will resort to option 1 when it seems more appropriate or when they run out of steam. However the author and DE agree to proceed, it's best to do a trial run with a single new passage before either party invests a lot of energy in writing new material. That way, you'll find out up front if your author is overly protective of the prose or if your DE is a frustrated author taking personal angst out on you.

The developmental plan called for thirty-two manuscript pages of new text. Eight pages were needed to flesh out the Asian detention center myth (chapter 9), which Rhodes had given short shrift; two pages apiece to introduce each of seven newly formed chapters (chapters 1 through 7); and ten pages of foreword by a local notable to help to sell the book.

The foreword was Perry's task. He approached Armistead Krasney, the local radio talk show host, whose serial tongue-in-cheek soap opera, *Bernal Nights,* had run weekly for five years before turning into an HBO miniseries. Despite this national exposure, Krasney remained enough of a Bay Area insider to strike the right note of suspended disbelief, and he would surely point out all the insider jokes that made the Querida myth so popular in the local imagination.

Because Rhodes was an adept writer with a folksy voice and an eye for vivid detail, Bud decided that he should not attempt to draft the seven new chapter openers for him. Instead, he embedded in the edited manuscript queries to the author (AQs) like the following:

AQ: Because this chapter now embraces all aspects of Querida's geology—from its birth as the lava of an underwater volcanic eruption, through your expla-

nation of how its composition allows it to float, to your extensive, fully cataloged collection of rock specimens—we need an opening passage that will
prepare the reader for this arc through time. Please draft no less than two
paragraphs, and no more than two pages. Perhaps begin with yourself on the
beach, picking up pumice specimens after a recent storm?

AQ: Here we need no more than two pages introducing the concept of island
biogeography and its effects on Querida's botanical diversity, from lichens
to kelp to pollinators. You might open with your personal drama of the
flesh-eating lichen, or describe in detail the strange, inverted kelp forest that
rudders the island. Other thoughts?

Then, against his better judgment, Bud drafted a model flashback for the first
chapter, clearly labeling it, "Copy for Example Purposes Only." He sent the queries in an email and attached a draft sample, heard nothing for two days, and
got the answering machine when he tried calling. A week later, the fax machine
twittered and there emerged a five-page diatribe, liberally dosed with STATE-
MENTS SET IN ALL CAPS FOR EMPHASIS. The gist of the author's objections was
that Bud had cast Rhodes as some sort of "mad scientist running an outpost of
Ripley's Believe It or Not." Since Perry had been cc'ed, Bud awaited his call, taking his evening glass of port six hours early.

Perry diplomatically defended the quality of Bud's draft but allowed that a
few of his phrases might be rendered less acerbic: "When you're dealing with
material that you know is a little, well, off the wall, it's hard not to become playful." They agreed that Bud would forgo drafting the remaining flashbacks and
submit his queries to Perry, who would remove any potentially inflammatory
phrasing before sending them on to Rhodes. "Keep it light," he advised, "just
not *too* light." Fat chance of that, Bud thought. This author had taken the play-
fulness out of him.

## Balance Chapter Weights

On commercial airlines, we're told to be careful opening overhead compart-
ments, as "contents may have shifted during flight." Similarly, chapter contents may have shifted since you initially resituated them. While restoring
bits of timeline or argument, you may have decided to leave out some pieces
that you'd saved "just in case." While rearranging the furniture, you almost
certainly moved certain passages to positions that you hadn't yet thought of.
And some of the new passages you'd drafted may have run longer or shorter
than anticipated.

RECALIBRATE CHAPTER BALANCE. To reestablish balance in the
weight of chapters, refer back to the guidelines in chapter 4. If a chapter is

running a few pages shorter or longer than initially projected, leave it be; but if chapters have gotten way out of alignment, now's your chance to reestablish the shape and symmetry of your discourse.

REVISIT THE LENGTH REQUIREMENT. Now is also your chance to meet any overall length requirement established by the publisher. If the publisher has mandated that the text be reduced by 25 or 50 percent, then the author and DE may already have been looking for opportunities to cut: instead of simply rearranging the furniture, they will have taken some of it out to the curb for Goodwill. But the method of "cutting as you go" can be hard on some authors. Each passage on the chopping block has significance or the author wouldn't have written it. At this later stage, however, the DE can remind the author of the overall length requirement, flag a variety of expendable passages, and allow the author to choose which ones to cut.

FLAG PASSAGES FOR DELETION. When looking for passages to cut, the DE and author should ask themselves the following questions:

· Are there side narratives or digressions that can be removed without detracting from the primary arc of the discourse? Digressions, however interesting, are usually expendable, their material readily recycled as a magazine submission, journal article, or speech.
· Are there places where the text gives several examples when one would suffice? With a minimum of effort, a single example can usually be generalized slightly so that the second and third examples can be cut.
· Are there passages that furnish more detail than is necessary to make the author's point? Eliminating such detail is harder work than wholesale cutting of passages, but in some texts this word-by-word line editing may be the only way to reduce length.

GRIEVE LOST PASSAGES. The DE should be sensitive to the author's feelings during the process of cutting large amounts of text. In poetry workshops, we call this kind of intervention "killing your babies." Each image and line has been lovingly crafted by the poet, who must be given a chance to grieve these losses. Authors may have an easier time of cutting if, instead of obliterating the material, they move it into a notebook for possible use in future projects.

Having roughed out the revised manuscript, placed old passages in their new order, and situated newly drafted passages, Bud was ready to edit for length. His Word table specified the number of pages to be excised from each chapter. About half the chapters needed no pruning (chapters 6 and 8 through 12), while the other half had to be cut by a third or more (chapters 1 through 5 and

7). Although the author had agreed to these reductions in principle, Bud was worried that he'd balk when the time came to cut. The heaviest editing would occur in chapter 1, where 119 pages of railing against the establishment would be compressed into twenty brisk pages of biographical sketch. The success of the whole developmental intervention would rest on this one chapter, so Bud figured he'd better start there.

First up on the chopping block were stories that did not contribute to the book's core narrative. The original chapter 6, "Querida at First Sight," told of the author's crucial first encounter with the floating island, but it embedded this key moment in forty-six pages of picaresque wanderings along the Lost Coast. Similarly, the original chapter 7, "Establishing a Beach Head," at twelve pages long, lingered with vivid detail and touching nostalgia over his first few seasons bivouacking along the bluffs, building his lighthouse, and finding a wife to install in it. Together, these two chapters formed the foundation of a charming memoir, but they contributed little to the story of Querida. Bud summarized these events in a dozen pages—a massive amputation that was sure to leave the author breathless.

Next Bud turned to the task of compressing the original chapter 8, "The Naysayers"— Rhodes's sixty-one-page conflict with the scientific community—into a scant eight pages. This turned out to be easier than he'd expected. Each of Rhodes's battles with his detractors followed the same narrative arc: Rhodes would discover a new piece of scientific evidence supporting the existence of Querida, submit his findings to the relevant scholarly journal, receive a rejection slip, hold a press conference publicizing his findings, and then appeal to the journal's editorial board for reconsideration that was never given. By describing this arc only once, Bud could dispense with most of the author's blow-by-blow descriptions of institutional warfare.

With great trepidation, Bud attached the new chapter 1 to an email message, which he routed first to Perry. He explained in his cover memo that the chapter's editing was still rough; the pacing would be smoothed out once Rhodes approved of the major revisions. This time, Bud was prepared for the author's silence, but the wait for his response was nerve-wracking nonetheless. Over the next few days, Bud cooked a big pot of chicken soup, proofed several chapters for another publisher, and went about his daily routine with studied nonchalance.

On the fourth day, when he returned from the gym, the inevitable fax, addressed to Perry Groenig, had unfurled like a carbon-paper scroll onto the floor. In it, Rhodes objected to Bud's "assumption of expertise in fields he knows nothing about," like paleobotany; he also dunned Bud for "having the audacity" to rewrite his personal history—"I don't remember Mr. Zallis being there at the time." Thankfully, Bud's chicken soup only got better over time—he ate three bowls of the comfort food before rereading the vituperative missive.

On Bud's computer, a completely revised version of chapter 1 was attached to an email message with no greeting or subject line. Because Rhodes insisted on "correcting" the file personally, Bud would have to edit the chapter from scratch. Delving into the new version, he discovered—with vindication and chagrin—that the author had actually accepted about 90 percent of the proposed revisions. As a DE, Bud was accustomed to seeing his contributions go unacknowledged. But to be accused of incompetence and then have his "shoddy" work adopted wholesale, without thanks or apology—that was a new experience for him.

Bud called Perry in a state of great agitation. "I understand where you're coming from," Perry said, "but this is an important book for our region, however cantankerous the author. . . . I know you're strong enough to handle this guy." To help Bud regain some enthusiasm for the assignment, Perry played his ace: "I'll double your hourly fee."

## Edit for Pace

A friend attempting to break into Hollywood with a script recently told me the basic rules of screenwriting. Evidently, agents, directors, and studios won't read past the title page if the manuscript is not set in twelve-point Courier type, single spaced, with fifty-six lines per page, and with characters, settings, and dialogue all handled in prescribed manners. More important than all of these trappings, however, is the pace of the narrative: the option buyer expects to encounter a new scene every third page, come hell or high water—literally, in the case of some occult and disaster films. For the scriptwriter, this means establishing character and setting with a few choice phrases and trimming all fat from dialogue until even the fustiest politician and sloppiest drunk speak with the economy of Zen masters.

Happily, nonfiction book publishing has no stringent requirements about shifting scenes or starting new topics after a certain number of pages. The author's own style may establish a brisk or leisurely pace. But now that the DE has done so much shuffling of text, it is time to step back and scan the pace of the discourse to make certain that there are no passages that proceed in slow motion or fast forward. (For use of fictional techniques to modify pace, see sidebar, "Scene and Plot Summary.")

QUICKEN THE SLOW SPOTS. Look for passages that feel plodding and mark them for condensation. The pace of a passage may have felt appropriate in its previous location but in its new position may feel belabored. Con-

## Scene and Plot Summary

In today's culture, primacy is given to the scene. The stories we consume via film and television are made up of scenes with little or no plot summary between. Our critics laud directors for their ability to evoke vivid scenes, splice them together in dizzying sequences, and invest each detail of the location, dialogue, and action with significance. Occasionally, the disembodied voice of a character speaks directly to the audience, summarizing events as a montage wheels by on the screen. We have little patience, however, for such theatrics, which violate the so-called invisible fourth wall of the stage.

But language is more supple than celluloid. We all summarize the plots of our lives every day: over dinner to our families, on the phone to our friends. So the technique has a psychological authenticity in prose that it usually lacks in film. Consider these three opening paragraphs from short stories by Isaac Bashevis Singer:

Amid thick forests and deep swamps, on the slope of a hill, level at the summit, lay the village of Frampol. Nobody knew who had founded it, or why just there. . . . Legends were current among the people, tales of wicked intrigue concerning a mad nobleman, a lascivious lady, a Jewish scholar, and a wild dog. But their true origin was lost in the past. ("The Gentlemen of Cracow")

Houses sometimes bear a strange resemblance to those who inhabit them. Leizer, my uncle Jekhiel's former brother-in-law, owned such a house. Beila, Leizer's sister, was Uncle Jekhiel's second wife. She was no longer alive and my uncle had married for the third time after my parents brought me to Shebrin. ("A Dance and a Hop")

Herman Gombiner opened an eye. This was the way he woke up each morning— gradually, first with one eye, then the other. His glance met a cracked ceiling and part of the building across the street. . . . It took a few seconds to realize that he was no longer in Kalomin, or in Warsaw, but in New York, on one of the streets between Columbus Avenue and Central Park West. ("The Letter Writer")*

Singer is justly celebrated for his modernization of ancient narrative techniques, chief among them plot summary. In the first example, he manages to establish a village's entire history in a handful of sentences, with no fewer than four legends compressed into a single sentence. In the second, he opens with a trademark proverb and then summarizes a family's history of deaths and marriages before placing the narrator uneasily in their midst. In the third, he es-

---

*Isaac Bashevis Singer, *The Collected Stories* (New York: Farrar, Straus, Giroux, 1981). "The Gentlemen of Cracow" translated by Martha Glicklich and Elaine Gottlieb (page 15); "A Dance and a Hop" translated by the author and Ruth Schachner Finkel (page 396); "The Letter Writer" translated by Alizah Shevrin and Elisabeth Shub (page 250).

Scene and Plot Summary (*continued*)

tablishes a proper scene, with the action unfolding in "real time," but uses his protagonist's state of mind to telescope a history of immigrant wandering.

Nonfiction authors naturally tend toward plot summary and should not strive to construct scenes merely for cinematic effect. However, if information about pivotal scenes in the narrative is available, authors may wish to portray a scene every so often to bring the historical or theoretical discussion alive for the reader. Such set-pieces are often effective as chapter openings or section transitions. Of course, memoirists and other authors who figure prominently as characters in their own narratives may favor scenes over plot summary. (The techniques of scene writing are beyond the scope of this handbook, but interested readers will find useful sources under "Further Reading.")

For DEs and authors of most nonfiction works, the key consideration regarding scenes and plot summary is their effect on the pace of discourse. Scenes slow down the action; summary speeds it up. Thus, if a chapter's pace is bogging down, the DE should look for opportunities to summarize the action further. Alternatively, if a chapter's pace is markedly more brisk than that of surrounding chapters, the DE may prompt the author to expand a few plot details into full-fledged scenes.

densing text is itself a minor art form: *Reader's Digest* employs a battalion of condensers (once staffers, now freelancers and offshore vendors) to boil down whole books to article length. The skill combines an eye for ruthless cutting, an ear for summative paraphrasing, and a knack for mimicking authors' voices.

SLOW DOWN THE QUICK SPOTS. Conversely, some passages that were intentionally brisk in their old positions may require expansion in their new ones. The DE can help the author to beef up these passages by revisiting the three strategies used to draft whole new passages. Usually, the DE employs a combination of techniques that includes prompting the author, demonstrating what is needed by example, and actually drafting new material.

ALLOW FOR SYNCOPATION. While marking passages for condensation and expansion, the DE should guard against imposing an artificial pace. The DE's goal here is to help realize the author's own natural rhythm, which may be the precise march of a Sousa band or the feints and shimmies of a Brazilian carnival *bloco*.

Eventually, the development of the Rhodes manuscript settled into a pattern. Each time a chapter was revised, Bud passed it on to Perry, who added his own endorsements and second thoughts to Bud's queries directly in the redlined

EXAMPLE 26. Editing for condensation in the Rhodes manuscript. The DE's queries to the author summarize the goals of condensation (AQ1), explain how specific edits support those goals (AQ2, AQ3, AQ5), and propose (AQ4) or request (AQ6) new connective material.

It is worth noting that most passages will not be queried so heavily as here and in example 27. Sustaining this level of inquiry throughout a manuscript would slow the editing to a snail's pace and risk authorial apoplexy. Most DEs query densely like this for a few pages, to give the author a sense of their approach, then allow the queries to taper off.

The third week of May, news of my discovery broke in the scientific community.[AQ1] ~~Although my paper had been rejected by both *Nature* and *The Journal of Vertebrate Zoology*, staffers there evidently felt it worthwhile to get the rumor mill going.~~ [AQ2] On Monday, the director of the Royal Academy dismissed my find as a cheap knockoff of the original fossil from which T. H. Huxley identified *Palaeeudyptes antarcticus* back in 1848. Until now, no other fossil of this species (or genus!) had ever been unearthed, and it was my bad luck to find the same damned bone as Huxley. On the bright side, the ankle bone or tarsometatarsus is the single most distinctive bone in penguins, so there's no doubt it's from a giant penguin.[AQ3] Back in the 1850s, the newspapers were overflowing with speculation about a species of penguin eight feet tall and warlike as the Maori; we now realize they ~~In reality, this species~~ stood only between four and five feet high and lived as sociably as extant species today, their only competition[AQ4] ~~and was surely no more violent than the penguins we know today. Many a time I've imagined what my penguin, whom I've named Carlos, would have experienced while standing on the rough black surface of Querida. He would have known the island was moving—all birds have an internal compass—and would have enjoyed a varied diet depending on the island's position in the California Current. He and his mate probably only spent part of the year on Querida, and knew where to find it each year for breeding season. They would have competed fiercely for food with~~ the abundant sea lions and seals, who would likewise ~~lived centuries before the fur trade brought them near extinction; they too would~~ have found Querida a convenient raft to fish from. ~~Carlos, did you have the regal plumage of the emperor, or the modest markings of the chinstrap?~~[AQ5] On Wednesday, the Smithsonian issued a statement condemning my find as "the latest stunt in a career of fraud that sullies the cultural memory of the First People." By Friday, I'd been implicated in the debate about the speed of the so-called molecular clock. ~~In 2002, researchers from Massey University in New Zealand had extracted DNA from penguin droppings 8,000 years old and deduced that the rate of mutation was two to seven times quicker than previously thought; since then, biologists have been arguing like drunken sailors about how to apply these findings to various orders in the fossil record.~~[AQ6] The lava in which my fossil was embedded indicated an age of no more than 600 years, which suggested that Huxley's bone may not have been as ancient as previously thought. The Guano Landing group wasted no time in calling me "a dreamer who has spent too much time alone in his tourist-trap lighthouse."

AQ1: In the edits that follow, I've compressed three paragraphs into one for two reasons: (a) to match the brisker pace of surrounding passages and (b) to heighten the sense of files. With Perry backing Bud, the author took the queries more seriously, argued less frequently, and responded by making most of the revisions requested. Perry had Rhodes return his responses to the Peregrine office rather than directly to Bud; that way, Perry could shield Bud from the author's lapses in civility.

Once the major cutting and drafting was done, Bud focused on tinkering with the narrative pace. For instance, in new chapter 4, "The Fauna: The Epoch of Giant Penguins," the developmental plan had called for reducing sixty-five pages to twenty-three. Bud had achieved this reduction by wholesale cutting, and the resulting text read well overall but still felt slow in places. Even though he'd already reached his length goal, Bud condensed these passages so their pace would match that of the leaner, meaner chapter (example 26).

Less frequently, the opposite problem surfaced. The original manuscript furnished a scant eight pages of narrative for new chapter 9, "Driftwood Haiku: The Secret Detention Center"; weighting this section as a full chapter had required an equal number of pages of amplification. Again, the "rough cut" of the new chapter had jerky pacing. Here, Bud needed to prompt the author for some additional elaboration in order to smooth out the rhythm of the prose (example 27).

Ultimately, Bud made his peace with a certain amount of variety in the book's pace. In some chapters, a paucity of concrete evidence kept the pace relatively brisk, while in others a trove of findings required that the narrative slow down for a careful forensic review. So long as the content was dictating these changes in tempo, Bud reasoned, readers would adjust without complaint.

EXAMPLE 27. Editing for amplification in the Rhodes manuscript. The author queries prompt the author to write new material (AQ3) and invite him to revise draft amplifications as he "sees fit" (AQ1, AQ2, AQ4).

To solve the first mystery, I visited my old hashish-smoking buddy Ed Closky, who now lived an ascetic life in a hermitage in the Sierra foothills outside Nevada City. He ran his fingers over the runes and confirmed my suspicion that the characters were Japanese *kanji*, in a modern calligraphic style. When he asked where I'd come by the planks, I told him "never you mind," knowing that it would be unbecoming of a Buddhist to press for answers. He just nodded his white fringe of hair and began translating:

| riding the back | the wind carries | marooned on this |
| of this heartless whale | a seal's distant bark | dried mushroom |
| going nowhere | deaf ears hear | asphalt cloud |

"These are in the old haiku style, but they use a vernacular that didn't enter Japanese literature until the Meiji, so they're clearly done in the 1920s or later," Ed surmised. The reference to a mushroom cloud might even suggest the bombings of Hiroshima and Nagasaki; if so, the poems could be dated to the week in 1945 between the August 7 bombings and the release of detainees shortly after VJ Day, August 15. "Probably these poets were good friends who enjoyed poetry-writing parties during peacetime," Ed said. This would have made them middle-class members of Japanese society who had gone to America to seek their fortunes.[AQ1]

My next visit was to another friend, who shall remain nameless, at the Phoebe Hearst Museum on the Berkeley campus. We met there at two in the morning and ran tests to determine the age of the planks. Embedded nails were from the 1940s, made of poor wartime iron,[AQ2] but the wood itself was at least three hundred years old, and the toolmarks shaping the plank were those of the First People.[AQ3]

On my long predawn ride back from Berkeley to the lighthouse, I tried to imagine what it must have been like to be detained on a flat, barren island of volcanic rock. Crude barracks would have been their only shelter from the strafing ocean winds. They probably felt seasick all the time—Querida is more stable than a ship, but the ground would have undulated subtly under their feet. And[AQ4] large swells would have created a treacherous surf along the island's edges. There would have been no need for guards, so they probably were given dried goods and water and left to fend for themselves. If they lived to see VJ Day, then they may have been liberated—or would the United States leave them there to rot in order to keep the secret of Querida?

AQ1: Okay to spell out implications a bit further? Revise as you see fit.
AQ2: How did your friend determine the nails were from the 1940s? Is my guess correct?
AQ3: This paragraph ends too abruptly. The paragraphs fore and aft are vivid and evocative, but this dramatic moment—breaking into a museum, as it were, in the wee hours to conduct a secret experiment—is hardly evoked at all. No doubt you're concerned about blowing your friend's cover, but won't familiars of the museum guess his or her identity anyhow? I suggest adding several sentences to include the reader in the suspense of the moment.
AQ4: A correct assumption? Or is the island really small enough to rock back and forth with the swells? Please clarify.

EXAMPLE 28. The final TOC for the Rhodes manuscript. The narrative outline is now clear, running from geological prehistory to the present, with the author's own story as a frame.

*Isla Querida: Sonoma's Mythical Floating Island*

Foreword: Isla Querida as a Site of Cultural Longing, by Armistead Krasney

1. Keeping Querida
2. The Geology of Desire
3. The Flora: Prehistoric Pollens, Kelp Rudders, and Man-Eating Lichen
4. The Fauna: The Epoch of Giant Penguins
5. Querida as Sacred Ground

6. European "Discovery" and Disbelief
7. Hearst's Hideaway
8. A Fate Worse than Alcatraz
9. Driftwood Haiku: The Secret Detention Center
10. An Ounce of Querida Gold
11. The Crooked Lighthouse
12. Seven Hair-Raising Sea Rescues

Final Inconclusive Thoughts

Several years passed after Bud's completion of the Rhodes assignment. Every so often, he would run into Perry, who would say, "Don't even ask," from which Bud inferred that Harvey was making the copyediting, design, typesetting, and indexing of the book as difficult as he had its development. Then, on a day trip to Mendocino, Bud saw the book displayed prominently in the windows of each of that hamlet's ninety-three gift shops. To his great surprise, the table of contents was as he'd last seen it (example 28). The front cover was a close-up of Querida as depicted in one of the First People's cave paintings; from the back cover, Harvey grinned disarmingly, a charming old salt.

By all accounts, *Isla Querida: Sonoma's Mythical Floating Island* was a great success. Perry eventually recouped his investment, and Peregrine Press gained prominence by the book's coverage in the local media, including a half-hour segment on *Bay Area Backroads*. That year, a popular Querida calendar displayed imaginative renderings of the island by a local artist, interleaved with well-produced photographs of the artifacts: the pumice collection, the gilded chunk of Hearst's swimming pool, the redwood planks carved with poems, the penguin bone. January featured Harvey's crooked lighthouse and December his red-nosed, seemingly affable mug. Bud's friends, who had listened to him complain about Rhodes for the six months he'd worked on the book, all bought copies and hunted, without success, for Bud's name in the acknowledgments.

Isla Querida, Bud realized, was forever ruined for him. No longer a source of fascination, it showed up in his dreams as a barren rock on which he was stranded, with only a fax machine for company.

In writing, as in life, transitions come in all kinds—geographical, temporal, intellectual, spiritual. And varying degrees: a book telling a story in three parts, with each part taking place on a different continent, will also contain a series of smaller shifts, from bedroom to bathroom, from home to office, from one side of the street to the other. The importance of such transitions may bear no relationship to the distance traversed, if, for instance, a protagonist crosses the street to avoid a woman he once loved. With practice, an author becomes adept at transitions; in the meantime, the DE can help to fill in those gaps.

In our case study, the author has made the ultimate transition, and his survivors are left to glean his intentions from a piecemeal draft. The editing job is further complicated by the literary executor's intention to publish the manuscript out of her garage, so to speak—though in this case, her garage is an office in a sleek high-rise occupied by the deceased author's foundation. If this situation seems like a stretch, be forewarned: most freelance DEs find themselves dealing with a posthumous editing assignment at some point in their careers, and most take on the occasional well-funded vanity project to make ends meet.

### Author Profile: The Dead Author

Anyone who has worked in book publishing for a while has encountered the difficult circumstance of an author dying before she or he has had a chance to finish the manuscript. The author may have completed an entire draft but intended to revise, or may have reached only the halfway mark in the story or argument. If written under the strain of physical pain and disorienting medication, the manuscript may not represent the author's thinking at its most cogent or style at its most lucid. Raw research notes may be scrawled in a code understood only by the author, or an assistant long since gone. The publisher is free, of course, to dissolve the contract for lack of a complete manuscript, but most will make a good-faith effort to see the project into print. Often, the author's will bequests funds for just that purpose, or funds are raised by the author's survivors and colleagues.

Over the years, I have learned that most people choose for their literary executors not the most accomplished writer among their friends, nor the colleague who shares their area of expertise, but the person closest to their hearts, the one soul they can trust. Thus, the DE who takes on a posthumous assignment must allow the stages of grief to influence the developmental process. Most literary executors start out hesitant to alter the language of their recently departed loved one; over time, they realize that they will fulfill their custodial role best if they allow improvements that the author would surely have embraced.

Paul Chandler wasn't your average author. Son of a real estate tycoon, he had spent his life fighting against the urban sprawl his father helped perpetrate, using his trust fund for the purpose. As a boy, he'd lived in San Francisco's East Bay hills among chaparral and oak savannahs teeming with wildlife, but by the time he had finished high school the wilderness beyond his backyard had become a suburban maze. As much as the deer, bobcats, hares, coyotes, and owls, he had missed the stars. He'd dreamed of becoming an astronomer, but soon his bedroom telescope could pick out only the brightest celestial bodies through the thickening light pollution.

In college at Chico State, Paul had led a somewhat dissolute life. Then one night out camping and smoking weed with his friends, lying on his back on a picnic table, he got an idea—he'd mount a crusade to "save the stars" by reducing light pollution. His first environmentalist activities looked more like frat shenanigans than serious protests, and they drew public attention for the wrong reasons. Initially, his father threatened to cut him off, but during the Clinton administration, as the consequences of urban sprawl became a hot topic in the media, the elder Chandler found it useful to condone his son's activities publicly. Paul, for his part, never directly challenged his father's real estate projects, although he came under fire from environmental groups for not lying down with them in front of bulldozers.

Paul's first "protests" were actually techno-music dance raves held spontaneously during the rolling brownouts that began plaguing California's urban areas in the late 1980s. These illegal events landed him in jail several times and made him a countercultural hero, but it wasn't until a decade later—when Paul donned a business suit to announce the results of his foundation's research into the negative social and environmental effects of artificial light—that the utilities and developers took notice. As did Washington: Vice President Al Gore invited Paul personally to testify in front of the House Committee on Energy and Commerce.

Chandler had another distinctive quality as an author—he was dead. In the early 2000s, he had decided the best way to fight light pollution was to make a high-profile tour visiting the "ten darkest spots on the globe," a journey he would document for the Discovery Channel. He was taping a nighttime walk-about deep in the Australian outback when a poisonous snake bit him and ended his life. The infrared video clip played on the Web for weeks afterward.

Now his almost-finished memoir was in the hands of Gwen Troth, his long-time personal secretary. She had discouraged his tell-all approach: he was bound to make enemies of many powerful people, not the least of whom was his own father. But the writing had given Paul an immense sense of liberation, and now that he was gone, Gwen would publish the book in the form he'd intended, using the foundation's funds. No one could harm him now.

### Client Profile: The Self-Publisher

The term "vanity press" has pejorative connotations, and with good reason. One needn't look far to see print advertisements for books making wacky claims, and many of these bear the names of vanity houses. These publishers handle production and marketing for a fee, and some take advantage of authors with unrealistic hopes for their ill-conceived and poorly written books. With the advent of desktop publishing, more authors are typesetting and printing their own books, then selling them via post office boxes or Web pages. Some are skipping the printed page altogether and publishing in electronic format only. These phenomena, like the Web itself, foster rich diversity and democratic access at the expense of quality control.

For a DE, taking an assignment from a self-publisher is risky business: the project may have been overlooked by agents and publishers because it is inherently flawed; authors can be slow or capricious about paying bills; and the DE may spend much time educating the author about basic publishing realities. On the flip side, some self-publishers have ample resources, and they may be circumventing the usual channels simply to avoid the groupthink censorship imposed by our market economy. Occasionally, self-publishing is the first step toward a bestseller or literary canonization: witness Whitman's *Leaves of Grass*, Joyce's *Ulysses*, and Redfield's *The Celestine Prophecy*.

Most DEs prefer to avoid self-published projects but will take them on when the vagaries of freelance income dictate. DEs should be sure to size up the author, and the author-as-publisher, using the advice in chapter 2. DEs would do well to specify an hourly rate, partial payment up front, and a cap on the number of hours or months they are willing to commit. And because no publisher is available to serve as buffer, DEs should set firm limits about what work they will do, and which hours of the day or week they will be available.

Hedda wasn't enthusiastic about so-called vanity publishing jobs, but the Darkness Foundation was a well-known philanthropic entity in the West, so although she might be in for some tough rounds of editing, she wouldn't have to worry about getting paid.

The author's literary executor, Gwen Troth, assured Hedda in a telephone conversation that the foundation would sell paperback rights to a major trade house promptly. Gwen was following Chandler's own wishes by publishing the hardcover edition out of the Darkness Foundation's coffers to ensure that the book did not get censored. The finished draft had vanished from his study within hours of news of Paul's death, and the grieving family insisted that Paul had not been writing a memoir. What they didn't know was that Paul had backed up the manuscript every night on the foundation's FTP server; Gwen then nightly downloaded a copy onto a jump drive, which she kept on her person.

Wow, thought Hedda. This woman was a dedicated assistant.

"He wrote it in installments," Gwen said, after a pause. "He always intended to, you know, smooth over the rough spots. The whole story is there, but the connections are missing. That would have been his wish, to fill in the gaps."

Hedda promised to take a look and get back to Gwen in about a week. "Any editing we do," Hedda said, "is going to require your full participation. He obviously trusted you deeply, which tells me that you know better than anyone how he thought, and how he expressed those thoughts." Gwen didn't reply, but her silence was eloquent.

## Assignment: The Memoir with Lapses

Gwen had represented fairly the manuscript's strengths and weaknesses. Chandler's story unfolded in straight chronological order and crisp prose, true to its simple table of contents (example 29). Nevertheless, a few adjustments seemed desirable. For one thing, Chandler's "Opening Words" would serve better as "Closing Words," since he would now have no chance to write the latter. Also, the two chapters about Chandler's dissolute youth could be combined. Finally, the last chapter about Chandler's global tour would need to be constructed from a miscellany of materials, including interviews he'd given while promoting the trip, entries from his travel journal, and Gwen's epilogue. With these adjustments, the text could remain structured as it was.

Gwen had put her finger on the manuscript's main problem: from chapter to chapter and subsection to subsection, transitions were sorely lacking. The book had been written out of temporal order, with each passage told as a complete story in its own right. Sitting down with his drafts each morning after breakfast, Gwen had never known whether she'd be reading about Chandler's childhood, his wild days in Chico, or more recent events that she'd witnessed personally. "It seemed like a vivid memory would take hold of Paul and he'd want to get it written down right away," Gwen told Hedda over the phone.

"Are you certain he wanted the passages to end up in strict chronological order?"

"Yes, I'm sure," she replied curtly. "He was always saying, 'This piece will go before the one we did about the Richmond Brownout Rave' or whatever. You think I would make up a thing like that?"

Hedda didn't respond.

"I'm sorry," Gwen continued. "I don't know what's gotten into me."

"No need to apologize," Hedda said. "We knew this process would be difficult for you, especially at first. We'll get there."

"I feel like I should be paying you extra for therapy," said Gwen, a hint of a smile audible in her voice.

"Say no more. It goes with the territory."

## Create Opening Transitions

In the previous chapter, the author and DE focused on cutting up the cloth of the text, rearranging the pieces, and finding new patches to cover gaps. Now it is time to stitch the pieces together with transition statements. Each seam will require some needlework, but the most important transitions will occur at the beginning and end of each chapter.

As in the drafting of whole new passages, the duo has three ways to proceed. Option 1 has the DE prompting the author (or author's surrogate) to do the drafting with little writing assignments. Option 2 involves the DE querying the author for raw material and then drafting the transitions on the author's behalf. In option 3, the DE drafts all new transitions without prior author involvement. Whichever method is chosen (and all three can be used in turn), authors should be empowered to reword the transitions in their own voice.

SPLIT THE THESIS INTO HALVES. The easiest way to create an opening transition is to split the chapter's thesis statement in half. A thesis contains an implicit question and answer; an opening transition should pose the question but defer the answer to the end of the chapter, creating suspense:

*Thesis:* The increase in reckless driving on American highways stems from the advent of a generation who has learned to drive from videogames.
*Question:* Can the increase in reckless driving on American highways be attributed to the popularity of videogames?
*Answer:* Yes, because an entire generation of drivers now experiences the road as a virtual reality, makes lane changes that defy the laws of physics, and expects to simply "start over" after causing a crash.

To put it differently, a chapter's thesis is the sum of its opening and closing statements.

TWEAK THE QUESTION HALF. Opening transitions need not always be explicit. Anecdotes, dialogues, set-pieces, and even jokes can introduce a thesis dramatically and subtly:

By the time your sixteen-year-old has gotten behind the wheel of a car, she or he has already logged hundreds, if not thousands, of hours in the driver's seat.

The best books vary their chapter-opening strategies, mixing explicit statements with implicit ones—but this plan can be overly ambitious for a DE-author team. The safest strategy is to break the chapter thesis in two and explicitly state its interrogative half.

CONSIDER A FUSED OPENING. Another variant is to fuse the answer half from the previous chapter with the question half from the present chapter. This may be necessary in works with very complex plots or arguments, or when the previous chapter has ended in a cliff-hanger. For a more detailed discussion of how to create such fused closing-and-opening transitions, see the next section.

Hedda began by drafting a thesis for each chapter. For chapter 1, which she'd retitled "Trust Fund Baby" (a favorite self-deprecation of Chandler's), she wrote

*Thesis:* From my earliest years, darkness was not a realm of monsters but a safe place in which to create the fantasy worlds of my imagination.

As an opening statement, this thesis would tell too much. She tried breaking it into its "question" and "answer" halves:

*Question:* Why didn't I fear darkness, like other children?
*Answer:* Because for me darkness was not scary but a safe place in which to create the elaborate fantasy worlds of my imagination.

Having isolated the ideas that she wanted to open and close with, Hedda looked for sentences in Chandler's text that might serve the purpose:

*Opening:* I was never one of those kids who asked for the light to be left on.
*Closing:* So it was that, from my earliest years, darkness was a calming presence, a friend I played with after supper in the wild chaparral behind our house.

Now the chapter opened vividly by immersing the reader in a homey detail of Chandler's childhood, while at the same time foreshadowing the centrality of darkness to the author's life. And it closed with Chandler's own assessment of darkness in his boyhood as "a calming presence."

On to chapter 2, which Hedda titled "Boy Astronomer." Here, the main thrust of the narrative was something like this:

*Thesis:* As I entered puberty, subdivisions developed around us, the night sky became less populated with stars, and I lost my boyhood interest in astronomy.

As an opener, this statement would rob the chapter of its narrative suspense. But expressed as a question and answer, the statement set up a dynamic passage through the rites of youth:

*Question:* Why did I lose my interest in astronomy at age thirteen?
*Answer:* As an adult, I came to realize that my loss of interest in astronomy resulted not so much from the onset of puberty as from the gradual dulling of the stars.

Better, but the answer was still a bit ham-fisted. Hedda now looked for phrasing in the chapter's text that might be promoted to opening or closing status; this time she came up empty handed. The best she could do was draft a pair of statements for the literary executor to revise into the author's voice:

*Opening:* By age thirteen, although my bedroom looked like a planetarium, I was losing interest in the stars.
*Closing:* Years later, I realized that, despite my father's claim to the contrary, I left astronomy behind not because of the onset of puberty but because so many stars had left the sky.

Now the chapter opened on an evocative note and closed with a strong perception of personal motivation. Hedda continued to draft openings and closings for the remaining five chapters and then emailed the list to Gwen. Did she think they would work?

## Create Closing Transitions

Closing transitions are no less important than opening ones. An opening transition engages the reader's interest in the present chapter, while a closing transition engages their interest in the *next* chapter.

CONSIDER FUSED TRANSITIONS. Picture your discourse as a length of chain, with each link a chapter. Each link has two points of intersection, and only two, with the rest of the chain. Where two links meet, the first link's "answer" meets the next link's "question." These can be stated separately, with the answer at the end of one chapter and the question at the beginning of the next, or they can be fused in a single statement that occurs at either the end of the first chapter or the beginning of the second:

*Answer:* In summary, this survey of over a thousand depositions taken from drivers under thirty years of age suggests that their accidents were caused by a cognitive gap, a fundamental lack of awareness of the consequences of reckless driving.
*Question:* Can millions of American drivers be "reprogrammed" to appreciate the dangers of the highway by a campaign of public service announcements?
*Fused:* As millions of American drivers career about the highways with cognitive gaps that blind them to the consequences of their reckless driving, some advocacy groups are calling for a campaign of public service announcements on the order of those launched in past decades against drunk driving and domestic violence.

CONSIDER CLIFF-HANGERS. When a single fused statement appears at the beginning of the next chapter, the previous chapter has ended in a "cliff-hanger." This term comes from the serials of early cinema, in which the hero was inevitably left dangling one-handed from a cliff or window ledge to ensure that moviegoers returned the following week. Usually, cliff-hangers are narrative, but they can be expository as well: that is, a theoretical argument can be interrupted at its apex for dramatic effect:

As millions of American drivers careen about the highways with cognitive gaps that blind them to the consequences of their reckless driving, advocacy groups are marshalling their forces to make the roads safer.

The key to using cliff-hangers effectively is restraint—pick up any novel from an airport book rack to see how mind-numbing this device can become when used repeatedly.

Gwen called when she got the draft transition statements. She was upset. Until now, the prospect of putting words into her deceased friend's mouth had been hypothetical, and now she wondered whether engaging Hedda's services hadn't been a mistake. Hedda assured her the draft transitions were meant only to demonstrate the kinds of statements that would be needed—they could work together to ensure that the statements were expressed in Chandler's voice.

"You did say he would not want the book published without polishing," Hedda reminded Gwen. "By doing this work you are executing his wishes. You're enabling the book to be published."

Wherever possible, Hedda had already pulled phrasing from Chandler's own text. When Hedda pointed out that nine of the fourteen statements were minor variations on Chandler's own words, Gwen began to relax. They spent the next few days emailing revised versions of the statements back and forth until Gwen was satisfied with all of them. It seemed that Hedda's draft statements, whether on the mark or off, would elicit strong memories of talks between Gwen and Chandler. In this way, over a period of several weeks, Hedda watched Gwen's editing gain confidence. She was stepping into her role as literary executor.

It was chapter 3 that inspired Gwen to use cliff-hangers. Hedda's draft closing statement for that chapter was less summative and more forward-looking than the others:

*Closing:* No one who saw me in those days—unshaven, high on pot, and full of pranks—would have guessed I would soon become an influential figure in the civic arena.

This sentence had been adapted from one of Chandler's own, and Gwen liked the dramatic effect of the foreshadowing. The statement summarized the waywardness of Chandler's college days, which had been the focus of chapter 3, while intimating the developments to occur in chapter 4.

Soon Gwen had redrafted all seven closing transitions as cliff-hangers. Some of these worked remarkably well, but the overall effect was too formulaic, too mechanical. A more serious problem was that a couple of her cliff-hanging closures made the following openers redundant:

*Chapter 4 closing:* When I saw how effective the Brownout Raves were at grabbing media attention, I decided it was time to put some hard science behind the message.
*Chapter 5 opening:* Now it was time to get serious about demonstrating the facts and misconceptions surrounding light pollution.

By intimating the opening of the Darkness Foundation Laboratory at the end of chapter 4, Gwen stole the thunder from the opening of chapter 5. She also strove so hard to create dramatic chapter transitions that she sometimes put unconvincing thoughts in Chandler's mind:

*Chapter 7 opening:* When we first approached the Discovery Channel about doing a documentary series on the world's ten darkest places, I hoped to find cultures that valued the darkness as I do.

As far as Hedda could tell, during preparations for the trip, Chandler had been fixated on locating each continent's darkest spot, period. The cultural insights he had gained via his sherpas and hosts had come as a surprise; Gwen's edits were romanticizing the biographical record.

When Hedda pointed all this out, Gwen quickly understood the problems and corrected them. "I can't help seeing new things in this material," she told Hedda, "but I can put all those observations in my editor's note and let Paul tell his own story." Not bad, thought Hedda, for a young woman with the weight of the world on her shoulders—or at least, the weight of a substantial fortune. By the time the transition statements were finalized (example 30), Gwen's and Hedda's contributions were thoroughly intermingled.

## Draw Conclusions

Now is when you deliver on the promise of your main thesis. If you've restructured the entire manuscript (see chapters 4 and 5), you'll already have found positions for the author's conclusions. If, however, your intervention is limited to providing connective tissue between chapters and passages, you'll want to check that all of the promises implied by the main thesis have been kept.

EXAMPLE 30. Seven pairs of transition statements for the Chandler manuscript, reflecting the literary executor's revisions. The bona fide cliff-hangers are the closings to chapters 3 through 6, with chapter 5's the most dramatic.

Chapter 1. Trust Fund Baby (1960–1972)
*Opening:* I was never one of those kids who asked for the light to be left on.
*Closing:* So it was that, from my earliest years, darkness was a calming presence, a friend I played with after supper in the wild chaparral behind our house.

Chapter 2. Boy Astronomer (1973–1978)
*Opening:* By age thirteen, although my bedroom looked like a planetarium, I was losing interest in the stars.
*Closing:* Years later, I realized that, despite my father's claim to the contrary, I left astronomy behind not because of the onset of puberty but because so many stars had left the sky.

Chapter 3. Dropping Out and Getting High (1979–1982)
*Opening:* My strongest memories of college are the days I spent cutting class, getting high, and frolicking nude among the glacier-hewn boulders of the Yuba River.
*Closing:* No one who saw me in those days—unshaven, high on pot, and full of pranks—would have predicted I would soon become an influential figure in the civic arena.

Chapter 4. Brownout Raves (1983–1993)
*Opening:* "Wouldn't it be cool," said my friend Vic one night by the campfire, "if we could hold a rave during one of these rolling brownouts they're having?"
*Closing:* When I saw how effective the Brownout Raves were at grabbing media attention, I decided it was time to put some hard science behind the message.

Chapter 5. The False Security of Light (1994–1996)
*Opening:* My professors wouldn't have recognized me, so diligent became my studies of the phenomenon of artificial light.
*Closing:* "I look forward to seeing you, then," said Vice President Gore, leaving me stunned with a dial tone in my hand.

Chapter 6. The Prince of Darkness Goes to Washington (1997–2001)
*Opening:* Ironically, all those years listening to my dad boast over supper about his successes in Sacramento had given me a deep understanding of how lobbying works.
*Closing:* My job done in Washington for the moment, I turned my attention to the world at large.

Chapter 7. The World's Ten Darkest Places (2002–2005)
*Opening:* Seen from space at night, Earth's artificial lights look like fallen stars swept into piles and clinging like dust to the edges of continents.
*Closing:* My journey had started out as a publicity stunt with a political agenda, but it ended as a kind of spiritual awakening to the value of darkness in preserving the cultural diversity of our species.

UNPACK NESTED CONCLUSIONS. To draw conclusions, you need to go through the process of thesis selection in reverse. In chapter 3, you placed smaller theses within larger theses like nested Russian dolls; now you'll unpack those dolls until you have a freestanding answer for each nested question.

DRAFT CONCLUSIONS AS NEEDED. Note the operative word "free-standing." It denotes a key difference between how a discourse begins and how it ends. Whereas a main thesis has greater impact if its subordinate theses are nested, a main conclusion has greater impact if its subordinate conclusions are treated separately. Why is this so? At the beginning of a book, readers are impatient to know what the book is about and what they might expect to learn if they commit valuable time to reading it. By the end of the book, readers have been won over by the author and have both the patience and the curiosity to see each line of inquiry through to its finish. These readers want to be sure that all the loose ends have been tied up properly; they want closure.

So, if your main thesis A contained smaller theses B through E, you'll want to draft separate conclusions for E, D, C, and B before delivering the final blow, main conclusion A.

RECYCLE CLOSING TRANSITIONS. Often you won't have to start this process from scratch: some of your chapters' closing statements will probably serve well as conclusions. In fact, because most books have more chapters than theses, your conclusions may all be drafted already. The author and DE should survey their closing transitions, earmark those that double as conclusions, and draft any conclusions that don't yet exist. Chapter closings doubling as conclusions may need emphasis added to ensure that readers don't miss their special relevance.

Each chapter was now a coherent narrative that linked seamlessly with the chapters preceding and following it. "But something's still missing," Gwen said, and Hedda had to agree. They put aside the project for a couple of weeks.

Then, on one of Hedda's morning cardiovascular hikes, she had a sudden realization. Here she was supposed to be the DE for this book, and she'd completely forgotten to look for the main thesis. True, Chandler's backmatter "Closing Words" spelled out a moral for his life story, but this short section seemed hasty and tacked-on, the conclusions too convenient. The manuscript had been so well written that Hedda had neglected to think it through from the ground up. Now she would have to perform her usual procedure in reverse—instead of culling a set of thesis candidates from the manuscript and combining them into a grand overarching thesis, she would need to identify the main thesis first, smash it into corollaries, and then sow those shards into the text.

What was the moral of Chandler's story, anyway? It comprised two parts. Hedda tried putting into a single statement the gist of the book as she understood it:

In modern times, ubiquitous light has been equated with safety and progress, but such light actually hampers the growth of human potential by providing a false sense of security and by blinding and starving the fellow species on whom we depend for the richness and diversity of our lives.

The sentence was a bit overblown, but it would serve its purpose until she could get Gwen to recast it in Chandler's cadences. In the meantime, she broke it down into its component parts by trawling the manuscript for sentences that reflected facets of the whole:

*Nature:* To love nature is to love the darkness, because more than half the biodiversity on our planet comes alive at night.
*Society:* That first Brownout Rave, with thousands of city dwellers peacefully celebrating the night sky, gave me a belief in the essential goodness of humanity that would carry me through my future political battles.
*Crime:* In studies we conducted from Calgary to Manchester, from Tucson to Singapore, the results were the same: all-night lighting gave residents a sense of greater security but failed to reduce crime and more frequently accompanied a slight increase in assaults and crimes against property.
*Politics:* Lobbying a senator was like praying to a Greek god: you had to appeal to the flaws in his or her character to get your way.
*Culture:* More and more, I saw foreign cultures as falling into two global camps—those that fought against darkness as an enemy and those that lived peacefully in its shelter.

Although one of the statements was Gwen's and another Hedda's, most were Chandler's own words. In a few cases, Hedda had needed to tease out an explicit theme from phrasing that only hinted at it. But much of the power of these conclusions was lost because they were buried in the middles of chapters. They needed to be moved to places of prominence so that the reader would notice a progression of insights.

## Place Those Conclusions

To switch metaphors again, the main thesis is like the starting line of a footrace, with each sprinter a line of inquiry. The runners leave the starting line all at once, but at the moment the race is won they are staggered along the length of the track. The main conclusion overtakes the subordinate conclusions one by one; the slowest sprinter is the most easily proven of those subconclusions.

STAGGER CONCLUSIONS. Similarly, the author and DE should expect to place their conclusions at various points along the last third of their discursive line. This staggering avoids a confusing "photo finish" in which the reader is forced to absorb all the conclusions at once.

EMPLOY INVERTED ORDER OF IMPORTANCE. Writing isn't a mathematical science, but the use of sets in math is a useful analogy. Just as you wouldn't have an open square bracket without its closing mate, so you shouldn't introduce a thesis at the beginning of a book without a conclusion near its end. As with sets, the statements fall in nested order, with conclusions generally in inverse order of importance:

{Thesis A [Thesis B (Thesis C {Thesis D [Thesis E (Thesis F
Conclusion F) Conclusion E] Conclusion D} Conclusion C) Conclusion B] Conclusion A}

Because discourse isn't governed by mathematical laws, an occasional disruption of this order is permissible, but these lapses should be exceptional, lest chaos ensue.

Hedda looked for ways to move the conclusions she'd identified into the more prominent closing positions of their respective chapters. In chapter 4, she took the "society" conclusion from the middle of the chapter and fused it with the closing statement. What began as two separate statements

*Society:* That first Brownout Rave, with thousands of city dwellers peacefully celebrating the night sky, gave me a belief in the essential goodness of humanity that would carry me through my future political battles.
*Chapter 4 closing:* When I saw how effective the Brownout Raves were at grabbing media attention, I decided it was time to put some hard science behind the message.

became a single powerful closing:

*Revised closing:* Emboldened by my newfound belief in the essential goodness of humanity, I decided to make the most of the media attention drawn by the Brownout Raves and put some hard science behind the message.

Because this formulation referred back to the "society" conclusion, Hedda decided to leave the original statement in the middle of the chapter.

In chapter 5, Hedda and Gwen had come up with a dramatic ending, but the chapter's main message was buried. Hedda decided to pull the "nature" conclusion from chapter 1 and massage it into the Gore phone call. The discrete statements

*Nature:* To love nature is to love the darkness, because more than half the biodiversity on our planet comes alive at night.
*Chapter 5 closing:* "I look forward to seeing you, then," said Vice President Gore, leaving me stunned with a dial tone in my hand.

became a surprising hybrid when cross-pollinated:

*Revised closing:* "I look forward to seeing you soon," said Vice President Gore, leaving me stunned with a dial tone in my hand. I hung up, and the sounds of nightfall rushed in on me, as more than half the planet's species began to awaken.

Although this new closing resembled the "nature" conclusion closely, Hedda decided that the statements were far enough apart, with three chapters between them, that a little repetition wouldn't hurt. So she left the "nature" conclusion in its original place.

Finally, Hedda situated the author's most mature insights at the end of the last chapter. This was easily accomplished because his "culture" conclusion and his final closing resonated deeply with each other:

*Culture:* More and more, I saw foreign cultures as falling into two global camps—those that fought against darkness as an enemy and those that lived peacefully in its shelter.
*Chapter 7 closing:* My journey had started out as a publicity stunt with a political agenda, but it ended as a kind of spiritual awakening to the value of darkness in preserving the cultural diversity of our species.

---

EXAMPLE 31. The final TOC for the Chandler manuscript, which retains the simplicity of the original but imparts the narrative's contours much more concretely.

*Light Pollution: One Man's Crusade to Save the Night Skies*

Editor's Note
1. Trust Fund Baby (1960–1972)
2. Boy Astronomer (1973–1978)
3. Dropping Out and Getting High (1979–1982)
4. Brownout Raves (1983–1993)
5. The False Security of Light (1994–1996)
6. The Prince of Darkness Goes to Washington (1997–2001)
7. The World's Ten Darkest Places (2002–2005)
Closing Words

---

The closing required the merest tweaking:

*Revised closing:* My journey had started out as a publicity stunt, but it ended as a kind of spiritual awakening to the value of darkness in forming diverse human cultures, whether it was seen as an adversary to be fought or a sheltering ally.

This time, Hedda decided that the revised closing's thunder should not be stolen by a mid-chapter revelation, so she removed the "culture" conclusion from its original position.

✳

When Hedda received her copy of *Light Pollution: One Man's Crusade to Save the Night Skies,* she wished she'd advised Gwen to hire an experienced book designer. The table of contents read beautifully, if she did say so herself (example 31), but the jacket was a horrid collage of images that dutifully represented the periods of the author's brief life. Fortunately, the cloth run sold out instantaneously and Visigoth redesigned the cover when they picked up the paperback rights. The first, self-published printing had been reviewed in the trade journals, but it was the publication of the paperback that resulted in a blizzard of media retrospectives of Paul Chandler's life. The elder Chandler found the attention of the press irresistible and eventually made public appearances to help sell the book he'd once tried to destroy.

One warm moonless June night, Hedda turned out all the lights, went out behind her farmhouse, and lay down on the picnic table, just as the young Paul once had done. An orangish haze haloed the trees to the south where downtown Lancaster lay, but she was far enough away to have a pretty clear view of the stars. It was true, she realized, there'd been more of them when she was a girl. Still, she was grateful for the chance to see them again before they were altogether obscured.

**9** ✳ S T Y L E ✳ *Training the Voice*

Each of us writes using diction, syntax, and rhetoric developed over thousands of years by millions of speakers and writers. As children, we absorb these inventions of others like sponges; as young writers, we ape the style of the master whose work has most recently dazzled us. Gradually, these disparate influences meld into a single mature voice, a dialect spoken by a population of one, our idiolect. We achieve originality of style not by avoiding the influences of others but by blending them into a combination that has not been heard before.

By the time authors have achieved a book contract with a reputable publisher, their style should have matured enough that their influences are pleasingly integrated. Having reached this level of achievement, some authors try to protect their style by avoiding further influences. Their style becomes set in stone, and before long they offer parodies of themselves. The best writers know their style is a living thing that will encounter and absorb new influences until the day they die; thus, even the best writers risk betraying recent infatuations in their prose.

This chapter assumes a familiarity with grammar, usage, and the rules of composition. These "elements of style" have been addressed definitively elsewhere (see "Further Reading"). Although some DEs intervene at the word, sentence, and paragraph levels, others leave much of this stylistic cleanup to the copyeditor. Our focus here is on the elements of voice, those qualities of style that define an author's unique stance among the host of published writers. These elements convey the author's personal blend of attitudes toward subject, audience, self, the world of ideas, and society. For our purposes, we'll group them under the headings of tone, rhetoric, abstraction, and irony.

In our case study, a talented but impressionable young journalist suffers a malady that frequently afflicts first-time authors: she allows too many prose styles to influence her own. The client is a book packager operating on a thin profit margin: its overworked staff cannot take the time to "train" a new author. The manuscript's structure is simple and sturdy, and its subject is a sure bet, but the author needs the help of a DE to modulate and integrate her clashing styles into a single effective voice. What makes this case study instructive—if a bit farfetched—is the unique opportunity it affords the DE to meet in person the author's stylistic influences.

## Author Profile: The Journalist

Reporters and feature writers are generally among the easiest authors for DEs to work with. Accustomed to slash-and-burn editing, they routinely see paragraphs cut from their newspaper or magazine articles for no better reason than to make room for another advertisement. Most know how to collaborate—their editors will assign two or more of them to a major story—and the better ones prize factual accuracy to a degree that rises to the level of scholarship. Perhaps best of all, they rarely miss a deadline, importing their fast daily or weekly pace into the comparatively sluggish stream of book production.

Journalists can face special challenges, however, when they segue from assignments of 300 or 3,000 words to a book contract for 130,000 words or more. The book project probably draws on a series of in-depth reports that have already been published; if so, the author will be tempted to splice the material together rather than to recast it as a fresh seamless narrative. The habit of writing short articles may not transfer well to the larger canvas of a book-length manuscript. Often reporters, who may have done a dissertation's worth of research, have trouble, like postdoctoral authors, stepping back from their subject to see its essence.

Some freelance journalists develop a knack for pitching their voices to widely varied audiences, but others have a limited stylistic repertoire that becomes apparent only when sustained over the length of a book. Still others have developed habits as bloggers or commentators that are self-indulgent or idiosyncratic. It is the DE's job to demonstrate why stylistic choices that pop and sizzle in articles turn to static in the longer form of the book.

At twenty-seven, Dorian Riley was over the beauty beat, tired of writing about acne and prophylactics. She'd been writing her column for *Girlfriend* magazine for three years now, and she wanted to put her journalism degree to use on more newsworthy subjects.

Maybe that's why she felt such a deep connection with the book project she'd stumbled on last year. As a well-known role model to teenagers, she'd been engaged by a book packager to write a teen makeover book for a major trade house specializing in beauty that would surreptitiously encourage American adolescents to think twice before getting tattooed, pierced, botoxed, or surgically altered. Dorian had liked the original idea well enough: she was something of a crusader against the supermodel aesthetic that resulted in epidemics of anorexia, bulimia, and teen suicide among today's boys and especially girls. But her research had taken a surprising turn toward harder journalism when she happened upon the Mug Shot Module at Jerry Garcia High School in the heart of San Francisco.

The module was the brainchild of a quartet of teachers who'd convinced Animar—the local computer animation studio whose recent hits *Stone Age* and *Ostrich Story* had propelled them to the upper stratum of the entertainment industry—to provide seed funding and computer graphic interface (CGI) technology for their experiment. Mug Shot combined lessons in graphic arts, health education, cultural studies, and biology to help tenth graders look critically at their newly developing self-images. The premise was simple: students' video portraits were fed into their workstations in the computer lab, and then their images became "virtual pets" that either thrived or languished depending on how well the students nurtured them.

The digital wizardry was cool, but what enthralled Dorian were the instructors themselves. Two were her age and two older, but all four were gutsy pioneers who didn't just talk about the problems of today's youth but risked their careers trying to solve them. They taught health, science, computers, and art, and their personalities were as different as can be, but they shared a commitment to their students and the module. Her book contract had started out as a self-promotional move, but now she had a higher purpose: to see that the vision of these four educational trailblazers reached a wider audience.

### Client Profile: The Book Packager

Book packagers fall into three main categories. The *production packager* is a full-service vendor that picks up overflow work from publishing houses, providing the services of editing, design, composition, and sometimes oversight of manufacturing. These packagers often work closely with a small number of client publishers and are usually staffed by former employees of their largest client. The relationship is mutually agreeable: the publisher has the flexibility to take on extra work without hiring permanent staff, and the packager's staff enjoy the advantages of being their own bosses. The *agenting packager* is a production packager that also comes up with the idea for the book, commissions the author, and shops the proposal around to its major clients. The *copublishing packager* is an agenting packager that sees itself as a publishing house: it publishes the book jointly under its own imprint and that of its publishing partner, whose role is usually limited to distribution, sales, and fulfillment.

It is the agenting packager who most frequently requires the services of a DE. Assignments tend to be last-minute jobs with high earning potential—that is, the stress is high but the pay good. Trade packagers often handle surprisingly high-profile books: these are the "instant" books that most publishers dabble in, books whose success will be determined by whether they make it to market first to take advantage of a recent news event. Book packaging isn't for everyone, but packagers can be a regular source of lucrative assignments that will look good on the resumé of a freelance DE.

This is why I don't work with first-time authors, Irma Cherise reminded herself. An experienced author would not sign a contract and then turn in a draft bearing no resemblance to the work stipulated. True, the Riley manuscript was a valuable property—the story it told was a fascinating one that could sell well if produced and marketed properly. The question was which publisher to place it with.

Irma had started Sachet Books, a copublishing packager, after burning out in her staff position at Glamour Eyes Publishing. She had tired of doing the same old books and felt that, with Glamour Eyes as a bread-and-butter client, she'd be able to branch out into other subject areas. All had not gone as planned: after eleven years, the Eyes (as she and her staff called their main client) still accounted for 90 percent of her business. Teen beauty was what she knew, and the vulnerability of self-employment had caused her to favor the safe route. Now, with six full- and part-time staff members relying on her for income, she felt less free than ever to take a risk in a sector of publishing that she didn't know well.

She'd pitched the original Riley assignment to the Eyes and signed Riley's contract on the strength of a letter of interest from them. Now she had two choices: reject the project on grounds that it did not meet contractual obligations, or rouse her entrepreneurial spirit and find the book a suitable publisher. She was obligated to offer the project to the Eyes first but hoped they wouldn't like it: the book would get lost on their list, which was strictly lipstick and bubblegum. Fortunately, the current draft had major stylistic problems: Irma decided to leave these gaffes *in flagrante* to make the text less appealing. Once the Eyes demurred, she'd hire a DE to clean up the text before pitching it to a major house. The Animar logo would go a long way toward opening doors.

EXAMPLE 32. The unrevised TOC for the Riley manuscript. The narrative thrust is deftly handled overall, but subtle lapses in tone indicate deeper stylistic problems in the main text.

*Mug Shot Makeovers: Life Lessons in a Virtual Classroom*

## Assignment: The Story with Too Many Voices

Bud was glad when Sachet Books called. He'd done a few projects with the book packager before, and they paid well, although their schedules were killer. Usually, the subject matter was not his cup of tea—the smart remarks of his gay friends notwithstanding—but this time he was intrigued by the idea of the teachers' high-tech approach to students' self-esteem. Irma had thought of him because of the local angle—Garcia High was only about a dozen blocks from his apartment. Once the package arrived, Bud saw that Irma's assessment was dead on: the content was fascinating and the structure sound, but the style was all over the place.

The table of contents (example 32) mirrored the course outline of the Mug Shot Module exactly. During the first four weeks of the ten-week module, the students experimented with choices in diet, exercise, study, work, and play habits. Through the use of CGI technology developed for the criminology units of police departments, they were also able to try out different clothing, hairstyles, tattoos, piercings, and surgical alterations.

Then at week 5, the real life lessons began. Each Monday, the students entered the lab to find that their virtual selves had aged, with the repercussions of their youthful choices etched on the faces of their adult, middle-aged, and senior selves. Students who had chosen to set their alcohol intake at high levels found themselves with bloodshot eyes at age twenty-eight and W. C. Fields noses by age forty-eight. Students who got tattoos were surprised to find they couldn't "undo" them and then watched the sexy designs melt and splay on their sagging flesh. With each new stage of life came new adult choices such as career changes, marriages and divorces, child-rearing, and retirement. In week 9, the students were forced to consider how a generation making the choices they'd made for their virtual selves might affect global trends in population, politics, and the environment. And by week 10—after "journaling" throughout the module—they were asked to tell the stories of their virtual lives to their own teenaged grandkids.

Dorian Riley had done a good job of reporting. She selected four "representative" students to spotlight throughout the module and supplemented their detailed accounts with colorful anecdotes from the virtual life histories of other classmates. Much of the book's appeal would be in the art program: the publishing plan allowed for 100 color photographs captured from the Mug Shot user interface, including ten composite "yearbook pages" showing all twenty-four students at thumbnail size at each of the course's intervals. Amazingly, she'd managed to procure parental consent forms for all but one student, whose story would appear under a pseudonym and whose photos would be blurred like those of passersby in television news footage.

But the writing style was a mess. Irma had sent along clippings of Riley's magazine articles, which had an appealing and consistent voice: sassy, post-9/11 jaded, conversant with hip-hop slang but not enslaved to it. She wrote about emergent teen fads with a sharp critical eye, expressing her wry intelligence in language that spoke effectively to her peers and juniors. She'd tackled tough subjects like sexism in gangsta culture and last year had been voted one of VH1's "top 100 role models." But the complexity and sophistication of the Mug Shot Module had overwhelmed her. Her text had somehow become a patchwork quilt of New Age transcendentalism and various kinds of jargon, from biomechanics to postmodern theory to videogamer speak.

This dissonance was evident even in the table of contents, where Riley abutted knowingly hip section headings like "The Boss from Hell" with clunkers like "Transience and Flexibility in the Workforce." In chapter 2, the section headings were boringly scientific, in chapter 3, hip and colloquial. Clearly, Riley hadn't been able to assimilate so much new information into her own psyche and voice. Where were these undigested influences coming from? That was what Bud would have to figure out.

## Set the Tone

Tone is that dimension of style which conveys an author's attitudes toward subject, audience, and self (see table 2).

RESPECT THE SUBJECT. Lapses in tone are, simply put, lapses in respect. A biographer, for instance, may treat her subject with such disdain that the reader wonders, why did you bother devoting years of your life studying this general if he was so horrible? Another may treat his subject so worshipfully that the reader distrusts every word of the saintly portrait. Because most authors are motivated by a deep interest in their subjects and a genuine desire to engage their audiences in meaningful conversation, these lapses of undercriticism and overcriticism are generally unwitting. The DE can help the author to avoid putting off readers by querying bad jokes, inept metaphors, and remarks made in poor taste.

RESPECT THE AUDIENCE. Worse off are authors who misgauge their tone toward the audience. What these authors intend as enthusiasm or wit comes off as overwriting on the page. Readers pick up on the faintest whiff of condescension, they shun overfamiliarity, and they're alienated by an air of entitlement or proselytizing, however well meaning. If pervasive, these defects can be the kiss of death to an author's prose. When these attitudes come naturally to authors, DEs may have difficulty getting them to see what's wrong.

Conversely, some authors who love their subjects passionately can become intimidated by the prospect of writing a book and fail to communicate their ardor. The honor of making an immortal contribution to the annals of print puts some authors on their best behavior—which makes them downright boring. To break this spell, DEs can flag telltale signs like passivity, euphemism, overqualification, and equivocation to get these authors to lighten up.

ESTABLISH A PERSONA. One of the trickiest aspects of tone for a DE to address involves an author's attitude toward herself or himself. The classic style guides advise writers to place themselves in the background and avoid editorializing; this strategy yields prose that is quietly authoritative. But some writers in the postmodern era have balked at this guidance, which they see as restrictive and artificial—for them, this false modesty is the nonfiction equivalent of third-person omniscience in fiction, or the "fourth wall" in theater, both of which have been dismantled in recent decades. These

TABLE 2. Examples of tonal lapses

| LAPSE | DEFINITION | EXAMPLE |
|---|---|---|
| **TOWARD SUBJECT** | | |
| Undercriticism | A tendency to idealize in lieu of balanced critical thinking; when the subject is a person, called "hagiography." | Repeating the word "despair" in each stanza was a stroke of genius. |
| Overcriticism | Reflexively negative judgment in lieu of balanced critical thinking; when the subject is a person, called "a hatchet job." | Repeating the word "despair" in each stanza is the most overt sign of the laziness that pervades this poem and threatens our national values. |
| **TOWARD AUDIENCE** | | |
| Overwriting | An excess of enthusiasm, particularly toward the author's own use of language. | Repeating the word "despair" in each stanza has a hypnotic effect, coaxing the reader out onto the window ledge beside the distraught poet, hovering on the lip of the abyss. |
| Condescension | An air of superiority, as if having waived the privileges of rank. | By repeating the word "despair" in each stanza, the laureate takes a lick from youth-oriented "slam poetry"— a sly gesture that has gone unappreciated by most older Americans. |
| Overfamiliarity | Chumminess; the suggestion of a degree of intimacy beyond what exists between author and reader. | If you missed the inaugural address, pull up the laureate's hilarious poem "Despair" on YouTube; you'll get a kick out of it. |
| Entitlement | An air of possessing rights and privileges beyond those of the average person. | Repeating the word "despair" in each stanza rings false: the state of our nation isn't nearly so bleak as the poem suggests. |
| Proselytization | Preaching with a goal toward converting the listener to one's viewpoint. | We may hope the poet will avoid such verbal chicanery as the "despair controversy" during the rest of her tenure; the function of the laureate is to uplift our nation's spirits, not cast them down. |
| Passivity | The lack of human warmth or a discernible point of view. | Repetition of the word "despair" in each stanza is a notable feature of the poem. |

*(continued)*

TABLE 2 (*continued*)

| LAPSE | DEFINITION | EXAMPLES |
|---|---|---|
| Euphemism | The understatement of disagreeable truths to avoid offense. | The poet's repetition of the word "despair" in each stanza is a note of disquiet in an otherwise stirring poem. |
| Overqualification | The layering of a decisive viewpoint with caveats and cavils. | Perhaps the poet meant to invoke an air of suffocating oppression by repeating the word "despair" in each stanza— in which case, she has succeeded. |
| Equivocation | An indecisive or wavering point of view. | The repetition of the word "despair" over so many stanzas is both wearisome and hypnotic. |
| TOWARD SELF | | |
| Editorialization | The expression of opinion in discourse presented as unbiased reportage. | At the inauguration, when the laureate read her poem, the president elect flinched each time she repeated the word "despair," enacting an impromptu comedy sketch worthy of the Marx Brothers. |
| False modesty | Unconvincing expressions of modesty that betray the speaker's egotism. | Those of us without training in versification may be forgiven for not enjoying the laureate's inaugural piece. |

days, more and more writers are speaking directly into the camera, and the DE's role is not to quarrel with this stance but to judge whether the author has executed it effectively.

Bud began working his way through the manuscript, taking notes on his yellow legal pad and assigning abbreviations to the types of problems he encountered: TONE for tone, DIC for diction, SYN for syntax, MM for mixed metaphor, FI for false irony, and so on. The flags for tone were by far the most prevalent. About a third of the way in, distinct strains of tonal problem began to emerge, and he realized he'd need to subdivide those problems marked TONE.

Before he did that, however, he decided to give the author a call. On previous jobs, he'd found that the tone of an author's conversational voice could yield insights into problems with voice on the page. He called "just to introduce myself," asked about the author's availability over the next several months, and wondered aloud whether she had any questions about his involvement with her book.

"I mean, I get why Irma brought you in. This book is something new for me, and I agree with her that the prose is all over the place. I just don't know where to begin to fix it."

"Was it hard for you to write this draft?"

"Yes and no. I mean, in some ways it was the easiest writing I've ever done because I was so *into* the subject. But it's also the most complex thing I've ever tackled. It's been a struggle to juggle so many characters with so many stories, and then make sure all of the educational theory is clear."

"Well, we'll smooth things over. You've structured the book beautifully, and you're great at evoking the characters and interweaving the storylines. The only problem, really, is the unevenness in the style, which is very fixable. One last question, just out of curiosity: who are your favorite authors?"

"Oh, I don't know. Five years ago I would have said Jane Austen, Dorothy Parker, Colette, Willa Cather—you know, the women in the canon. But now I'm really into Joan Didion, Margaret Atwood, Louise Erdrich—women who reach large audiences with strong messages. And I read more men now, too—Dave Eggers, Jonathan Lethem, Michael Chabon. Why?"

"No reason. Just trying to get a sense of your taste."

Dorian thought it important for Bud to experience the Mug Shot Module himself, so they made an appointment to meet at Garcia High the following Monday morning.

Off the phone, Bud replayed the conversation in his head. Surely Dorian Riley was reading younger women like Zadie Smith and Lauren Weisberger, but she wasn't mentioning them among her potential influences. Her literary aspirations may have become more realistic since college, but they were still quite high and emphasized classic values represented by mature writers. She was best when she wrote in the inherently ironic argot of her own generation; when she strove for a more literary effect like Erdrich's New Age spirituality (example 33), subtlety went out the window.

Perhaps the most revealing of the author's statements, Bud thought, was her emphasis on getting the pedagogy right. That concern could undermine her confidence in her own voice. For now, he decided to postpone refining his notes and read on to see if he could unearth some more clues.

## Parse the Rhetoric

As an expression of tone, rhetoric also conveys the author's attitudes toward audience, subject, and self, but it does so with dramatic flair. Rhetorical devices are those gestures that authors make to keep their audiences alert and entertained. The smaller gestures come automatically, like facial expressions or talking with one's hands. The larger ones tend to be chosen more

EXAMPLE 33. Editing for tonal lapses in the Riley manuscript. Queries that flag lapses in the author's respect for her subject include AQ8 and AQ11. The New Age expressions targeted by queries AQ1, AQ4, AQ5, AQ6, and AQ10 convey a lack of respect for the audience by committing the sins of condescension, overfamiliarity, overwriting, and proselytizing all at once. The author's distrust of herself comes to the fore in her editorializing, a problem addressed most directly by AQ4.

As noted earlier, most passages will not be queried so heavily as here and in examples 34 through 37. Most DEs query densely like this for a few pages, then allow the queries to taper off.

## Picture Day, with Measles

Sassy Sutherland was ~~the archetype of an old soul in a supple young body.~~[AQ1] a self-proclaimed proud Baby Mama, a child who herself had already given birth.[AQ2] That first day of the module, when instructed to adhere paper dots to her ~~flawless~~ flawlessly made-up[AQ3] face, ~~her peaceful warrior spirit rose up in protest:~~ she balked:[AQ4] "Hell no, I ain't lookin' like no raggedy-ass clown." Ms. Simmons, ~~sensitive to the change in Sassy's aura,~~ knowing Sassy's fiery temperament,[AQ5] pulled the young woman aside and let her watch ~~her witness the transformation on~~[AQ6] the screen as the glowing dots turned each of her classmates' still portraits into living, breathing, blinking~~, smiling, smirking~~ faces.[AQ7] "Okay, I'm next," Sassy said, ~~ready now to begin her own journey of self-discovery. "But~~ "but you gotta do Zach, too. Who ~~supposed to~~ got Zach?"[AQ8] Aisha stepped in ~~materialized~~ from the hallway and handed him over to Sassy with great nonchalance, as if she hadn't noticed a boy child was fastened to her hip. Little Zach ~~commenced to~~ began [AQ9] fussing when his mother daubed him with paper dots, but she calmed him with ~~the low murmurs of a mountain stream~~ soothing murmurs.[AQ10]~~, anointing his face for this virtual rite of passage. "Lookatchyoo, lookatchyoo!"~~ "Look at you! Look at you!"[AQ11] Sassy sang, and for a few moments I saw her cares slip away. The huge hoops in her earrings jangled with joy.[AQ12] ~~like dinner bells, and she settled her head back on her neck like the proud Baby Mama she proclaimed herself to be.~~

AQ1: This passage is heavily inflected with New Age expressions, which I've tried to soften throughout. In this sentence, the Jungian analysis seems vague and irrelevant.
AQ2: I've moved up the Baby Mama reference to situate Sassy more precisely in the cast of characters, okay?
AQ3: Okay to clarify? "Flawless" is slang in this context and may confuse your more mature readers.
AQ4: More New Age editorializing; okay to remove?
AQ5: Here, I've recast the pseudospirituality in more journalistic terms; okay?
AQ6: Transformation, journeys of self-discovery, and rites of passage are all understood by the reader in this context without being explicated, so I've stricken these phrases here and below.
AQ7: Okay to reduce series from five to three items? The full set felt melodramatic.
AQ8: Reproducing a speaker's pronunciation and grammar in dialogue can make the character more vivid, but overdoing this can invoke ugly stereotypes. The "raggedy-ass clown" rejoinder pegs Sassy beautifully, but further transcriptions of her grammatical errors seem petty. Here, "gotta" is okay because most English speakers use this contraction, but "supposed to got" verges on caricature.

EXAMPLE 33 *(continued)*

AQ9: "Commenced to" strikes an odd note here in the narrator's tone—too formal.

AQ10: A nice metaphor, but too self-conscious and intrusive here. Again, a bit New Agey . . .

AQ11: Very few English speakers say, "Look / at / you"; we all make the little "chew" sound. Yet generations of white English authors have transcribed the "chew" sound when quoting black characters and omitted it when quoting white characters. Use with care.

AQ12: Okay? Or revise as you see fit. Because I stole your Baby Mama reference from here, you need to conclude the paragraph on a different note. The earring simile didn't work—maybe "like wind chimes"?

---

deliberately, like an actor's stride to center stage before delivering a soliloquy. In writing, rhetoric is where structure and style meet: the smaller gestures serve as transitions from passage to passage, the larger ones as frameworks for entire passages (see table 3). The DE can help the author coordinate these stylistic and structural efforts for maximum effect.

MAKE FEW BIG GESTURES. To make their larger rhetorical gestures, authors draw on a fund of strategies rooted in oral tradition, among them analogy, irony, humor, enumeration, interrogation, declamation, and repetition. Most of these strategies cannot be deployed too frequently or they lose their usefulness as devices for clarifying complex systems of thought. For example, a single apt, recurring analogy can help a reader to fathom an esoteric subject like supply-side economics, but comparing that economic theory in quick succession to a seesaw, glacier, and conveyor belt—and then mixing those comparisons when referring back to them—will prove more confusing than illuminating.

STOP COUNTING. The single most overused rhetorical device in serious nonfiction may be enumeration. Authors love to enumerate the three causes of this and the five effects of that. The tendency is understandable: authors have taken some trouble to put their thoughts in order, and they want to be certain readers perceive that order. But overuse of enumeration undermines its usefulness: by the tenth list of "three crucial points," the reader is swimming in enumerations and mixes up the points from the various lists.

MAKE MANY SMALL GESTURES. The writer's smaller rhetorical gestures should be more plentiful, varied, and colorful. Aphorisms, jokes, similes, and metaphors are particularly helpful in spicing up passages, but only if they're done well: clichés passing as aphorisms, jokes that aren't funny, and mixed metaphors do more harm than good.

Paradoxes and oxymora must be true to add value to a text. Because most

TABLE 3. Examples of rhetorical gestures

| GESTURE | DEFINITION | EXAMPLE |
|---------|-----------|---------|
| **LARGE** | | |
| Analogy | Comparison between two things that are different but share many qualities; an extended simile or metaphor. | When I encounter writer's block, I am reminded of a backup in morning traffic: it comes when I least expect it, its cause is nowhere in sight, and it elicits a range of responses in my psyche, from stoic patience to dangerous lane-changing, to relief on those days I'm avoiding my desk. |
| Irony | Traditionally, a statement that unveils truth by seeming to say the opposite; in contemporary parlance, a tone of voice that confronts the paradoxes of life with detachment. | Writer's block is the marble from which we carve our masterpieces. |
| Humor | The quality of incongruity or absurdity that causes mirth. | Get away from me with your writer's block! I don't want to catch it. |
| Enumeration | Subdivision of a topic into its parts; may or may not employ numerals explicitly. | Writer's block can be caused by many things: a change of heart about one's subject, an acute awareness of deadline pressure, or unrealistic expectations of the quality of one's prose as one produces it word by word. |
| Interrogation | Exposition that proceeds by asking questions and then answering them; only when the answer to the question is obvious or unanswerable is the question said to be "rhetorical." | Does writer's block really exist, or is it only imagined? If writing is an act of imagination, isn't a block also imagined by definition? Yet if both writing and the state of being blocked are imaginary, why can't the author imagine the block away? |
| Declamation | Writing using the effects of oratory, including exclamations, exhortations, and other forms of direct address. | Come to me, writer's block! And stay a while, so I may rest in your company. |
| Repetition | Restatement for emphasis, sometimes verbatim, sometimes by rephrasing. | Go, writer's block, leave me be—go back to the circle of hell that spawned you. |
| **SMALL** | | |
| Simile | The explicit comparison of two different things that share at least one quality. | Writer's block is like a relationship that has stagnated—you've invested too much in it to abandon it, but staying only increases your frustration. |

TABLE 3 (*continued*)

| GESTURE | DEFINITION | EXAMPLE |
|---|---|---|
| Metaphor | The implicit comparison of two different things that share at least one quality, usually by treating one thing as though it were the other. | Writer's block forms in the uppermost reaches of the mind, creeps a few feet forward or back in due season, and seems—unlike other, more tangible glaciers—impervious to global warming. |
| Joke | A humorous word, expression, or brief story. | If Sisyphus had my writer's block, he'd be flat as a pancake. |
| Pun | A play on two or more disparate meanings of the same word. | My answer to writer's block is writer's block-and-tackle. |
| Paradox | A pair of truths that seem contradictory and irreconcilable yet remain equally true. | When writer's block comes, I write masterpieces in my mind; when it goes, I eke out my prosaic thoughts on the page. |
| Oxymoron | A paradox compressed into two words. | The worst form of writer's block is the soft block, which seems to give way before enveloping you. |
| Aphorism | A terse formulation of sentiment or truth. | Writer's block is the art of wishing you had something to say. |
| Understatement | A statement that emphasizes its point by consciously diminishing its force; used for irony or tact. | Writer's block can cause some authors uncomfortable moments. |
| Hyperbole | A statement that emphasizes its point by consciously exaggerating its force; used for irony or dramatic effect. | Writer's block is the scourge of an author's existence. |
| Amplification | Restatement of a point for clarity or emphasis; a kind of repetition. | Writer's block sucks; there's nothing worse than sitting in your favorite café and staring at an empty page of your notebook. |
| Personification | Comparison between an inanimate thing and a person; a kind of metaphor. | When writer's block moved in with me, he ate me out of house and home and left dents in the living room furniture. |
| Synesthesia | An observation of one of the five senses in terms of another sense; a kind of metaphor. | I pick at my writer's block like a scab, savoring its salty itch. |

*Note:* Rhetorical devices have been taxonomized since Aristotle and number in the hundreds; those in this table are the ones most frequently abused by today's writers. Fluent writers can create rhetorical effects deftly without knowing their technical names. For a discussion of useful sources on rhetoric, see "Further Reading."

of life's contradictions have already been observed, fresh paradoxes are hard to come by. A paradox can sometimes be central to an author's thesis, in which case it is more than a rhetorical gesture.

Understatement and hyperbole are both forms of emphasis, achieving the same result by opposite means. In general, the yin of understatement can be used more liberally than the yang of hyperbole. But the modesty implied by understatement can become obsequious through overuse. Conversely, some authors can sustain hyperbole to create an informative and entertaining "tall tale."

The brilliant pun is exceedingly rare. What is it about cutting hair, human or canine, that attracts punsters? My local yellow pages yield Bushwhacker, Shear Magic, Groomingdales, Woofgang's, All Fur Love, and Pawsitively Groomed among many others. The more forced the pun, the louder the groan.

When the author's prose was not drowning in New Age sentiment, it often explored the drama inherent in the students' stories effectively (example 34). In these passages, the only recurring distraction was a tendency toward excessive self-consciousness: Bud would need to prune the rhetorical flourishes, which seemed largely the result of a youthful tendency to strive a bit too hard for originality. He could relate—he was old enough to know better, yet his own prose tended to run a bit purple, as his writing group never hesitated to point out. How easy it was to see the motes in another's eye.

When Monday arrived, Bud found his author every bit as appealing as her publicity photos. They met in the high school's muraled portico, and the security guard greeted "Miss Riley" cordially. They were scheduled to visit with each of the Mug Shot teachers and to watch the module itself during third period. First up was Eartha Simmons, an older, lithe woman in a shimmery running suit with lantern jaw, huge blue eyes, and Angelina Jolie lips. While we spoke, she backed up onto her desk in a seated lotus.

"Fix your book?" asked Eartha. "What on earth for? The parts I read were magical. Why does it need to be rewritten?" She directed her question at Bud with a gaze that was frank and a little wild.

"Well . . ." he began, but Dorian interrupted: "It's because I haven't written anything as long as a book before. My chapters all read fine on their own, but together they don't quite add up." She turned to Bud: "At least, that's how Irma explained it."

Bud redirected the conversation toward Eartha, asking how long she'd been at the school, what subjects she taught, and so on. She managed to sound brusquely practical and hopelessly idealistic at the same time—a useful pair

EXAMPLE 34. Editing for rhetoric in the Riley manuscript. Here, the DE tamps down the rhetorical flourishes in a passage that is well written overall. Note how AQ2 balances criticism and praise, and how AQ7 muses on a direct quotation without suggesting an editorial change. In these ways, the DE encourages open dialogue with the author while demonstrating that he has been reading attentively.

**Relocation Roulette**

Gustavo Mahalo was the class's ~~token~~ sex-change candidate.[AQ1] With long straight brown hair and slender hips, he got a thrill from passing as a woman at bars in the Mission, where mariachis strolled and *machismo* ~~dripped from the street signs and mariachis staggered from bar to bar like dying flies~~ reigned.[AQ2] It was a dangerous game, but so far the gangbangers hadn't discovered his secret. Sometimes these knights in shining bling even slow-danced with Gussie, never guessing they were in the arms of another man.

So last week, when the Mug Shot students were given the choice of staying "homebound" or going "outward bound," Gussie didn't think twice. ~~What choice did he have, really?~~[AQ3]He was already living on the streets, more or less: the streets were his finishing school, he liked to say—"they will finish you *off.*" But he felt safer there than at home, where his father ~~flew into violent rages and~~ used Gussie's own rhinestone belts and stiletto pumps to beat him ~~to a pulp.~~[AQ4] ~~Remarking on~~ Aware of the economic tyranny of beauty,[AQ5] Gussie chose to panhandle for his necessities: clothes, jewelry, and cosmetics. ~~How ironic that food and shelter did not make the list.~~[AQ6] "Only the fabulous die young,"[AQ7] he intoned over the keyboard, freshening the makeup on his virtual image before selecting "runaway" status and watching the screen fade to black.

This week, Gussie entered the computer lab to find his virtual self suddenly aged to twenty-eight. ~~In the footlights of his imagination, he'd~~ He'd always ~~seen~~imagined himself maturing into ~~as~~a gorgeous woman,[AQ8] but the feminine softness of his adolescence had given way ~~to a voluptuous~~ instead to a surprising virility.[AQ9] The CGI program had morphed him into a mascara'ed version of the men he wanted to attract: he was still flawlessly beat out, but his huge adam's apple and the blue beard under his skin clashed with the lashes, rouge, and lip gloss. ~~How could this be?~~[AQ10] "Aye!" Gus squealed, "Who's that thug in drag?"

AQ1: Okay to delete? The word "token" has pejorative connotations.
AQ2: Okay as revised? I recognize that you're taking off on the Spanish idiom "los moscas muertas" (dead flies) here, but the metaphor doesn't work in translation. In contrast, "knights in shining bling" works quite well two sentences later.
AQ3: This rhetorical question seems implied.
AQ4: Okay as edited? The deleted phrases are less fresh than the rest of the sentence, which is heartbreakingly vivid.
AQ5: "Remarking on" implied that Gussie used the paradoxical "economic tyranny of beauty," but I'm guessing that's your language; correct?
AQ6: The omissions will be obvious to the reader, so you don't need to remark on that irony explicitly, okay?
AQ7: Not sure what this statement means, but maybe that's okay. I never understood the phrase, "Only the good die young," either! Appropriating an aphorism and inserting a word like "fabulous" feels true to Gussie's drag-queen character.

(*continued*)

EXAMPLE 34 (*continued*)

AQ8: The "footlights" metaphor seemed a bit over the top; okay to delete? A bit more understatement here actually helps the reader register surprise along with Gussie.

AQ9: The word "voluptuous" is usually reserved for female sensuality; you may have intended this as an oxymoron, but it seems more distracting than helpful. Okay as revised?

AQ10: Again, a rhetorical question intrudes; this one steals thunder from Gussie's much more dramatic response in the next sentence.

of contrasting qualities in a career spent working with inner-city youth. Before Bud knew it, the period ended and they had to move on to the next teacher. It had been years since he'd heard a school bell ring; he'd forgotten how loud they could be. They found Caleb Force in Room 321, fingering a piano keyboard he'd ballpointed into the surface of his ancient desk. He dressed like a teenager himself—wrinkled vintage shirt worn too short, careful ringlets of dirty blond hair, strategically placed holes in his jeans. But the hair was thinning; he was an aging version of the waif look then in vogue. Dorian and he seemed mutually smitten.

"There she is," he declared, shaking Bud's hand. "Dorian is going to make our module famous. She's going to spread the Mug Shot gospel, and the education system in this country is going to rise up from its ashes."

Okay, thought Bud. This fellow gave new meaning to the term "drama coach." Still, Bud couldn't help liking him; after a while, he realized that Caleb's saving grace was a sense of irony. Each time he mixed a metaphor or posed a rhetorical question, his eyes twinkled as if to say, "I know, that was over the top." When he used hip-hop slang, his vowels slouched like a gangbanger's; and when he used a postmodern term, he assumed a stuffy, almost British accent. These impersonations lasted only the length of the word in question, and they acted like spoken italics or fingered "air quotes."

On their way to the computer lab, jostled by teenagers, Bud had a realization. He'd been assuming that the vocal disharmony in Dorian's prose was caused by unassimilated literary influences—that is, the styles of published authors. But the rhetorical excesses he'd noted in Dorian's manuscript sounded just like Caleb Force. The difference was that Dorian failed to transfer to the page Caleb's ironic tone. And Eartha, she must be the muse behind the author's intermittent New Age persona. Bud wondered which of her personalities he'd be meeting next.

## Master Abstraction

Authors' attitudes toward the world of ideas are conveyed by their mastery of levels of abstraction. The classic style guides advise writers to favor concrete words and simple sentences; this counsel yields prose that is clear and vivid, but sometimes at the expense of complex thought. Rather than automatically enforce the dictum "Be concrete," DEs do better to assess the role that abstract language plays in the public discussion around a book's subject. If an author's prose is markedly more (or less) abstract than that of other works on the subject at the local bookstore, then the DE must consider whether that difference is part of the author's contribution to the field. The goal of editing for abstraction is not simply to swap out concrete words for abstract ones but to bring out the *relevance* of both abstract concepts and concrete details.

HARNESS THE JARGON. Abstract language can be precise. There exist entire dialects of precise abstract terms: we call these arcane languages "jargon." Promotional blurbs often tout an author's text as "jargon-free," but this quality is a virtue only in books aimed at lay readers. Jargon is the best way for fellow specialists to discuss their subject with precision, and DEs should support the use of a term when it is the most appropriate word available. Take, for instance, the word "discourse," whose meaning—defined by Webster's as "connected speech or writing"—has been attenuated by postmodern theory. I was advised to avoid using it in this handbook, but I've found no alternative to serve as an umbrella term for both narrative and exposition. So "discourse" it is.

SLING THE SLANG. The English language constantly renews itself with fresh idioms. We perceive this slang as concrete because it is usually invented at street level; but the meaning of a slang word can be as conceptually sophisticated as a piece of jargon—and as incomprehensible to the uninitiated. Consider the word "feening," which I misheard as "feeling" for years until it was defined for me as a corruption of the heroin junkies' term "fiending," meaning "to crave that which is bad for one's physical or emotional health." Slang can be off-putting when it overtakes a written text, but its occasional use, when apt, can add much color and immediacy to an author's prose.

MANAGE THE SHIFTS. Most style manuals counsel authors to write consistently at a single level of formality that suits the audience and occasion. This advice is sound, and authors who hew to it will write in a coherent, distinctive voice. But this precept does not acknowledge the growing ranks of authors who mix levels of diction inventively to achieve dramatic, comical, and other literary effects. DEs should keep an open mind toward these experiments, giving authors constructive feedback when they succeed, and steering them back to the mainstream when they fail. (For a full discussion of levels of diction and syntax, refer to the resources under "Further Reading: Style.")

SWEAT THE DETAILS. Some manuscripts lack sufficient concrete detail, while others abound in concrete detail but fail to convey their relevance. Thus, editing for abstraction can involve both putting details in and drawing meaning out. (For use of narrative detail, see sidebar, "Character and Setting.") The DE can demonstrate the need for more detail, or the need to clarify the relevance of an existing detail, by willfully misreading the author's intentions:

*Text Lacking Detail:* The tiger's Christmas Day attack galvanized the whole community.

*Query A:* By "galvanized," do you mean the community was simply excited, or stimulated into action? Clarify?

*Query B:* Were there protests, then? And if so, by whom and toward what ends? If not, perhaps use a word other than "galvanized," which denotes "excited as if by electric current" but usually connotes active consequences, as in the phrase "galvanized into action."

*Detail Lacking Relevance:* On Christmas Day, three young men were attacked by a Siberian tiger that had maimed a zookeeper only last year.

*Query A:* Clarify the relevance of the earlier attack to the later one?

*Query B:* Are you arguing, then, that the tiger should not have been allowed to live after the first attack, and that the second one is therefore the fault of the zoo?

In both examples above, query A might well be met with an authorial response of "stet," or "Okay as is." If an author has not foreseen the potential for misreading a sentence before now, she or he is not likely to do so without some help from the DE. This strategy should be used sparingly: the disingenuous tone of such queries can undermine an author's trust in the DE if used too frequently. Willful misreading is also an effective technique for "breaking through" an author's resistance to editing for tone, rhetoric, or irony—but it's particularly useful in clearing up issues of vagueness and relevance.

In the computer lab, Chuck Vance moved among the workstations like a NASA director at Mission Control. The kids called him "Chucky" behind his back because he looked like Charlie McCarthy: reddish hair, freckles, and pronounced

## Character and Setting

In back-panel blurbs, it's become commonplace to extol an author's vivid writing by saying that the landscape serving as backdrop for the narrative is "a character in its own right." However hackneyed, this praise is often true: Dublin is a pal in *Ulysses*, New York a disappointing benefactor in *The Age of Innocence*, the barren winterscape an adversary in *Ethan Frome*. What's left unsaid by the blurbers is how this alchemy is achieved. These authors did not anthropomorphize their settings but gave them the emotional depth and complexity of a personality; they also allowed them a role in the plot, helping and hindering the protagonists' activities along the way. For these reasons, the methods for vividly evoking a historical setting—that fertile brew of place and time we call "milieu"—are the same as those for conjuring a believable character.

TELL WITH DETAIL. Physical and psychological details may be used to convey personality traits and ephemeral states of mind without stating them directly. The war veteran's nonchalant carriage of his amputated leg can convey bravery or denial: "He swung the stump up onto the chair bottom and leaned into it as though chairs were meant for standing." The sounds of the jungle surrounding a gated community on Maui can bode ill: "With dawn came the incessant song of the francolin, whom we call the car-alarm bird."

KNOW THE BACKSTORY. Depth of character can be established by subtle allusions to a person or place's history. Authors should resist the urge to rehearse an entire history simply because they have done the research. In the war veteran, this backstory might crop up as a facial expression or passing thought: "He winced, thinking of another chair that he'd been bound to for many hours." In the Hawaiian jungle, it might surface as the physical evidence of a layered past: "Beyond the reach of the lawnmowers and leaf blowers, the ruins of a longhouse moldered under the vines."

SUPPLY MOTIVE. The actions of characters and settings must have an underlying psychology of purpose, whether malevolent, benign, or otherwise. For the war veteran, "Standing here before her now was painful, but he tried not to break a sweat." For the jungle, "The gates of this quiet exurb posed no challenge; next monsoon, the island's vegetation would scale the walls, ply the swimming pools, and engulf the garden sheds."

overbite. Not that they knew Edgar Bergen's famous puppet: to their generation, he was the possessed dummy of the horror-movie series.

"Here," he said, "I'll pull up an old file so you can see how the module works." Dorian and Bud watched as he summoned the virtual Rocki Harris.

"Hey, we know this young lady," Bud said. "I just read about her in Dorian's manuscript. She's the one who went AWOL, right?"

Chuck went on to tell Rocki's story, and Bud began to recognize the source of another of the manuscript's stylistic motifs, the voice of bureaucratic jargon. Chuck himself was as unpretentious as they come, but he spoke like a police officer on the evening news, saying "deceased" for "dead," "apprehended" for "caught," and "witnessed" for "saw." Chuck played with Rocki's face to show how the Mug Shot program worked.

"Watch this. See how Rocki's virtual self would have manifested if she'd only managed her risk factors better. I'm decreasing her ingestion of unhealthy dietary components, increasing her aerobic activity, deselecting nicotine, raising her sleep level to the age-appropriate threshold. Look how her affect optimizes. Now she's a high achiever in school and career, marries well, positions herself for success as a working mother. She still resembles her own mother—but now she's a healthier, happier Mrs. Harris." A nice enough guy, but the kids must tease him mercilessly, Bud thought. No doubt Dorian found this language attractive because of its intellectual heft, but often its intentions were undermined by vagueness. If he hadn't seen it with his own eyes, Bud would have wondered what an "optimized affect" looks like.

As the period wore on, Bud was able to piece together the rest of the Rocki Harris tale by asking specific questions. It turned out that when Rocki ran away, her story made the local papers, prompting a school board member to attempt to shut down the Mug Shot Module on grounds that it threatened the students' mental health. Bud didn't remember this important information from Dorian's narrative; the next day, back at his desk, he confirmed that it wasn't there. Evidently, Dorian, like Chuck, was so concerned about the success of the module's educational mission that she hid this "bad press" under a veil of police-blotter euphemism. Bud would challenge her to come clean on grounds of journalistic pride and use details from his interview with Chuck to flesh out the story with concrete details.

Bud had to admit, though, that he too was becoming enamored of the module's potential to revolutionize secondary education, to get adolescents to *think* about their lifestyle choices. So he would suggest that Dorian use a quote from his notebook that countered the board member's argument (example 35). Nodding toward the soccer-mom version of the thirty-eight-year-old Rocki on the computer screen, Chuck had said, "We still don't know how the real Rocki's story will end. It may be Mug Shot was just the wakeup call she needed."

## Gauge the Ironies

In classical rhetoric, irony was a device in which the speaker said the opposite of what she or he meant and what the listener expected to hear. The effect was to underscore a contradiction or tension in the subject. In his famous essay "A Modest Proposal," Jonathan Swift argued for the institution-

EXAMPLE 35. Editing out abstraction in the Riley manuscript. The author has soft-pedaled a painful episode, her reticence marked by bureaucratic jargon and a lack of concrete detail.

**Career versus Kids**

Rocki Harris lived in ~~humble circumstances somewhere south of the city.~~ a trailer park in South San Francisco.[AQ1] Her mother, who worked ~~for the school district, made inquiries~~ in the cafeteria, pulled some strings[AQ2] and got Rocki transferred to Garcia High. She had a pretty round face with a strong jaw line and freckles over a nose that had once been broken, but somehow that bump only added to her charm.[AQ3] Rocki always said she hated her mother, but the other students knew she was just ashamed to see Mrs. Harris in a servant's smock. "I'm never going to embarrass my kids," she said again and again.[AQ4]

When Rocki came into the computer lab on week 7, she ~~was shocked to find her mother looking out of the~~ stared in horror at her computer's screen.[AQ5] The other students saw the same thing: "Hey, check it out, it's Mrs. Harris! I'll take the chili dog, Mrs. Harris! Cool piercings, Mrs. Harris!" Beneath the blue mohawk, eyebrow piercings, and nose post that Rocki had given her virtual self in previous weeks, it was Mrs. Harris all right: a pudgy woman with prematurely thin hair and circles under her eyes shining like bruises.[AQ6]

~~When Rocki asked Mr. Vance,~~ "How'd this happen to me?" Rocki asked. Mr. Vance ~~he~~ told her to think about the variables she'd constrained at the start of the module. [AQ7] ~~module: her diet was high in transfats, she had poor aerobic fitness, and she made recreational use of illegal substances.~~ She ate the same burgers and fries as her mother, had the same couch-potato habits, smoked just as heavily, and slept just as erratically. [AQ8] Her mom may have fought Rocki's use of illegal drugs, but Mrs. Harris's tranquilizers and sherry were just as detrimental to her health as Rocki's hash and cuervo—as Rocki herself had often pointed out.[AQ9] ~~When he suggested there might be a correlation between Rocki's personal habits and her mother's own health status, Rocki expressed disbelief.~~ Mr. Vance said, "Maybe you're not so different from your mother after all."[AQ10]

Rocki fell silent. A week later, she dropped out of school and no one heard from her again. Mrs. Harris continued working in the cafeteria, but when students asked about Rocki, she said she didn't want to talk about it. We later learned that she'd run away from home, disappearing for several months before showing up on her father's doorstep in New Mexico. In the module, she had decided to delay becoming a parent to pursue a career in cosmetology, but now it was likely she'd succumb to her father's pressure to marry young and give him lots of grandchildren. Still, the jury's out on Rocki, according to Mr. Vance. "It may be Mug Shot was just the wakeup call she needed."[AQ11][AQ12]

AQ1: This section on Rocki is short on detail. Per our visit with Mr. Vance yesterday, I'm supplying some specifics here and throughout. Your single paragraph becomes three. Feel free to revise as you see fit, so long as you retain the concreteness of detail.

AQ2: Why use such officious language (i.e., "made inquiries")? You need to specify that Mrs. Harris works in the Garcia cafeteria, else the students' chili dog remark (see below) makes no sense.

*(continued)*

EXAMPLE 35 (*continued*)

AQ3: Here, I'm adding physical descriptions from direct observation of Rocki's photos in the computer lab. Okay?

AQ4: This detail establishes Rocki's psychological motivation for responding so dramatically to the CGI image of herself at age thirty-eight. It also hints at the relevance of her story to a section about "Career versus Kids."

AQ5: Here, I suggest withholding the revelation of Rocki-as-her-mother so that it comes across more dramatically a few sentences later. Okay?

AQ6: Again, physical description is taken from direct observation in the computer lab.

AQ7: Inadvisable to begin two paragraphs in a row with the same syntax ("When . . . When . . .") Okay as revised? Also, sentence was a bit run-on in a passage that is otherwise direct.

AQ8: "Constrained variables" is abstract and vague, and references to transfats, aerobic fitness, and drug use are all generic. I've made up some details here to demonstrate how they might read, but you need to interview Rocki's former girlfriends for actual details.

AQ9: From your notes; but, again, I'm pulling the particulars of alcohol and drugs out of thin air. More research needed.

AQ10: Here, I'm quoting Mr. Vance from notes I took during our visit to the school. Okay?

AQ11: These details are from our meeting with Mr. Vance yesterday. As written, the Rocki story ended too abruptly. As rewritten, her story now leads into a larger discussion of the section's topic—the challenges of delaying childbearing.

AQ12: A final thought on Rocki's story. In the interest of full disclosure, shouldn't you tell about the board member's move to shut down the module? Reviewers will attribute your omission to biased reporting.

alized cannibalism of Irish children, employing irony in every sentence to expose the falseness of English charity toward the Irish underclass. But the term *irony* has broadened in recent decades to encompass an author's attitude toward society as a whole. Now when we say "That's ironic," we mean something on the order of, "That's emblematic of the paradoxes inherent in the human condition." Quite a mouthful.

These days, the classic device of irony is rarely used. Few authors have Swift's ability to sustain in serious prose a voice that says the opposite of what it means and genuinely reverses readers' expectations. The best most of us can do is fire off an ironic salvo now and then: when the tone is light-hearted, we call it *wit*, when bitter, *sarcasm*. But the deeper dimensions of irony, the so-called ironies of life, have only become more important in a world bereft of the certainties once afforded by closed systems of religious belief and social tradition. Grappling with these ironies is the work of all writers.

FLAG FALSE IRONIES. A DE can help an author identify attempts at irony that ring false or trite. When irony isn't working, it often veers toward sarcasm, conveying a mean-spiritedness that the author may not intend. For example, in a book about contemporary nuns finding their individuality within convent walls, one author described in excessive detail the cell of a hippie-era sister with a penchant for patchouli, tie-dyed curtains, and incense. What the author meant as gentle ribbing came across as jeering.

ACKNOWLEDGE TACIT IRONIES. The DE should also be on the lookout for ironies that the reader will apprehend but that the author seems to have overlooked. I recall one memoirist who, early in his manuscript, took a famous friend to task for not appearing at the bedside of a dying mutual friend. Late in the manuscript, when the famous friend was himself dying, the author refused to visit that deathbed. He reported this information without remarking on the irony of his decision—until his editor prodded him to.

Back at his desk, Bud thought about the last of the four Mug Shot teachers. From the computer lab, he and Dorian had proceeded to the science wing, where they caught up with Mrs. Madge Gracie, a linebacker of a woman. With her beauty-parlor hairdo and flowered dress peaking out from under her white lab coat, she had looked like June Cleaver on steroids. At the front of the classroom, she'd made Bud's acquaintance with polite tea-and-biscuits chatter, her head swiveling occasionally to bark out an order like a drill sergeant.

"We love Dorian, she's such a good egg. We've all wanted to document the Mug Shot Module but never seemed to have the time, and then along comes this angel to do it for us.—*Benji, if you don't turn that bunsen down you're gonna singe those pimples right off your face*—Anyhoo, when we dreamed up this experiment in the teachers' lounge one day, we never knew how important it would become to all of us. It's been so rewarding to watch these little ones—*Taylor, if I have to come over there*—watch them blossom, first in the virtual world and then in the real one. It's so crucial to catch them at this early, innocent stage—*Rachel, did we leave our brains on our pillow this morning?*—when they can really establish healthy habits that will last the rest of their precious lives."

Geez, Bud thought, this woman's a trip. At first he'd been uncertain whether her Jekyll-and-Hyde routine was intentional, but now he saw that it was. The kids understood the affection in her rough threats, and her otherwise ladylike mien allowed her to pay compliments without making the kids, or Dorian, blush. By playing these polar personae off each other, she made both tones ironic.

In the manuscript before him, Bud saw only sporadic evidence of an attempt to mimic Madge, but he did find the use of irony somewhat inept, vacillating between too little and too much subtlety. Dorian underscored small ironies heavily and then seemed to miss the larger ones altogether, as in a passage about student Angel Manzanarez (example 36). Angel was a class clown intent on turning the module into a running joke, but his efforts backfired: the monstrous virtual self he created eventually confronted him with some of his own deep insecurities. It may be Dorian was aware of this broader irony, but because she didn't acknowledge the irony explicitly, she risked seeming clueless. Bud made a note for his next pass to look for ironies that required softening or bolstering.

## Harmonize the Voices

Some texts have multiple personality disorder. They read beautifully at the word, sentence, and passage levels; they are free from tics and small lapses in tone; but from passage to passage, or chapter to chapter, they vary so distinctly in voice that the reader is left with a confused sense of the author's persona and point of view. The DE's goal is to help the author harmonize that choir in her or his head.

If you're wondering how authors develop this syndrome, you're asking the wrong question. Imagine taking a decade to write a book: the forty-year-old who finishes chapter 22 is in many ways a very different person from the thirty-year-old who started chapter 1. An author who suffers trauma halfway through drafting a manuscript may find that a new self, with altered emotions and insights and politics, picks up the pen to resume writing. Young authors encounter and absorb new influences so frequently that their voices can change from day to day. Given how long it takes to write a book, the real question is how so many authors manage to maintain a consistent voice for the duration of their labors.

FLAG TONAL SHIFTS. DEs can help an author to integrate disparate voices in two ways. First, they can point out passages styled in a manner that deviates from the book's dominant tone and prompt the author to rewrite those passages from scratch. Second, they can flag abrupt shifts in style between passages and suggest rewording to smooth over the rough edges.

CONSERVE TONAL RICHNESS. DEs should avoid, however, undermining the richness and variety of tone in an author's voice. Each time a dissonant note surfaces, the DE must reflect, "Will the reader intuit a reason for this quirk?" If the answer is yes, then the author has successfully absorbed the source style into her or his own. If the answer is no, then the note is false and the DE should suggest a different way to achieve the author's desired effect.

Once Bud had completed an editing sample of fifty pages or so, he forwarded it to Dorian with a developmental plan. Because she and he had developed a rapport during their day trip to Jerry Garcia High, Bud felt comfortable treating the multiplicity of voices in her prose in a somewhat lighthearted manner: he

EXAMPLE 36. Editing for irony in the Riley manuscript. The author underscores some ironies too heavily (AQ5) while failing to acknowledge the fundamental irony of the anecdote (AQ6). In the other queries, the DE modulates the author's use of irony in more subtle ways.

**Custody Smackdown**

Angel Manzanarez had a mustache by age fourteen and a wisecracking manner at birth. [AQ1] Like class clowns in previous semesters, he thought he'd get under the teachers' skin by making outrageous choices for his virtual self. He set his diet, exercise, and drug use patterns at the worst extremes available; he deprived his cyberself of sleep for weeks; he wore dreadlocks and army fatigues and tattooed SpongeBob Squarepants onto his forehead. The virtual Angel sagged and splayed like an image in a funhouse mirror. At the age of forty-eight, after three ~~After~~ decades without bathing, he was covered in sores and black with human soot. The other students thought his antics were hilarious.[AQ2]

But despite himself, Angel couldn't resist making a few appealing choices for his other self.[AQ3] He gave his despicable creation an unlikely way with the ladies, ~~also made himself a lady-killer~~ bedded a B-movie starlet named Lotta Lux, married her, and fathered several children.[AQ4] He made himself a brilliant businessman who created ~~and a rich tycoon with a movie starlet for a wife. (Ironically, the fake Angel invented~~ a sonar device for cleaning teeth, its success belied by the inventor's own rotting, green smile. ~~teeth—ironic because the fake Angel's teeth were green and rotten.) Then~~ [AQ5] And so on week 8, when he ~~Angel~~ came to the lab, ~~he~~ the real Angel was stunned to find himself being divorced by ~~busty~~ Lotta ~~Lux~~ and engaged in a bitter custody battle. Suddenly, the module was no longer a game: Angel himself was the product of a broken home, and the battles between cyberhusband and cyberwife tapped repressed reservoirs of feeling.[AQ6] When Mrs. Gracie asked him if he thought he should clean up his virtual self a bit before going to court, Angel spewed obscenities and stomped out of the computer lab. Unlike Rocki, however, he returned the next day to try to salvage a wiser Angel from the wreckage.

AQ1: Okay? Not sure why you lead off with his mustache, but I infer that he came across as both older and wiser than the other kids, making his irreverent jokes cool. My addition underscores this point a bit.

AQ2: I'm making this more explicit to heighten the contrast when his mood shifts.

AQ3: Okay as revised? Your original poses a contrast here but doesn't offer any psychological insight into his contradictory actions. My guess seems likely, but you should confirm against your notes.

AQ4: I'm moving Lotta's name up here where she's first mentioned, and making the children more explicit, so that Angel (and the reader) can feel their loss more acutely a few sentences later. Okay?

AQ5: Until now I've been pointing up ironies in the Angel story, but here you underscore the irony too heavily by naming it as such. "Belied by" okay? If not, please put in your own words.

AQ6: The reader already knows this from chapter 3, but I think it's important to insert a reminder here. Otherwise, you give the impression that you've missed the irony of the situation.

dubbed them the Guru, the Hipster, the Bureaucrat, and the Drill Sergeant. This shorthand allowed his queries to be succinct (example 37); it also kept the tone of his editing playful in a way that he hoped would make Dorian's review less grueling for her.

Bud did not, however, point out the correspondence between these four voices and those of the Mug Shot teachers. Doing so would only embarrass Dorian, he felt, and served no purpose in promoting the goals of editing. He remembered the professor who once wryly admired an early poem of his and then said, "Been reading some Hopkins, have we?" He had been devastated by the revelation that his work was so obviously derivative.

In fact, Dorian was extremely receptive to Bud's editing—so receptive that he became concerned about *his* influence over her. Had Bud become a fifth mentor, a fifth voice in her head? He noticed some of his own favorite words cropping up in her rewrites. So he began to backpedal a bit, allowing her greater leeway with phrases like "gangbanger paramour," which combined levels of diction in a novel, knowing way. Maybe this was her new voice coming through, struggling to emerge from its chrysalis. In which case, who was Bud to impede its birth?

※

Irma Cherise was pleased with the revised manuscript (example 38). As she'd hoped, Glamour Eyes had turned down the unedited version, so she was free to shop the project around. She found it a home with ViaLife, who'd been courting Animar for several years to create a line of serial novels based on their block-buster movies. The Animar founders were a pair of twenty-something geeks who believed in promoting "social justice" with their work—while making loads of money, of course—and *Mug Shot Makeover* gave the folks at ViaLife an opportu-nity to impress Animar with their commitment to serious educational values.

Much to the surprise of all involved, when the book came out, it added fuel to the firestorm surrounding high-school exit examinations in states like Califor-nia. Proponents of the exams used *Mug Shot* as an example of the widespread misuse of school resources, while opponents heralded the module as a beacon of hope in an educational system that had lost its social relevance. When the San Francisco school board succumbed to pressure from the state to shut down the module, the four Mug Shot teachers became celebrities. Madge Gracie told Larry King that she'd like to "get a hold of the Governator and shake him till his teeth rattle." And Eartha Simmons was picked up by the Lifetime channel as a Life Coach. Lost in the scuffle, Dorian Riley quietly married and switched to the women's health beat, which allowed her to reach out to expectant mothers like herself.

A few months after the Mug Shot experience, Bud came across a photo from

EXAMPLE 37. Harmonizing voices in the Riley manuscript. Here, the DE removes the more jarring notes of the disparate voices while allowing the author to retain some multivocal richness.

**Stories You Tell the Grandkids**

"I look like the granny in *Roots*," Sassy said when she came into the computer lab and ~~invoked~~ booted up her virtual self. She looked ~~fly for an old lady,~~ young for sixty-eight, with ~~radiant~~ glowing cheeks, chin, and forehead,[AQ1] but her crow's feet ~~were huge,~~ had reached her temples, and her jaw line and neck sagged pendulously.[AQ2] Far from disturbed by this vision of her ~~old-ass~~ geriatric self, Sassy seemed to ~~get a kick out of turning ancient and wise.~~ relish the prospect of becoming an elder.[AQ3] "Look, I got no worry lines," she pointed out, evidently quoting sources from a neighborhood beauty shop. "All my wrinkles are ~~is~~ power lines."

In the past nine weeks, Sassy had ~~brought to the module her radically disciplined spirit:~~ entered into the spirit of the module with enthusiasm: instead of experimenting with her virtual life, ~~her calibrations were reality-based and wise beyond her years.~~ she chose honesty and hard work. [AQ4] She set her study and after-school job hours high and then watched her virtual self achieve success in college and graduate to become a child-care specialist, working with ~~at-risk~~ children from ~~post-millenial~~ at-risk households like the one she grew up in. ~~and thus completing the circle of life.~~ [AQ5] She fed her virtual self the ~~identical high-transfat diet~~ same food she ate in real life, and she set her ~~aerobic and anaerobic activity~~ exercise levels at the minimum thresholds. "I love me some French fries, and I can't stand aerobics," she explained, unfazed as her virtual hips ~~achieved hippo proportions.~~ got bigger.[AQ6]

Of course, she included her year-old son Zachary in her virtual life: "No way I want to think about a life without him," she said. "He's my soul mate." This was a telling ~~revelation,~~ admission, because her virtual love life soon ~~fluctuated in sync with~~ paralleled the ups and downs of her real love life. Sassy was prone to periodic romances and breakups because no ~~gangbanger paramour~~ young man could compete very long for her ~~heart~~ affection with Prince Zachary.[AQ7] At the end of the module, telling her virtual life story to future grandchildren, Sassy decided this lesson was the most valuable one she had learned—that a woman must ~~apportion her~~ give equal affection ~~equally between~~ to mate and child or she'll end up ~~dying~~ single. ~~for life.~~[AQ8]

AQ1: Your Guru voice ("invoked," "radiant") seems to have picked up some jarring slang (is "fly" still au courant?): okay to regularize a bit?

AQ2: Physical details remained a bit vague: okay to make them more concrete? Revise as you see fit.

AQ3: Again, your Guru voice tries to be hip—and fails. Okay as revised?

AQ4: This long sentence began as the Guru ("radically disciplined spirit") and ended as the Bureaucrat ("her calibrations were reality-based"), with cliché ("wise beyond her years") thrown in for good measure. Better now?

AQ5: Again, a mix of the Guru and the Bureaucrat, this time with the Hipster making an unscheduled appearance. Not sure what "post-millennial" has to do with anything; the conditions of Sassy's upbringing are very twentieth century.

AQ6: More of the Bureaucrat. Also, "hippo" may be intended as humor but strikes me as hurtful—avoid?

AQ7: More veering between the Guru ("revelation," "heart") and the Bureaucrat ("fluctuated in sync"). "Gangbanger paramour" has a certain cachet—it melds two of your voices in a single coinage—but draws too much attention to itself. Revisions okay?

AQ8: "Dying" seemed a bit melodramatic here—better to end on an up note? Irony here handled nicely, by the way.

EXAMPLE 38. The final TOC for the Riley manuscript. Traces of official language (Weeks 2, 5, 6, and 8), hipster slang (Week 3), and New Age metaphysics (Week 7) have been removed, but the TOC shows little evidence of the extensive editing that has occurred at the paragraph and sentence levels.

*Mug Shot Makeovers: Life Lessons in a Virtual Classroom*

Introduction: The Big Idea
    The Mug Shot Module
    Meet the Teachers
Week 1. Let the Games Begin
    Picture Day, with Measles
    Your Trust Fund
    Reality Checks
    Experimenting with Your Life
Week 2. Care and Feeding of the Virtual Self
    Cheeseburger Cheeseburger Cheeseburger
    Training for the Big Leagues
    Staying Up and Sleeping In
    The Virtual Tutor
Week 3. The Social Game
    Hair and Clothing
    Tattoos, Scarification, and Piercing
    Cliques, Gangs, and Best Friends
    Smoking, Drinking, and Getting High
    Baby Mamas, Deadbeat Dads
Week 4. Kickin' It: Environment as Choice
    During Free Period
    After School
    At Home
Week 5. Sudden Graduation (Age 18)
    Time-Travel Sickness

    The SAT Blues
    Homebound or Outward Bound
    Friendship Turnover
Week 6. Career Moves (Age 28)
    What Color Is Your Collar?
    Politics on the Job
    Relocation Roulette
    The Boss from Hell
Week 7. The Parenting Trap (Age 38)
    The Wedding Planner
    Career versus Kids
    Babies Having Babies
Week 8. Mid-Life Crises (Age 48)
    Switching Spouses
    Custody Smackdown
    Career Change
    Pause, Meno and Andro
    Your Elderly Parents
Week 9. Futureworld (Age 58)
    The Population Explosion and You
    Geopolitics and You
    The Environment and You
Week 10. Stories You Tell the Grandkids
    (Age 68)
Acknowledgments

his own high school prom and tried to remember what it felt like to be that young man—the adrenaline, the appetite, the fear and loneliness, the hair in his eyes. If his high school had offered a Mug Shot Module, how much would his virtual self have resembled the man he eventually became? He supposed the computer would have gotten right his receding hairline and the white in his goatee, and maybe even the general direction of his career. But it could never have guessed at the adventures and heartaches that awaited him, much less the sequence of literary crushes that had given rise, while he wasn't looking, to his earnest, fractured voice.

Think of a department store in a shopping mall. The outer display windows draw your attention, providing a sense of the style, range, and quality of the wares within. You step inside, and smaller displays are the gateways to each department. If you're lucky, a map near the escalators gives you the store's floor plan, and large signs hang over each department in clear view. A book's display matter functions in much the same way. Good display entices and guides readers on their stroll through the text; bad display confronts readers with a snootful of perfume and leaves them dazed to wander an obstacle course of racks and counters.

In bookmaking jargon, "display" is any element that is not a part of the author's running text. Display matter includes typographical elements like frontmatter, chapter titles, subheads, epigraphs, tables, and sidebars; illustrative elements like photographs and drawings; and hybrid elements like maps, charts, and graphs. In chapter 6, we thought about chapter titles; in this chapter, we'll focus on the remaining elements of display and briefly consider ancillary components like text boxes, sidebars, and Web sites.

Display matter is especially important in travel guides, cookbooks, how-to manuals, natural history guides, and other reference works. In cookbook publishing, for instance, a series with a reader-friendly format for illustrating difficult culinary techniques can edge out its competition, so a new series format is thoroughly tested for usability. By applying a trademark formula to every book, reference publishers draw devoted readerships; they become expert in the needs of that audience; and they achieve economic efficiencies by following a single house style in writing, fact-checking, illustration, cartography, and design.

Of course, no display format works equally well for all subjects. In our case study, a large travel house faces new challenges when it applies its patented formula to the first in a series of "diaspora" travel guides. The author is a veteran contributor to the publisher's list who knows series style by heart, but she's unsure how to manage the cultural content of host country and diasporan enclave that makes her new book unique. The DE's role is to help her develop new display elements in keeping with the publisher's trademark approach.

### Author Profile: The Author-for-Hire

Work-for-hire authors receive no royalties for the books they write—they are paid by the word, the page, or the project. In lieu of the creative freedom and potential literary glory afforded by a royalty arrangement, they receive a more reliable paycheck and the knowledge that their work serves a practical purpose. Some authors are happy to make a career of writing for hire in one subject area, sometimes for one publishing client. Other authors consider working for hire the first rung on their ladder to literary success. Publishers who hire authors are usually willing to train them in the subject area so long as the applicants have demonstrated writing skills. Thus, at face value, it would seem unlikely that a freelance DE would ever work with an author-for-hire.

However, when a for-hire author does fail to deliver an acceptable work, the publisher may have little leeway to reject the material. A new software application cannot be rolled out without its manual; a travel series on Central America cannot skip over Guatemala. When these crises occur, the publisher turns to the most experienced members of its authorial pool to provide emergency intervention. Often, that pool consists of freelancers who make ends meet by a combination of writing and editing assignments. And because the author has forfeited copyright in exchange for a fee, the DE usually has complete freedom to alter the text.

Jagreet Raj Kaur was ready for a change. After almost a decade of traveling the world as a contributor to travel guides, she'd finally gotten what she wanted: a solo writing assignment. It was the first time her name would appear alone on a title page. But she'd come to realize that this book was no more hers than any of the writing she'd done thus far for Famous Footsteps Travel Guides. She'd stuck it out, but the final pages of the draft had taken her last ounce of creative juice. And now Footsteps was saying the manuscript "would need work."

What she wanted to do was write great novels. She would be the Anita Desai of American-born Sikhs. As a girl growing up in the tiny town of Iselin, New Jersey, Jagreet had come to understand how special her religious tradition was. Like most expatriates, the Indians of Iselin were ecumenical by necessity: Muslims watched Hindi films from Bollywood with Arabic subtitles; Sikhs ate Muslim baked goods; Hindus wore Sikh fabrics. But this solidarity was superficial. The other Indian kids made fun of her brother's *patka,* his "weeny beanie." Worse, they teased the siblings for having different surnames, calling their mother terrible things, no matter how many times Jagreet and Balvinder explained that all Sikh men were named Singh and all women Kaur.

This most recent writing assignment should have been a step toward her literary goal. "We're a new religion, kind of like the Mormons," she would explain to her friends in college, and even now she believed that Sikhism held the key to Indian unity and peace, combining as it did the spiritual elements of Hinduism and Islam, while rejecting their rituals. But traveling around the globe to visit the ghettos and gated communities of the Indian diaspora, Jagreet had found her faith shaken. Everywhere she went, Indians had recreated the fragmented society of the motherland, and everywhere Sikhism was in the minority—a drop of holy water in the bucket. The trip had confronted her with contradictory thoughts and feelings, and her confusion had surfaced in the manuscript's structure.

"Stand by for a call from the DE," her managing editor had said. Which Jagreet didn't mind, really: she suspected the person revising her text would be her old Footsteps travel buddy, Hedda Miller.

### Client Profile: The Trade Reference House

Trade reference houses are niche publishers. By focusing all of their resources on books in a single subject area, they streamline project development, production, and marketing. By maintaining an elaborate system for keeping their books up to date, they can provide useful new editions to their audience, in effect realizing "repeat" sales of the same book. The publisher's highly formatted approach to content allows it to hire less experienced authors whose mistakes can be corrected by a crack production team of editors, fact-checkers, cartographers, designers, and compositors. For staffers, it is as though they are working on the same endless manuscript; many eventually burn out and "go freelance" in hopes of varying the content of their work lives.

Trade reference houses can be among the most stable clients of freelance DEs. Once they've established their market share, their "brand" sells new titles and editions with a reliability that other trade houses envy. But establishing that market share can take years; the publisher usually has to unseat a competitor already considered the definitive resource in the subject area. And this extensive, long-term investment means that the reference publisher guards the quality of its imprint jealously. A book perceived by the publisher's audience as "beneath the dignity" of the imprint can create an opening for the next competitor to drive a wedge into. Thus, while authors are less empowered in the for-hire environment than in the royalty arena, staffers and loyal freelancers are correspondingly more crucial to the imprint's continued success.

The Famous Footsteps office was the place where University of Michigan dropouts went to die. In a sea of stained carpet and cubicles that filled a former Vulcan Rubber plant in Ann Arbor, the staff members looked more like bike messengers than editors, designers, and cartographers. Most continued to nurture as-yet-unrealized career aspirations in art, music, or Eastern health therapies, but Deb Brown was the rare lifer. She thrived on the fast pace and admired her colleagues' ability to blend professionalism with bohemianism. Because the "overlords" of the home office were in far-off Dublin, the Ann Arbor office was free to create its own collaborative, horizontal reporting structure.

Deb also enjoyed working with the authors and photographers, although they were sometimes hard to keep in line. Jagreet Kaur had always been utterly dependable, but her latest effort was a muddle. At the time, Deb had considered Jagreet a natural for the first volume of their new diaspora series. After all, Jagreet was herself a product of diaspora who had picked up the Footsteps format effortlessly a decade ago and had consistently churned out sharp, accurate, clean prose on deadline. India's diaspora was Dublin's choice for the inaugural volume in the series because it had such a broad base of devoted constituents, and because in recent decades its members had median incomes well over those of their host countries.

In retrospect, Deb realized it had been a mistake to delegate the important work of planning the new series to an out-of-house author, even one as familiar with the imprint as Jagreet. Deb herself should have conducted the market analysis to define the new audience with clarity, then thought through the format changes that the diasporan emphasis would entail. At the time of the assignment, Deb had been overwhelmed with another project, so she'd given Jagreet an extra stipend to combine market research with travel research. It was a plan born of desperation, and Jagreet's intimate knowledge of the subject only made matters worse: far from lending depth to her analysis, her family heritage had clouded her judgment with strong emotions.

Unfortunately, Deb was no freer now to rework the manuscript and art program—she was knee-deep in elephant sign, wading through the latest edition of *The Famous Footsteps Guide to Hannibal's Trek,* one of their bestsellers. So she turned to her list of Footstep alumnae, former staffers who'd gone freelance and moved to exotic locations like . . . Lancaster, Pennsylvania.

## Assignment: The Guidebook with Poor Signage

Hedda didn't do too many jobs for Footsteps anymore. She'd been a stringer for them briefly after graduation while traveling in Southeast Asia, and had worked in-house in the rubber plant for just under a year before deciding that she needed to return to her Pennsylvania Dutch roots. During her first years as a freelancer, Footsteps—or Lockstep, as it had been affectionately nicknamed by its staffers—had been a bread-and-butter client, allowing her to pay the bills while she courted the New York houses. On the strength of her knowledge of series format and the needs of the Footsteps audience, she had even been invited to become a volume editor for a guide to Southeast Asia—but she'd declined. Gradually, the Ann Arbor office's stable of authors and freelancers matured, and Hedda's services were required less frequently, though Deb still called her once in a while to shove a rectangular manuscript into the round hole of Lockstep format.

This manuscript, however, required a deeper level of intervention. Until now, all Famous Footsteps guides had fallen into one of two categories, single country or multicountry. The premise of the series was to allow guidebook users to hew as closely as possible to the route taken by a famous explorer, conqueror, missionary, or other trekker. The hallmark of the series, aimed at the history-buff leisure traveler, was continuity: no reader should ever find herself wondering how to get from point A to point B on the featured trail. The single-country guides were easier because they dealt with only one government, language, monetary system, and culture: the Lewis and Clark Trail guide was a good example. But most of the world's famous historical treks crossed national borders, so the multicountry format had been developed with the first three guides, which followed the peregrinations of Marco Polo, Dr. Livingstone, and Che Guevara.

Now, the new diaspora focus added unforeseen complications (example 39). There was no linearity to the story of a diaspora, especially one as large and complex as India's. More important, the usual Footsteps book emphasized sights and services of interest to a traveler, but the diaspora guides needed to provide information on topics of concern to potential immigrants, including jobs, schools, and quality of life. Someone in the Ann Arbor office should really have pounded out a new template for this series before contracting the first volume—now Hedda was being asked to "reverse engineer" a new series format from a completed manuscript.

One thing was certain: Jagreet was the right author for the inaugural volume. She and Hedda had known each other since their paths crossed in Singapore and they indulged in a three-day marathon of shopping and laughter in one of the world's most colorful Little Indias. Jagreet had done her homework: she had not stinted on coverage of some of the less romantic destinations, like Myanmar

*The Indian Diaspora: A Travel Guide*

and Suriname; she had even researched a section on Fiji, despite the exile of many Indo-Fijians after a coup in 2000. The question was how to massage all this present-day political intrigue and economic advice into a format designed for history-buff leisure travel.

## Consider Subheads

Subheads are mile markers that keep readers encouraged along the discursive journey. Subheads periodically let readers know where they've been, how far they have left to go, which points of interest are along the way. Subheads can be an integral part of the author's organizational strategy, or they can simply entertain. The best subheads serve both purposes.

DECIDE WHETHER TO USE SUBHEADS. Subheads are like a voice-over in a film: the more frequent the intrusions of the voice, the more documentary-like the tone of the text. Each time a subhead appears, the reader is reminded of the author's presence as omniscient narrator. For this reason, subheads are more common in nonfiction than fiction. That said, in this postmodern era it can be playfully hip to use subheads in novels, too.

REMOVE SCAFFOLDING. Some authors use subheads to organize their thoughts as they write. They reproduce their chapter outlines and then fill in the skeleton's flesh with passages of text. Sometimes the subheads are "written into" the flesh of the text, but other times they are made redundant by transitions in the text. Sometimes this practice results in bald redundancy:

*Anglerfish Reproduction*
Anglerfish reproduction includes some of the most unusual evolutionary strategies in the animal world. In many species, the male is much smaller than the female and attaches like a parasite during fertilization. His body fuses permanently to the female's, and his nervous system is thereafter controlled by her brain, rendering him an appendage.

In a narrative work, which is read cover to cover, subheads like the one above try a reader's patience and should be removed. In an encyclopedic work, which is consulted in nonlinear fashion, the subhead should be retained and the first sentence amended:

*Anglerfish Reproduction*
These denizens of the deep sea have developed reproduction strategies that are among the most unusual in the animal world. In many species . . .

DEs should strategize with authors about when and how to alleviate the redundancy caused by residual scaffolding.

STYLE SUBHEADS LIKE TITLES. In terms of style, subheads should follow the same rules as chapter titles (see chapter 4), but with greater leeway allowed in length and tone. Subheads can range from jokey to serious and from single words to full sentences, and can even have subheads of their own (i.e., sub-subheads). Consistency is desirable, however, in the intervals at which subheads appear: readers will be annoyed if they encounter subheads on every page of chapter 2 and only on every fifth or tenth page in chapter 3. It's perfectly okay to deploy sub-subheads in a single chapter or passage without imposing them on the rest of the book, so long as the rationale for their selective use is apparent. No chapter should contain a lone subhead.

VET TRANSITIONAL SUBHEADS. Some authors use subheads in lieu of transition statements. This strategy can be effective, but it's tricky to pull off because the subhead is doing double duty as both transition and signpost.

Authors who have trouble writing transition statements will likely have even greater trouble with transitional subheads. DEs should help authors to resist the temptation to skip the writing of formal transition statements.

CONSIDER ORNAMENTS AND CAESURAS. Two other subhead-like tools are the ornament and the caesura. An ornament is a graphic symbol that indicates a firm break in thought but without labeling the content of the new passage as a subhead would. This type of break is often favored in fiction or metafictional narratives. (Authors should use three asterisks to indicate an ornament in the manuscript—the book's designer will choose the graphic device that appears in the printed book.) A caesura is simply a line space. When ornaments and caesuras alternate in a discourse, the former indicate a firmer break than the latter.

KNOW WHEN TO MIX BREAKS. In general, it's wise to avoid mixing subheads with ornaments and caesuras; the use of both explicit and implicit breaks will confuse the reader unless handled deftly. Note, however, that subheads are not usually appropriate in brief frontmatter and backmatter elements such as forewords, prefaces, prologues, epilogues, and codas— here, ornaments and caesuras may be used even if the rest of the book contains subheads. Introductions, appendixes, and other backmatter elements may have subheads if they are substantive—that is, "chapter-like." Finally, a single caesura or ornament may be appropriate at the end of each chapter, offsetting a summary or denouement—as in this handbook, for example.

Like all travel series, Famous Footsteps had developed a signature organizational structure. Although she knew the Footsteps format by heart, Jagreet had been tripped up by the need to accommodate two types of readers: the tourists for whom the format had been developed, and the diasporans who were the primary audience for this book. Hedda wondered why Footsteps hadn't planned separate books for these two diverse audiences. It was just like Lockstep to struggle through several editions, losing buckets of money, before finally getting the audience defined properly. But her mandate was to mop up the mess, not wonder how it got there.

Hedda counted five kinds of subhead problems in the book's introduction, which was the first of the book's two major parts (example 40). The confusion started with underuse of subheadings in the manuscript's opening pages. Most Footsteps guides had a simple overview providing a brief biographical summary of the famous subject and outlining the progress of his most famous journey. But Jagreet's manuscript needed to sketch the thousand-year history of the Indian diaspora and define the readership for which the guide was intended. So Hedda created new subheads breaking the disapora's history into its three major waves: the exodus of the Roma (a.k.a. "Gypsies") in the eleventh century;

EXAMPLE 40. The subhead structure in the introduction of the Kaur manuscript. After editing, new subheads convey the history of the Indian diaspora more clearly and identify the book's readers more overtly. Changes to the order and wording of existing subheads place emphasis on the needs of the guide's primary audience, namely, Indians considering a move abroad.

| Introduction (before editing) | Introduction (after editing) |
|---|---|
| How to Use This Book | A Brief History of the Indian Diaspora |
|   Overview |   The Roma |
|   History |   Indentured Servitude |
|   Demographics |   The Emergence of Bollystan |
|   Coming and Going | Who This Book Is For |
|     Transportation |   Emigrating Indians |
|     Visas |   Touring Indians |
|   Changing Money |   NRIs and PIOs |
|   Places to Eat |   Non-Indian Tourists |
|     Markets | How to Use This Book |
|     Restaurants |   History |
|       Expensive |   Demographics |
|       Moderate |   Travel |
|       Inexpensive |   Visas |
|   Places to Stay |   Finance |
|     Local Housing |   Food |
|     Hotels |     Restaurants |
|   Places to Work |     Markets |
|     White-collar Jobs |   Lodging |
|     Blue-collar Jobs |     Hotels |
|   Places to Shop |     Local Housing |
|     Clothing |   Shops |
|     Dry Goods |   Sights |
|     Arts and Crafts |   Local Culture |
|     Religious Articles |   Employment |
|   Schools for the Children |   Schools |
|   Places to Worship |   Worship |
|   Travelers' Services |   Health Services |
|     Health Services |   Other Services |
|     Other Services |   Glossary |
|   Important Sights | |
|   Customs | |
|   Local Glossary | |

the period of slavery, euphemistically called "indentured servitude," throughout the British Empire in the late nineteenth and early twentieth centuries; and the current flood of Indian expatriates, many with advanced educational degrees, whose shared vision of a unitary Indian culture had been nicknamed "Bollystan." Similarly, she added subheads to draw attention to the paragraphs describing the guide's four main audiences: emigrating Indians; Indian tourists going abroad; persons of Indian origin (PIOs) and nonresident Indians (NRIs) either relocating or touring; and last, but not least, non-Indian tourists seeking "real Indian" experiences around the globe.

After the opening passage, Jagreet's subhead trouble swung from underuse to overuse. As in all Footsteps guides, the overview was followed by succinct descriptions of the information categories that would later appear in each destination entry. In this section, Jagreet tended to break out topics that were best left together. For instance, in the "Places to Eat" section, she correctly emphasized shopping markets over restaurants, acknowledging that the guide's primary readership, diasporans, would be more interested in cooking their own meals than in eating out every night. But she left in place the subheads for expensive, moderate, and inexpensive restaurants, despite the fact that each section contained only three to five entries. The result was that the book *seemed* weighted toward tourists. It took Hedda a while to catch on to this problem, which Dr. Worth had called "residual scaffolding," because the series format had been engrained in her, too. I'm still a Lockstepper! she thought.

A third problem with the manuscript's subheads was unintuitive order. Jagreet had consistently placed information of interest to diasporans first and tourists second, a plan that at face value seemed to correctly reflect the guide's priorities. But, to Hedda's way of thinking, this strategy did not reflect the actual experience of diasporans. As a traveler who had settled down in foreign countries for prolonged stays, Hedda had found that her method was to find a hotel room, sate her hunger at a restaurant, and then begin to explore her options for longer-term housing. Only after securing access to a kitchen would the markets become relevant. So Hedda reversed the order in the sections covering places to eat and stay. And she applied the same principle to the order of the main sections, placing "Shops" and "Sights" before sections on employment, schools, and houses of worship.

The fourth type of subhead problem Hedda encountered involved the phrasing of subheads. Jagreet had stuck closely to the Footsteps formula, "Places to Eat . . . Stay . . . Work," but some illogical nesting resulted. For instance, markets were not generally places to eat but rather places to buy food for preparation at home. Hedda decided to simplify the subheads overall, changing "Places to Stay" to "Lodging," "Places to Work" to "Employment," and "Schools for the Children" to "Schools," and distinguishing "Customs" as "Local Culture" so it would not be confused with laws governing ports of entry.

The last type of subhead problem Hedda stumbled on did not show up in the table of contents. A hallmark of all Footsteps guides was the use of a dingbat, or colophon (in the original sense of the word), depicting the house logo: a pair of bare footprints. The dingbat was employed throughout the guides as a kind of asterisk, to emphasize a place of particular interest, usually at a point along a road or trail that had no proper name. But Jagreet, wrestling with the sometimes contradictory demands of her dual readership, had applied the dingbat as a transitional mark between passages meant for diasporans and those for tourists, with the result that the text had more bare feet on it than the Jersey Shore. Hedda would have to remove these and provide in each place an explicit transitional phrase or clause.

## Consider Epigraphs

Good epigraphs are snippets of conversation overhead, letters intercepted, diaries plundered. Like vivid chapter titles and subheadings, they draw the reader into the text at the bookstore shelf and revive her curiosity at home in the armchair. Good epigraphs are sometimes also epigrams—pithy statements that render a truth with succinct wit, like an aphorism—but they need not be. A pair or trio of contrasting epigraphs can hint at conflicts to come in the ensuing chapter; a single epigraph can foreshadow the chapter's climactic event, creating suspense. An epigraph's source note alone can speak volumes about character, setting, or theme.

But bad epigraphs can have the opposite of these desired effects. The detritus of too much research, they betray an author unwilling to sacrifice items from her or his notebook. The worst are bland statements chosen as thematic umbrellas; these are often stacked three to five deep, each restating its predecessor in less remarkable language. Often they are pressed into service as thesis statements and topic sentences by authors too timid to speak for themselves. When they are used as crutches, epigraphs crop up under subheadings and even at the ends of chapters as erstwhile conclusions.

Even when epigraphs are apt, entertaining, and distributed evenly, they can be overused. An armchair guide to the natural history of birds may use epigraphs liberally, but a field guide to those birds should not. Epigraphs, like other text elements, should be evaluated in terms of how well they serve the overall goals of the book.

READ THE EPIGRAPH PROGRAM WHOLE. The DE should review a manuscript's epigraphs in a separate pass—skipping over the main text—and encourage the author to do so as well. Read this way, the epigraph program may yield redundancies, overuse of certain sources, or imbalances in the number and length of epigraphs per chapter. Keep in mind that epigraphs are display elements; their primary role is to enhance presentation, not provide crucial information. Source notes to epigraphs should cite only basic information: for a published work, the author and title; for a speech or interview, the speaker, date, and, if relevant, place or occasion. Full citations should be relegated to a backmatter reference list or—if there is none—supplied on the copyright page.

CHOOSE AN EPIGRAPH STRATEGY. Most books benefit from one of four epigraph strategies. The first is the "kitchen sink" strategy, which makes sure that epigraphs vary widely in tone and provenance throughout the book. This method provides the reader with many small pleasurable surprises and implies that the author's discourse has broad cultural relevance. The second strategy is the parallel storyline: the author uses a single source for epigraphs throughout, building suspense from epigraph to epigraph, with the reader correctly inferring that the intervening chapters connect the dots. This approach often serves well for biographers, who can draw on their subjects' diaries and letters. A third strategy is the round robin—a short list of sources among whom the author rotates, drawing them in as participants in an intimate conversation. This method best suits an expository text with a strong central thesis.

FACE PERMISSIONS ISSUES. The fourth strategy is to eliminate the epigraph program. This choice has several benefits: it forces the author to make her opening sentences interesting; it guards against the other abuses just described; and, perhaps most important, it avoids permissions headaches. Copyright law is open to interpretation on the matter of epigraphs, with the result that house rules vary among publishers. Some publishers defend epigraphs under the "fair use" exception; others require permissions documentation on grounds that epigraphs, like other display elements, serve primarily to entice readers into the text. All houses require iron-clad documentation for song lyrics and poems, because corporations in the music industry are notorious for exacting stiff penalties for the use of even single lines without permission. Before sinking time and energy into an epigraph program, authors should consult their publishers' written permissions policies.

Everyone knew Jagreet had a weakness for epigraphs. The Footsteps style guide allowed their use sparingly, especially when drawn from the writings of the famous explorer whose journey was shaping the text. But Jagreet always went overboard, submitting epigraphs for most of her subheads, and she never failed to express dismay when their number was dramatically reduced in print. So it was hardly surprising that in this, her first solo effort, she had developed a fulsome epigraph program.

Hedda made a separate pass, skipping over the main text and reading only the epigraphs. She found that Jagreet had chosen the "kitchen sink" strategy, which was appropriate for a book drawing its material from diverse societies. But it seemed as though Jagreet had tired in the execution of her plan, because many of the entries were pedestrian, redundant, or otherwise readily dispensed with.

In the section on the African island of Mauritius, for example, the epigraph program yielded mixed results (example 41). On the one hand, there was an admirable diversity reflecting the population's Hindi, Tamil, Telugu, Muslim, and African Creole minorities—the sources weren't identified by ethnic background, but a quick Web search on their surnames confirmed Hedda's hunch. On the other hand, the program was dominated by two voices, both male, and both presumably Hindu: a politician whose quotes were boosterish, and a journalist whose advice to potential immigrants was dourly pessimistic. The canned wisdom of a young customs officer, "Easy in, easy out," was hardly worth quoting. And several of the epigraphs featured platitudes heard on any island: for true insight into local culture, "you must go to the interior"; and worse, "The marketplace is where we all come together."

The stronger entries evoked unique facets of Mauritian history and culture, most involving the centrality of Hindu pilgrimages to island life. A guesthouse operator encapsulated Mauritian hospitality in the act of road cooling, a tradition in which villagers of all faiths run to the roadside with vessels of water to splash the road before the bare feet of pilgrims. A Port Louis cashier used local idiom to characterize Mauritian daily life: "Everything here moves at the pilgrim's pace." An elder, among the last of the indentured servants, spoke movingly of the impression that Gandhi's 1901 visit to the island had made on his parents' generation. And a high school student, with adolescent glee, took pleasure in comparing the charms of Mauritius to the trance-induced body piercings of the Kavadee festival.

In several places throughout the text, Jagreet used song lyrics as epigraphs. Hedda was certain that the "sega reggae" or "seggae" artist quoted in the Mauritius section would be impossible to track down for permission. Jagreet should have flagged those.

By Footsteps decree, the main text contained no other quotations, so Hedda could not nominate replacements for these weaker epigraphs. But she suspected that Jagreet's notebook would yield better choices. The text itself vividly evoked the island's largest festival, the Maha Shivaratri, a twelve-day event in which three hundred thousand people walked from their homes throughout the island to the Lake of the Ganges on the high plateau at the island's north end. Jagreet must have made this trek herself from Port Louis—her description of the journey's hardships and pleasures was too vivid to have come secondhand. Hedda felt her slumbering wanderlust stir with envy.

EXAMPLE 41. A portion of the epigraph program in the Kaur manuscript. The selection appears diverse but actually favors entitled Hindu males. Some epigraphs are evocative of Mauritian culture, but others are redundant or banal.

**MAURITIUS**

| SUBHEAD | EPIGRAPH |
| --- | --- |
| History | "We came as servants, but now we are our own masters."<br>—Dinesh Patel, 56, member of Parliament |
| Demographics | "Welcome to the true rainbow nation."<br>—Dinesh Patel, 56, member of Parliament |
| Travel | "Mauritian hospitality will cool the roads for your feet."<br>—Bandana Vivekananda, 33, guesthouse operator |
| Visas | "Easy in, easy out."<br>—Hussain ibn Rahil, 26, customs officer |
| Finance | "Don't expect quick service at the banks."<br>—BalaMurugan Padayachi, 41, newspaper editor |
| Food | "Every Indo-Mauritian has his favorite Creole dish."<br>—Lateefa Gounder, 36, sous chef |
| Lodging | "For true Indian hospitality on a tropical island, you must go to the interior."<br>—Tarla Mehta, 51, tour operator |
| Shops | "The marketplace is where we all come together, Hindu, Muslim, and Christian alike."<br>—Jawahar Bhatt, 64, shopkeeper |
| Sights | "This place gets its hooks in you, like the devotees at Kavadee."<br>—Maaran Reddy, 16, high school student |
| Local Culture | "When Mahatma Gandhi came to our port, he began a process of healing in the Mauritian heart."<br>—Manchu Chinuku Bal Gangadhar Tilak, 89, former servant |
| Employment | "No malaise no malaise / the creole is no malaise."<br>—Antoine Naidu, 76, seggae artist |
| Schools | "Don't expect your child's Mauritian degree to take him far."<br>—BalaMurugan Padayachi, 41, newspaper editor |
| Worship | "Our island has a temple in every sugar cane field."<br>—Tarla Mehta, 51, tour operator |
| Health Services | "Don't expect to use your insurance at medical facilities."<br>—BalaMurugan Padayachi, 41, newspaper editor |
| Other Services | "Everything here moves at the pilgrim's pace."<br>—Semantika Sen, 19, cashier |
| Glossary | "Our children speak at least three languages."<br>—Dinesh Patel, 56, member of Parliament |

## Draft an Art Plan

There is a natural tendency among authors to postpone planning their art programs until after they've finished writing their manuscripts. Not infrequently, publishers abet this deferral, saying, "Just get us the text; we'll worry about the art later." Unless the art is truly dispensable, this habit is self-defeating, because the project will remain in production limbo until the art program has been completed. And the result is often an art program that looks like an afterthought—which it is.

Ideally, authors move the art program forward in step with their writing; when they've finished writing chapter 3, they assemble, number, and place its art before moving on to chapter 4. Once they've drafted the entire manuscript, they write up a several-page memo that sets forth the goals of the art program, enumerates its components, and describes a vision for how the art will enmesh with the text. More often, however, in-house production staff or freelance DEs are left to compose the art plan. This "reverse engineering" has obvious drawbacks, but it's better than no art plan at all because the process identifies problems before the book enters production.

In the following sections, we consider how to evaluate existing programs of plates, figures, maps, and unnumbered "display art," along with programs of floating text elements such as tables, text boxes, and sidebars. (For guidelines in creating new art programs from scratch, see sidebar, "Art Research.") For each program, the following general principles apply.

READ EACH PROGRAM WHOLE. Each component program should tell its own story, like a motif in narrative or a supporting argument in exposition. In a program of strong historical shots, a few current photos may break the program's nostalgic spell. In a program of data tables supporting an empirical argument, a few tables listing subjective factors may cast doubt on the impartiality of the author's judgment.

CROSS-EXAMINE PROGRAMS AND TEXT. Each component program should be read against the others, the text, and the caption matter. This cross-examination—admittedly, a tedious set of tasks—ensures against redundancy, obvious omissions, and mismatched organizational principles. Maps require special attention: the DE should read the text against the maps, and then the maps against the text, to flush out gaps and contradictions.

PLAN FOR PLACEMENT. The author should indicate where each piece goes in the text by placing a bracketed callout: "[Figure 6 near here.]" Next, the publisher should supply the DE with a desired final page count for the printed book. By counting the floating elements and noting the placement of the author's callouts, the DE can then:

## Art Research

When an author is unwilling or unable to create a book's art program, a publisher may hire a freelancer to perform the task. Textbook and trade publishers who make frequent use of these services tend to engage professional art researchers; these specialists know the major stock photography collections by heart, have a firm grasp of the complexities of permissions law, exercise keen visual taste, and usually know certain subject areas especially well. Publishers who make only occasional use of these services are more likely to turn to DEs whose editorial skills they already trust. If you have taken on an art research assignment, be sure to follow these steps.

READ THE TEXT. The publisher should pay you enough to allow you time to read through the entire manuscript (at about fifteen manuscript pages per hour). The text will be your key source of ideas for illustrations. Working from a proposal or other brief synopsis of the book can result in serious divergence between the content of art and text.

MAKE A WISH LIST. If the author is alive and amenable, she or he should draft a wish list of images for you to amplify and edit. If you must draft the wish list yourself, insist on having it reviewed by the author or publisher before you begin securing images: there's no sense in putting effort into a photo that will ultimately be rejected. Your wish list should be at least 20 percent longer than the number of images you are contracted to provide.

STICK TO THE BUDGET. Make sure you have a clear understanding of how your fee breaks down per image. Most publishers offer a flat fee that includes both your hourly pay and the cash available for permissions fees. This arrangement gives you an incentive to bargain for good rates; it also allows you the flexibility to spend $500 on one image and only $50 on ten others. When you're asked for a bid, figure your hourly rate by the image: plan to spend half an hour on research, an hour on requesting options and returning rejects, and a final hour on permissions, for a total of 2.5 hours per image.

TRACK THE REJECTS. The most common mistake made by new art researchers is inadequate tracking of the images they reject. If you invite a photographer to submit ten images and select three, be sure to make printouts or photocopies of the ones you return, and write down the file names or catalog data from the slide frames directly onto the copies. Otherwise, the photographer may eventually return from the wilds of Borneo, misremember which photos were sent, and demand that you return photos you never possessed.

EDIT FOR BALANCE. As your program coalesces, keep in mind the goals set forth in this chapter. There's no sense in investing 2.5 hours of effort into an image that you will ultimately decide to cut because its subject has too much coverage or its text section is already too dense with callouts.

SECURE PERMISSION. Be sure you understand what constitutes free and clear permission to use an image. An entertaining, enlightening, and current reference on the subject is Susan M. Bielstein, *Permissions, A Survival*

- Break up dense clusters of floating elements so that the printed book doesn't end up with ugly mixtures of tables, maps, and photos.
- Advise whether a program should be gathered or scattered. Typically, art should be gathered if the text asks the reader to compare images carefully. Tables are sometimes gathered, too, for ease of reference. For color art, gathered "inserts" may be a matter of cost efficiency: a book with color printing throughout carries a much higher unit cost—and, ultimately, price—than a book with an insert.
- Advise the publisher if the art-to-text ratio will cause problems in composition. Books dense with floating elements incur special handling, longer schedules, and higher costs. Content issues aside, if the art-to-text ratio is prohibitive, the DE may need to suggest significant cuts.

EDIT FOR IMPACT. Images, tables, and other floating elements are detours from the main discourse. Too many side trips—even interesting ones—can test a reader's patience, the way pit-stops on a family vacation rile kids up when meant to simmer them down. Each detour should be memorable, a scenic overlook affording a fresh view of the landscape traversed. The DE should flag items that detract from the cohesive force of the author's story or argument.

Deb had asked Hedda to review the Indian diaspora art program in light of the text, and when Hedda downloaded the files from the Footsteps site—which took forever—she saw why. Putting aside problems involving reproduction quality, she found a serious imbalance in the content focus. Naturally, there was no written art plan, so her first task was to survey the art program's contents. While she was at it, she would consider the tables, text boxes, and sidebars, since these floating text elements would compete with the art program for the reader's attention.

Hedda found that the component programs favored certain destinations. The color plates surfaced mostly in tropical destinations, where strong tourist industries meant lots of free stock photography. Historical photos showed up in just a few destinations—Singapore, Trinidad, Guyana, and Suriname—where Indian populations had played a prominent role in local political life. Countries in which Islam was the official religion contained no art at all, presumably because of the prohibition against figurative art among fundamentalist sects of that faith. There were no charts or graphs, and a single mammoth table conflated the population data for all destinations. Text boxes describing the daily life of the average diasporan popped up only in the developed world—the United States, Canada, and Europe—where published sources would be easier to come by. And the manuscript contained only two sidebars: an oddly generic description of the "Little Indias" of the world in the introduction's shopping section, and a strained essay on assimilation of the burgeoning Indian population in Australia.

In short, Jagreet seemed to have pulled together only those ancillary items that made themselves readily available in the course of her travels. Hedda could sympathize. While conducting travel research, it was hard enough to stay "on task" with directions, addresses, and descriptive note-taking; prospecting blindly for images in out-of-the-way places was a full-time job of its own. For this reason, some of the best guides in the Footsteps series were coauthored by spouses, with one focused on text and the other on art.

Recognizing these constraints, Hedda would need to go easy on the art and floating text programs. She would suggest the strategic addition or removal of a photo, text box, or sidebar only where lopsided coverage risked offending a segment of the target audience. Even with her mission so narrowly defined, she had plenty to do.

## Illustrate Concepts

It is the rare picture that is worth a thousand words. Good descriptive language can accomplish as much as most pictures in fifty words or less. Language has the advantage of appealing to all our senses with concrete detail and adding nuance of thought. But photographs can convey a visual immediacy and particularity that words cannot match, and line drawings can evoke meaningful patterns from raw data. So authors must ask themselves whether a modest art program would contribute to their book's success.

Decisions about whether to include art, how large the program will be, and what kinds of images it will comprise should be made jointly by the author, publisher, and DE when the book is first conceived. Many publishers expect authors to cover permissions and illustration costs, though some allow those costs to be charged against future royalties. The publishers themselves foot the bill for insurance and reproduction costs, not to mention the significant cost of art management.

KEEP AN EYE OUT FOR ART. Authors, as you do research, take careful notes about the location of art that you might want to reproduce in your book. For art in published sources, record full publication data and note the museum or other holder of copyright mentioned in the source's credits. For art on the Web, secure a high-resolution electronic copy immediately or jot down the complete address and telephone number of the site's sponsoring agency. Most books take several years to write, and periodicals and Web sites often expire in the meantime. Even if the publisher has agreed to undertake development of the art program, your research will provide many crucial leads.

CHECK OUT THE COMPETITION. Some books require illustrations to compete in the marketplace. Biographies are considered lacking if they do not include a small gallery of the subject's personal and professional photographs; art history books require reproductions of the masterpieces they discuss, often in full color; cookbooks and other how-to books can edge out the competition with excellent illustrations; and scientific texts need diagrams to help readers visualize complex processes. Before signing a contract, the author and publisher should do market research to see how much art is included in competing titles, whether it appears in black and white or full color, and whether diagrams have been reproduced from other sources or freshly drawn.

EVALUATE DISPLAY ART. When bookstore browsers consider two competing books, they naturally prefer the one with more visual appeal, especially if the titles are offered at the same price. In two recipe books from the American South, the one that makes "down home cooking" look like haute cuisine will likely outsell the one that shows in gory detail how chitlins are prepared. Competing books often distinguish themselves by strategically placing "beauty shots" on the title page and at part and chapter openings. These programs of display art, or "window dressing," should be evaluated by DEs on three grounds: sales appeal, aesthetic integrity, and narrative cohesion. Yes, even these programs have a story to tell, however obliquely related to the substance of the text.

Turning first to the plate program, Hedda found many of the sorts of photos favored by Footsteps editorial policy: sunlit beaches, misty rainforests, vibrant festivals, chaotic outdoor markets. Most of these "brochure shots" Jagreet had simply dug up in the Footsteps repository, which contained images previously published in other guides. A second type of photo showed Indian diasporans performing the tasks of daily life in their adopted countries: these were taken by Jagreet and fellow travelers, and they were the heart and soul of the art program. But Hedda was concerned about a third class of photos in the program: images drawn from wire services and television news that graphically illustrated social unrest either within diasporan communities or between Indian and host populations. These journalistic shots—depicting horrors ranging from pot-bellied children in the Bangladeshi enclaves of Cooch Behar to the smoldering ruins of a Hindu temple destroyed as an "illegal building" by the Muslim state of Malaysia—were not going to sell those places as destinations.

Hedda understood Jagreet's impulse to warn her diasporan readers of dangers in places they were thinking of calling home. But the diasporan communities in these locations were laboring hard to grow their tourism industries, and they would cry foul if Famous Footsteps gave them bad press. Like all travel publishers, Footsteps walked a narrow line, recommending caution but also encouraging cultural appreciation. It was obvious that Jagreet had been horrified by some of her discoveries, and rightly so, but she would need some help in tempering her art program.

Take the United States section. Its photos contained many appropriate and candid glimpses into Indian disaporan life, with subjects ranging from a turbaned Sikh driving a taxi in Manhattan to a Hindu woman behind the counter of a corner store in Gary, Indiana. Other photos showed an Indian doctor's bedside manner with an American patient, an Indian engineer's face in the glow of a computer screen, a portrait of the lesbian civil rights activist Uvashi Vaid, and location shots of franchises dominated by Indian owners (Dunkin' Donuts, Patel hotels) as well as the usual temples, festivals, and Little India boulevards.

But there were also photos of a more disturbing nature. One showed Hindu white-collar workers in a Chicago sports bar raising their beers to toast the destruction by Hindu militants of a mosque "back home" in 1992. Another was the official police photo of a victim beaten by New Jersey's notorious "Dot Busters," gang members who targeted women wearing the red dot, or *bindi,* on their foreheads.

Hedda decided to establish a volume style allowing just one journalistic photo per destination. Where brochure shots were in short supply, she queried for additional images, knowing they'd be available in the Footsteps archive. For the display openers, she bypassed the tourist shots and instead chose from among the candid shots of contemporary Indians performing their daily activities. Bookstore browsers thumbing through the guide would encounter the human face of the Indian diaspora, young and old, smiling and serious, struggling and thriving.

Hedda embedded her suggestions for adding and cutting photos in the caption manuscript, wording them as sensitively as possible. Where a photo was too painful to include, she suggested Jagreet develop a verbal description instead — brief text boxes could be posted as "safety warnings," one per destination. The Dublin office would yank these boxes if they saw them before publication, but Ann Arbor would probably let them stay. The office staff, like Hedda, would be shaken by the sight of that bruised, swollen face of a sweet Hindu matron.

## Visualize Data

Our world is full of ill-conceived data displays, in books and newspapers, on television newscasts, in financial reports; we try to wrap our brains around them and give up in frustration. Yet hard data are often the foundation of the most original and convincing expository works, and well-made visual displays can reveal patterns in raw data that might otherwise bewilder. These displays can be either tabular or graphic.

CREATE CLEAR DATA TABLES. A table should be created whenever empirical data are crucial to text comprehension and that data cannot be readily summarized in descriptive sentences. A table should amplify but never supplant its corresponding text discussion. A good table performs the following functions (see table 4):

- Pits one set of variables in the leftmost column, or *stub*, against a second set in the column heads.
- Communicates clearly the relationship of the two variable sets in the table's *title*.
- Keeps the table's title, stub, and column heads simple, using a *table note* to amplify and clarify as needed.
- Uses *straddle heads* judiciously to avoid repetition in the column heads.
- Uses *cut-in heads* to indicate major divisions that would otherwise require separate tables.
- Uses the same unit of measure throughout the data cells if possible, and otherwise keeps units of measure consistent by row or column.
- Expresses numbers in the simplest form possible to illuminate patterns of meaning.

AVOID CONJOINED DATA TABLES. In developmental terms, the most common mistake made with tables is conjoining them. Authors, if the publisher has given you an upper limit for the number of tables, don't attempt to

TABLE 4. The parts of a table

| | Column straddle head | | | | |
|---|---|---|---|---|---|
| | Column head | Column head | Column head | Column head | Column head |
| | Cut-in head | | | | |
| Row head | | | | | |
| Row head | | | | | |
|   Row subhead | | | | | |
|   Row subhead | | | | | |
| Row head | | | | | |
| Row head | | | | | |
|   Row subhead | | | | | |
|   Row subhead | | | | | |
| | | Cut-in head | | | |
| | | | Column straddle head | | |
| Row head | | | | | |
| Row head | | | | | |
| Row head | | | | | |
| Row head | | | | | |
| Row head | | | | | |
| Row head | | | | | |

*Note:* The column of row heads (and row subheads, if any) is also called the "stub."

circumvent this constraint by pushing two tables together under one number and title. Even if the two tables have related content, don't conflate them unless each row head applies to all cells to its right and each column head applies to all cells below. Nothing frustrates a reader more than a column that changes meaning halfway down the page.

CREATE CLEAR LIST TABLES. Not all tables contain numerical data. In some cases, a list is too awkward to leave embedded in the text—maybe it is a taxonomical hierarchy with several levels of indention, or a list of instructions that should begin at the top of a printed page. These list tables usually look like data tables, but with just one column below the title. Readers should be able to intuit a common-sense rationale for why these lists get placed as floating tables; reasons include list length, complexity of the list format, and the reader's need to refer back to the table later in the manuscript.

DRAW CLEAR CHARTS AND GRAPHS. Data tables expressed visually to illustrate a data pattern, charts, and graphs are usually considered a part of the figure program, like conceptual line drawings. Like tables, *line graphs* arrange one set of variables vertically and a second set horizontally. However, whereas tables can readily display multiple levels of variables vertically by indenting in the stub and horizontally by using several levels of columnar heads, line graphs are wed to a simple format pitting x-axis against y-axis. The discipline imposed by this rigid structure is what gives line graphs their visual strength.

For this reason, avoid adding third and fourth axes to line graphs. This practice is rife in scientific publishing, where periodicals encourage conflation of graphs as a space-saving measure. A second x-axis is sometimes slapped onto the top of a graph, and a second y-axis to its right side, enclosing the data in a box. Unless the values along the two x-axes and two y-axes are truly parallel, this arrangement will only confuse the average reader with a serviceable memory of high-school algebra. When multiple levels of data are required along a single axis, turn your graph into a *bar graph*; when required along both axes, turn it into a table or two separate graphs.

Finally, for simple graphs and two-column tables, consider the venerable *pie chart*. This device is highly effective because it expresses visually the relative weight of data as pie slices of different sizes. These days, there's no excuse to use a flat circle—a flattened, cylindrical wheel, rendered in perspective, can be generated in Excel or other widely available software applications.

The manuscript contained only one table, but it was a doozy. Toward the beginning of the introduction, Jagreet summarized data in "Population of the Indian Diaspora," a table that was obviously a patchwork quilt of tables she'd found in source documents (example 42a). It looked reasonable at first glance, but on closer inspection revealed serious structural problems.

The table was divided in half by two cut-in heads, "Indian Majority" and "Indian Minority." The first category, Hedda assumed, would comprise nations in which Indians constituted more than 50 percent of the whole population. But a quick check of the math showed this was not so, and it was only by surfing the Internet that Hedda deduced that "majority" in fact meant "largest minority." She would have to clarify this fact in a table note.

Next she found that the table's two halves presented their data in different schemes. In the majority half, the Indian population appeared in the first column after the stub; in the minority half, the Indians showed up mostly, but not always, in the second column. In a way, this arrangement made sense, as the first column was always the largest population. But readers would be unable to compare Indian populations quickly by running their eyes downward.

The table's most pervasive problem was a lack of consistency in the units of measure. Some Indian populations were broken down by religion, others not; some national populations by ethnicity or religion, others not. Surfing the Web

EXAMPLE 42A. The Kaur manuscript's table, prior to editing. Boldfacing highlights the occurrence of Indian population numbers, which hopscotch down the table among the left, middle, and right columns. The data for individual countries has been imported from different sources in a variety of formats, and the author has simply grafted the table matter together.

Table 1. Population of the Indian Diaspora

| | INDIAN MAJORITY | | |
|---|---|---|---|
| | **Indian Expat** | Other Expat | Citizens |
| United Arab Emirates | **2,572,000** | 2,054,000 | 514,000 |
| | **Hindu** | **Muslim** | Other |
| Mauritius | **601,400** | **171,800** | 342,500 |
| | **Indo-Trinis** | Afro-Trinis | Other |
| Trinidad | **535,000** | 522,000 | 248,000 |
| | **Indians** | Africans | Mixed Heritage and Amerindian |
| Guyana | **323,000** | 240,300 | 187,700 |
| | **Hindu** | **Muslim** | Christian |
| | **Indo-Fijian** | **Indo-Fijian** | Polynesian |
| Fiji | **227,500** | **58,500** | 460,800 |
| | **Indians** | Creole | Other |
| Suriname | **166,500** | 139,500 | 126,000 |
| Javanese | | | 67,500 |
| Maroons | | | 45,000 |
| Amerindians | | | 13,500 |
| | INDIAN MINORITY | | |
| United States | Citizens and Residents | Population | Unauthorized Residents |
| White | 206,720,000 | 68% | |
| Hispanic | 45,000,000 | 15% | 6,960,000 |
| African American | 35,000,000 | 12% | |
| Asian | 14,600,000 | 5% | |
| **Asian Indian** | **2,600,000** | **1%** | |
| Native American | 2,950,000 | 1% | |
| Total | 304,270,000 | | 12,000,000 |
| | Malays | Chinese | Other |
| Malaysia | 14,105,000 | 8,137,500 | 4,882,500 |
| **Indian descent** | | | **2,331,000** |
| Indigenous | | | 2,551,500 |
| | Burmese | **Overseas Indian** | Overseas Chinese |
| Myanmar | 45,520,000 | **2,000,000** | 3,000,000 |

| | Black African | Other | | |
|---|---|---|---|---|
| | | White | Colored | **Asian Indian** |
| South Africa | 37,950,000 | 4,270,000 | 4,250,000 | **2,000,000** |
| | Arabs | **Indians** | Other | |
| Saudi Arabia | 27,100,000 | **1,400,000** | 3,600,000 | |
| | White | **Indian** | Black | |
| United Kingdom | 54,000,000 | **1,160,000** | 5,050,000 | |
| | White | Nonwhite | | |
| Canada | 27,390,000 | Aboriginal | 1,320,000 | |
| | | Visible Minorities | 4,290,000 | |
| | | **Indian** | **963,000** | |
| | Total Population | **Indian Population** | | |
| Singapore | 4,550,000 | **319,000** | | |
| Oman | 3,205,000 | **312,000** | | |
| Kuwait | 3,100,000 | **295,000** | | |
| Netherlands | 16,570,000 | **217,000** | | |
| Australia | 21,040,000 | **190,000** | | |

again, Hedda ascertained that the ethnic categories were drawn from the nations' official censuses, and she realized it would be difficult for Jagreet to obtain truly comparable data.

Hedda could, however, minimize confusion in the data's presentation. In the table's current incarnation, each country had its own organizational scheme: South Africa used a column straddler to create an additional column; Canada interjected a column straddler and three inset row heads; the United States added an anomalous percentage column, while also singling out the Hispanic population in a prejudicial column of "Unauthorized Residents." Hedda made a first editing pass over the table, pushing the ethnic breakdowns into the stub and offsetting the corresponding figures with parentheses. It was like herding cats—a phenomenon with which Hedda was all too familiar.

After a couple of hours, Hedda finally had a version of the table that was passable. Still, readers would have to work pretty hard to pick out the Indian and total population figures, and there was no overt comparison from nation to nation. What if she pulled the ethnic information out of the table altogether? She could suggest that the publisher express each nation's ethnic breakdown in a pie chart embedded in its country's demographic discussion. Hedda then knocked strings of zeroes off the figures by expressing them in millions and put the rows in descending order by size of the Indian population. These changes left the summary table spare and clean, with room for a third column expressing the Indian population as a percentage of each nation's total population (example 42b).

EXAMPLE 42B. The same table, after editing. The reader can now easily perceive the size of Indian diasporan populations relative to the total populations of the host countries. Ethnic breakdowns have been moved into the destination discussions, where they are expressed as pie charts.

Table 1. Population of the Indian Diaspora

| | Indian Population (millions) | Total Population (millions) | % Indian |
|---|---|---|---|
| **NATIONS WITH AN INDIAN MAJORITY** | | | |
| United Arab Emirates | 2.572 | 5.140 | 50 |
| Mauritius | .773 | 1.116 | 69 |
| Trinidad | .535 | 1.305 | 41 |
| Guyana | .323 | .751 | 43 |
| Fiji | .286 | .747 | 38 |
| Suriname | .167 | .432 | 39 |
| **NATIONS WITH AN INDIAN MINORITY** | | | |
| United States | 2.600 | 304.270 | <1 |
| Malaysia | 2.331 | 27.125 | 9 |
| Myanmar | 2.000 | 50.520 | 4 |
| South Africa | 2.000 | 48.470 | 4 |
| Saudi Arabia | 1.400 | 32.100 | 4 |
| United Kingdom | 1.160 | 60.210 | 2 |
| Canada | .963 | 33.963 | 3 |
| Singapore | .319 | 4.550 | 7 |
| Oman | .312 | 3.205 | 10 |
| Kuwait | .295 | 3.100 | 10 |
| Netherlands | .217 | 16.570 | 1 |
| Australia | .190 | 21.040 | 1 |

*Note:* The population of the Indian diaspora as a percentage of the host country's total population, taken from recent national census figures. Among nations listed as having an "Indian majority" but with Indian populations of less than 50 percent of the total, the Indian group is the largest of multiple ethnic minorities.

There, she felt better. There was a way to herd cats after all—just engage the high-pitched whine of the electric can opener.

## Test-Drive Maps

In this age of satellite technology, our automobiles have systems that guide us to our destinations, and every inch of the earth's surface seems to have been photographed and cataloged. But this deluge of data only makes the traditional mapmaker's skills more essential. Cartography is the selective presentation of geographical data to allow it to be read, understood, and navigated. The mapmaker shows us the path through the labyrinth.

Some authors assume that their publisher will "handle the maps," from conception through execution. But a map program's structure and emphasis cannot be divorced from the aims of the main text—an author provides crucial insight into the reader's cartographic needs. Moreover, as the book's primary (if not sole) researcher, the author is most likely to come across pertinent cartographic source materials. However, not all authors have a knack for thinking cartographically—which is where the help of a good DE comes in.

CONSIDER RELATIONSHIPS OF SCALE. The core organizational device for any map program is scale. Books with extensive map programs generally contain one overview map of the entire area of discussion, then regional maps at the chapter level, subregional maps at the section level, and, finally, specific location maps at the subsection or passage level. As the reader drills down from the largest region to the smallest, scale changes and the specificity of detail increases. A well-conceived map program keeps its relationships of scale simple and consistent for ease of comprehension; it uses scales at just a few regular increments and provides detail appropriate to each level.

IDENTIFY BASE MAPS. In some map programs, the same geographical region is viewed in various lights. In these cases, a single base map gets overlaid with different data patterns to highlight relationships among particular sites. In a book about the ecological history of the Great Lakes region, for example, a single base map might appear twenty times: once overlaid with former and extant wetlands, then with former and extant forests, then with urban sprawl, then with historical floods, and so on. Each map lifts a pattern out of the mire of available data, and readers who live in the region can flip among maps to compare the various ecological trends that have occurred in their neighborhood.

CAPTURE MOVEMENT. In addition to stationary features like towns, rivers, and landmarks, maps can contain information about ever-changing processes and behaviors: weather patterns, plant habitats, animal ranges, human traffic, even cultural developments like the spread of jazz. In these cases, the author does well not to get too bogged down in data overlays: it is the gist that matters.

CREATE A MAP SOURCEBOOK. To prepare a map program, authors should gather photocopies of base maps and other data into a binder and then list the features they want to appear on each map, specifying which are to be labeled and which unlabeled. For a single map, an author might supply as many as five sources, describing the strengths and weaknesses of each. Authors may use a colored highlighter on the photocopies to help the DE and cartographer find the features being picked up for the new map.

DO THUMBNAIL SKETCHES. Sometimes the sources for a map are so varied in scale and format that it can be difficult to visualize the final map. Authors can help convey their intentions by making small sketches. These can be quite primitive, with ovals for islands, upside-down v's for mountains, and so on. If the author cannot visualize the final map, then the DE should draw the thumbnail and run it by the author. Skipping thumbnails can result in an expensive extra pass of cartographic drafting.

CREATE A MAP PLAN. A several-page cover memo for the source book should explain the goal of the map program, the aesthetic desired, and the distinctive features of certain categories of maps. An in-house production editor will add nuts-and-bolts information about budget, schedule, type fonts, and map dimensions. Cartographers default to established traditions for features like water bodies and national borders, but the DE must decide how much information is too much, and which patterns to illuminate. For a four-color book, a DE may suggest a color scheme that organizes maps and their features by various types; for a black-and-white book, the DE may devise a system of icons, solid and dashed lines, and gray screens.

Following standard practice, Jagreet had prepared her map sourcebook by relying heavily on the Footsteps repository. Happily, most of the nations and cities in her manuscript had already been rendered for previous Footsteps guides; for these, Jagreet had only to include photocopies, striking some labels and adding others. Most of the new maps were at neighborhood scale: they showed the residential streets, shopping districts, and restaurant rows of the world's Little Indias. For these, while traveling, Jagreet had dutifully collected brochures put out by local civic organizations. Where those weren't available, she'd made sketches in her notebook and later transferred them onto zoom views from Google maps.

All of this work was well done. But the more Hedda thought about them, the more the maps shed light on a defect in the manuscript's organization: after moving plausibly from the Middle East southward to Africa and then eastward to East Asia, the text backtracked seven thousand miles westward to Europe. Hedda now realized that she had been bothered by this long jump when she edited the table of contents; the maps allowed her to see the problem more concretely. She played with several schemes before deciding to arrange the destinations so the text and maps moved in an uninterrupted flow westward from the Middle East via Europe to North America, southward to South America, eastward via Africa to Southeast Asia, and finally southward again to Australia.

There was one other aspect of the map program that deserved special attention. Jagreet had provided a category of map not usually found in Footsteps guides but that could well become a standard feature in the diaspora series.

These maps showed the patterns of Indian migration over time. In the introduction, the magnitude of the Indian diaspora was illustrated by a map of the globe with arrows radiating out from the subcontinent in all directions. Then in "Destinations," each country's history section was accompanied by a map showing where the first Indians had landed, how they spread from port towns to outlying villages, and—in many cases—how reverse migration was now causing villages to shrink and urban centers to sprawl. The source materials were of variable quality, but Jagreet had done a fine job of editing them to achieve a uniform level of detail.

Still, Hedda felt a nag of doubt. She checked the history maps against the population pie charts and saw that the ethnic breakdowns were not jibing between chart and map. In Mauritius, for example, the pie chart lumped together all Hindus, while the history map detailed movements by populations of Sanatanists, Arya Samajists, Tamils, Telugus, Marathis, Guarajatis, and Bengalis. Such discrepancies resulted from a lack of uniformity in the data available, and Hedda doubted Jagreet could find other sources. On balance, Hedda decided, the value of the information outweighed the inconsistency of format.

## Add Lagniappe

In Cajun country, lagniappe is that extra bit of added value, the gravy on the po' boy, the plastic baby in the king cake. In book publishing, where simplicity is a virtue, lagniappe should be added with caution. What follow are a few of the most common strategies for adding lagniappe that DEs and authors may propose.

DESIGN TEXT BOXES. Usually, text boxes are small digressions that don't fit in the body of the text and are too long to shoehorn into a caption or footnote. When a text box program is designed well, it leads readers through the text like a trail of bread crumbs. Text boxes of "fun facts" can relieve a dense intellectual argument; single-sentence text boxes, or pull quotes, can relieve the visual monotony in a book lacking art. Some dos and don'ts:

· Observe standard convention by ensuring that text boxes contain only "optional reading." Many readers routinely skip text boxes; if they discover they've missed a key piece of information in the process, they will be peeved.
· Avoid lone text boxes. A text box program should contain at least half a dozen pieces—otherwise, the odd box looks like a scrap of unassimilated story or argument.
· Keep lengths relatively equal. A program may contain up to three lengths:

single-sentence pull quotes, single-paragraph boxes, and multiparagraph boxes. A box that threatens to require a full page in the printed book should be moved into the sidebar program (see below).

· Include or omit box titles consistently. If a program contains some boxes that are untitled, they look like printer's errors.

· Avoid embedding art and tables in text boxes. A box that requires these elements should be moved into the sidebar program.

BUILD SIDEBARS. Sidebars are to nonfiction books what feature articles are to newspapers: they are longish digressions that provide an alternate, usually more intimate perspective on the subject at hand. I've seen authors' journal entries used effectively to enliven discussions of the evolution of birdlife in California, the stories of the makers of the first atom bomb, and the effects of modern media on traditional culture in Morocco. For authors-for-hire, sidebars may allow for creative expression outside of the bounds of series format.

Sidebars follow the rules for text boxes listed above, with two exceptions: they may run longer than a page if necessary, and they may contain art. Figures in sidebars should not be numbered in sequence with the rest of the art program. They should not have fat captions, nor may a sidebar comprise art and captions alone.

Because a sidebar program presents alternate views of the book's subject, it may be constructed using the same strategies as an epigraph program. The "kitchen sink" strategy vouchsafes that sidebars vary widely in tone and provenance throughout the book. The parallel storyline uses a single source for all sidebars (e.g., the author's journal), building suspense from sidebar to sidebar. The round robin passes the "talking stick" among several key sources: in a book applying gender theory to Japanese culture, for instance, a sidebar program might contain anecdotes that rotate among the shogun past, the influx of Western culture during the Meiji, and the market-driven culture of today.

CREATE A WEB PAGE. Web links are the simplest and cheapest way to add electronic value to a printed book. Most publishers today have sites with separate pages for each book in print; authors can set up their own sites for the cost of an Internet account. Materials best posted on a Web site include appendixes that would otherwise inflate the length and cost of the printed book; data that need to be updated frequently; audio and visual files that support comprehension of the printed text; color versions of photos that appear in black and white in the printed book; exercises, workbooks, and other course materials; programs that can be downloaded onto Palm Pilots or Global Positioning System units; and links to interactive features like list-serves and blogs devoted to the book's subject. Smaller publishers expect the author to cover the developmental costs of Web materials, while they provide a stable Web address and maintain current links.

Authors often need help thinking through the contents of a book's Web component. A link to a handful of ugly tables will do most books' reputations more harm than good. DEs should be provided with a list of ancillary Web components with the unedited manuscript so that they can look for opportunities to exploit the resources of the Web in service of the author's subject. DEs should keep their suggestions simple and submit them first to the publisher, who can determine economic feasibility before the author's hopes are raised.

Hedda took a day off from the project, giving the pantry a whitewash job that it needed badly. When she returned to the computer keyboard, dried paint on her hands, certain issues were clearer.

The text boxes fell into two categories. First were the "safety warnings" that Hedda was suggesting in lieu of more graphic photos of anti-Indian violence. The second group described a typical day in the life of the average Indian immigrant in different countries. Although these two types of boxes presented useful information, they were a bit downbeat. To lighten them up, Hedda decided to add a third category: favorite diasporan hangouts. Hedda went out of her way to keep these boxes light, drawing from online sources to add descriptive color.

The sidebars were harder to deal with. Because Jagreet had submitted only two, Hedda would have to decide between beefing up the program or omitting it altogether. But whereas she could pluck ideas for text boxes out of the existing text and flesh them out with minimal research, sidebars would require access to fresh material.

She called Jagreet. After trading gossip about fellow Footsteppers and updating each other about their own love lives, or lack thereof, they got down to business. Jagreet admitted that her plans to provide a fuller sidebar program had succumbed to deadline pressure. Now, after some rest, she could probably psych herself up to write the new mini-essays. Her journal was full of raw material: a visit by canoe to a jungle village of aboriginals in Malaysia; a trip with moneyed Indian tourists to the Disneyesque "Indian" village of Chaguanas in Trinidad; a walking tour of the Indian shops along Jackson Heights in Queens; and a vivid account of her pilgrimage to the Lake of the Ganges in Mauritius. Hedda and Jagreet agreed to limit the program to one sidebar per continent.

The last element of Jagreet's manuscript was a list of Web sites that would appear at the back of the printed book and be replicated with live links on a

Footsteps Web page. Hedda tested the links and found some were duds, but most filled her screen with a rich tapestry of colors, images, and type: the visual designs were as diverse as the populations they served. There were tacky virtual tours of the various Little Indias, tendentious blogs on which PIOs and NRIs debated the merits of the "masculinization" of Hinduism, fan sites for Bollywood stars, temple and school bulletins, resort sites offering Indian cooking classes, sites that arranged marriages, and sites that allowed users to make their own matches. The Indian government's online outreach to its diaspora was a model for other developing countries, Hedda learned. In short, Hedda found the Web component to be more than adequately developed—Jagreet would have only to replace or delete the dead links.

✳

Once Hedda had turned in the manuscript to the Ann Arbor office, she emailed Jagreet a copy of the final table of contents (example 43) and gave her a call.

"So, what happened with this project, anyway? Seems like it should have been a breeze for you."

"I know, but the more I got into it, the more resentful I felt. It's like Lockstep is the colonial power and I'm the indentured servant all over again. I mean, don't you feel that way as a freelancer? No benefits, no career ladder, no respect."

"Well, my career ladder may be more of a step stool, but I'm happy with where I'm at."

"Lucky you. I gave Deb notice: this was my last Lockstep job."

Hedda didn't know what to say. Later, she thought about the diaspora that had resulted in her own life. She was descended from a line of German serfs who had sought refuge from religious persecution in the New World. Since the turn of the twentieth century, her family had been resolutely secular, working in the American typesetting industry that had sprung up in a corridor ranging from Binghamton, New York, in the north to Fairfax, Virginia, in the south. Now those jobs had moved offshore, and a new corridor ran from Bombay to Bangalore.

Did she resent this loss of a life she'd grown up with? Maybe a little. But Hedda had built a career from the skills she'd learned as a young girl hanging out in the composition room, and she'd enjoyed a life of relative stability, freedom, and intellectual stimulation. Of course, it was understandable that Jagreet would make a connection between her freelance status and the historically recent memory of indentured servitude in her family.

An epigraph at the front of Jagreet's manuscript synopsized a story Hedda remembered her telling one chilly night in Nepal. It concerned how Nanak, the sixteenth-century divine founder of Sikhism, had handled the bickering of his converts on his deathbed. The Muslims wanted to bury him and the Hindus to

EXAMPLE 43. The final TOC for the Kaur manuscript. Note changes in the order of destination countries, which now proceed in an unbroken circuit of the globe.

*The Indian Diaspora: A Travel Guide*

cremate him, so Nanak instructed each group to place a bouquet on either side of his body. "They whose flowers are fresh in the morning," he said, "may have the disposal of my body." The next day, his body had vanished and both bouquets had taken root and bloomed. Sometimes Hedda felt like that, caught between authors and publishers. No magical truces for her, just the hard work of empathy.

# AFTERWORD

By now, it will have become apparent that the dichotomy between this handbook's right- and left-brained editors was a bit disingenuous. Bud, the "intuitive" DE, often used analytical tools to guide his interventions in structure and style, while "logical" Hedda found herself at regular impasses in the revision process, waiting for inspiration to strike. For both of these DEs, their mentor's analytical approach provided a framework within which to receive fresh insights. Both adapted the techniques freely to suit their purposes, skipping some steps and repeating others, using them as springboards for enhancing their own creative processes.

Publishers need to perform the same balancing act between inspiration and sound editorial analysis. They may ask, how can we justify the cost of developmental editing? It's a good question because, while a book may sell many more copies than it would have without a DE's intervention, there's no way to estimate those increased sales in advance. We can, however, identify several principles that should guide a publisher's forays into developmental editing.

KNOW YOUR PROFILE. Consider the extent to which developmental editing dovetails with your mission. Textbooks, commissioned reference works, and entries in highly formatted series all tend to require development; if these are part of your list model, you'll need to budget for DE services as either overhead or direct freelance costs. Trade publishers may need to develop the occasional title in order to ensure their voice is heard in an important public discussion; regional publishers may rely on DEs to compensate for inexperience in their author pools.

SEEK COLLABORATORS. Cultivate a reputation for creative collaboration. This buzz will draw authors open to working with DEs. As we've seen in our case studies, when developmental editing has poor or mixed results, it's usually because of a lack of author "buy-in."

FOCUS ON REVENUE. That said, you'll need to develop rigorous criteria for when DE costs are justifiable. No matter how tempting its subject or author, a book should not incur developmental costs unless its projected profits can comfortably absorb them. Honesty here is key—it will be tempting to inflate projected income to cover the DE costs of a title that an editor fervently wishes to publish. At the University of California Press, an editor must argue convincingly that DE intervention will increase a title's income potential by $40,000 to $60,000.

THINK BACKLIST. When weighing DE costs against potential revenue, consider backlist potential. If the title is certain, by virtue of its authority or lack of competition, to sell for many years, then DE costs can be viewed in light of that longer interval. Most publishers "write down" unsold inventory after three years—that is, they declare it a loss for tax purposes—but many wait five years to write down new editions of backlist staples.

INTERVENE STRATEGICALLY. Not every title with developmental needs requires "the full Monty." Consider setting up a budget line for limited interventions to meet strategic goals (see end of chapter 6).

For practical reasons, this handbook has focused on the relationship between DE and author, with the publisher cast as a quiet partner. In reality, the publisher often plays a crucial role in the developmental process as muse, matchmaker, sounding board, nursemaid, shuttle diplomat, or all of the above. It is the publisher who ensures harmony between the author's vision and the DE's advocacy on behalf of the book's future readers. I hope this handbook will go some small way toward encouraging more publishers to explore the use of freelance developmental editors.

# FURTHER READING

In this handbook, I have limited the discussion to serious nonfiction, techniques for editing completed manuscripts, and the vocal aspects of style. In the works listed below, readers will find much useful advice, including additional perspectives on developmental editing; fuller treatments of proposal writing, fiction techniques, and applied rhetoric; and comprehensive style guides. Closing the list is a trio of works that together serve as a primer in the history and culture of American publishing.

## Developmental Editing

Gerald Gross. *Editors on Editing: What Writers Need to Know about What Editors Do.* Third Edition. New York: Grove Press, 1993.

Jeff Herman. *Jeff Herman's Guide to Book Publishers, Editors, and Literary Agents.* Stockbridge, Mass.: Three Dog Press, 2007.

Mary Ellen Lepionka. *Writing and Developing Your College Textbook.* Gloucester, Mass.: Atlantic Path Publishing, 2003.

Beth Luey. *Handbook for Academic Authors.* Fourth Edition. Cambridge: Cambridge University Press, 2002.

Carolyn D. Rude, with David Dayton. *The Longman Guide to Technical Editing: A Comprehensive Reference Guide for Editors and Information Managers.* New York: Pearson Longman, 2006.

Judith A. Tarutz. *Technical Editing: The Practical Guide for Editors and Writers.* New York: Perseus, 1992.

Although this handbook is the first work devoted entirely to developmental editing, several useful reference works offer chapters or sections on the subject. Gross gathers advice and insights from editors working in trade and scholarly publishing, among them an essay on developmental editing during the writing of a manuscript and another on "book doctoring" a completed draft. Herman's book contains three perspectives on book doctoring, with an emphasis on avoiding scams. Lepionka's is the best treatment available of the role of staff DEs in textbook publishing, although her primary audience is authors. Luey gives special attention to the developmental effort involved in revising a dissertation into a publishable scholarly book. Two thorough handbooks focus on preparation of technical documentation: Rude provides useful chapters on collaborating with writers and on what she calls "comprehensive editing"; Tarutz offers a more comprehensive desktop reference for technical editors but gives less attention to developmental editing per se.

## Concept and Content

Pam Brodowsky and Eric Neuhaus. *Bulletproof Book Proposals.* Cincinnati, Ohio: Writer's Digest Books, 2006.
Susan Rabiner and Alfred Fortunato. *Thinking Like Your Editor: How to Write Great Serious Nonfiction—and Get It Published.* New York: Norton, 2002.

Among the large number of "writing coaches" who deal with proposal writing, two teams have produced books that are particularly useful. Rabiner and Fortunato offer sound advice on the proposal, drafting, editing, and marketing stages of the publishing process, with an emphasis on serious nonfiction. Brodowsky and Neuhaus focus exclusively on proposal writing for the lighter end of the trade spectrum, with an emphasis on how-to guides and trade reference; half the book contains a dozen actual proposals that sold.

## Narrative

Madison Smartt Bell. *Narrative Design: Working with Imagination, Craft, and Form.* New York: Norton, 1997.
John Gardner. *The Art of Fiction: Notes on Craft for Young Writers.* New York: Vintage, 1983.
David Lodge. *The Art of Fiction.* London: Penguin, 1992.
Noah Lukeman. *The Plot Thickens: Eight Ways to Bring Fiction to Life.* New York: St. Martin's Griffin, 2002.

Prospective novelists do best to seek advice from authors whose own novels they admire. Gardner places concrete tips about technique in the context of his personal brand of literary theory. Bell usefully anatomizes a dozen short stories for plot, character, structural design, and other elements before providing a concise philosophy of composition. Lodge's brief essays analyze passages from classic and recent literary novels to illuminate topics ranging from narrative techniques (suspense, dialogue, the unreliable narrator) to rhetorical devices (irony, symbolism, allegory). Less literary and more pragmatic, Lukeman prompts authors to allow plot to grow out of character development.

## Exposition

Edward P. J. Corbett and Robert J. Conners. *Classical Rhetoric for the Modern Student.* Fourth Edition. Oxford: Oxford University Press, 1999.
Kate Turabian. *A Manual for Writers of Research Papers, Theses, and Dissertations: Chicago Style for Students and Researchers.* Revised by Wayne C. Booth, Gregory G. Colomb, Joseph M. Williams, and University of Chicago Press Editorial Staff. Chicago: University of Chicago Press, 2007.
Anthony Weston. *A Rulebook for Arguments.* Indianapolis: Hackett Publishing, 2000.

A number of handbooks focus on methods of argument drawn from classical rhetoric. Corbett and Conners offer a thorough treatment, applying to contemporary discourse the five canons of rhetoric, three modes of persuasion, and classical figures of speech. Weston distills this material into a concise and practical set of steps for making an argument. Addressing students with research papers to write, Turabian provides sound advice on exposition, emphasizing the research and development on which good argumentation is founded.

## Style

Amy Einsohn. *The Copyeditor's Handbook: A Guide for Book Publishing and Corporate Communications.* Berkeley and Los Angeles: University of California Press, 2000.
John McWhorter. *The Power of Babel: A Natural History of Language.* New York: Perennial, 2001.
William Strunk, Jr., and E. B. White. *The Elements of Style.* Fourth Edition. New York: Longman, 2000.
Joseph M. Williams. *Style: Toward Clarity and Grace.* Chicago: University of Chicago Press, 1990.

Strunk and White deliver the dos and don'ts of English prose with unparalleled concision, although they don't say *how* to achieve those goals. That question is answered by Williams, whose hands-on text, replete with examples, boils down the tenets of the "new grammar" without pedantry. Einsohn addresses the nuts and bolts of style from a copyeditor's point of view. For readers nostalgic for iron-clad, prescriptive rules of style, McWhorter's brisk review of the development of human language should prove an effective antidote.

## Display

Council of Science Editors, eds. *Scientific Style and Format: The CSE Manual for Authors, Editors, and Publishers.* Seventh Edition. Reston, Va.: Council of Science Editors, 2006.

Edward R. Tufte. *The Visual Display of Quantitative Information.* Second Edition. Cheshire, Conn.: Graphics Press, 2001.

University of Chicago Press Staff, eds. *The Chicago Manual of Style.* Fifteenth Edition. Chicago: University of Chicago Press, 2003.

The *Chicago Manual of Style* remains the definitive work on bookmaking in the humanities and social sciences and gives comprehensive attention to display elements. Its counterpart in the sciences, the *CSE Manual*, is especially useful on elements prevalent in those disciplines, such as numbered headings, equations, and complex tables. Lepionka (above) contains useful discussions of heading structure, tables, figures, boxes, and sidebars. Tufte's elegant book will inspire some readers to express data visually in arresting and communicative ways but may intimidate the left-brained among us.

## Publishing

Ben H. Bagdikian. *The New Media Monopoly.* Boston: Beacon, 2004.

Jason Epstein. *Book Business: Publishing Past, Present, and Future.* New York: Norton, 2002.

John Tebbel. *Between Covers: The Rise and Transformation of American Book Publishing.* New York: Oxford, 1987.

For a short course in the history of American publishing, read these three books in the following order. Tebbel traces the development of the industry from its earliest beginnings, through its creative heyday, to its aggregation in the mid-1980s. Bagdikian picks up the story from there, documenting the further consolidation of American media, including book publishing, from fifty conglomerates into the current Big Five. Epstein offers a glimpse of the future informed by four decades' worth of experience at the center of the New York scene.

# ACKNOWLEDGMENTS

Whenever a reviewer asserts that a publisher has failed to edit a book, I wonder. Did the editing team really choose to ignore the book's alleged deficiencies? Or did the author decline to take the advice offered? This handbook has received the attention of no fewer than eighteen experienced professionals: you may safely assume that any errors reflect stubbornness on my part.

To say that this book would not exist without the efforts of Marilyn Schwartz is an understatement. She put the idea in my head, helped shape the proposal, nurtured the core chapters, and held my hand when the going got rough. As mentor, friend, and former boss, she has taught me much of what I know about editing and publishing. I am deeply grateful.

Others have contributed substantively to the development of this book. Beth Luey gently improved the chapters on which this handbook is based while compiling her edited volume, *Revising Your Dissertation*. Early encouragement and useful advice were supplied by Doug Abrams, Jesse Brodkey, Blake Edgar, Stan Holwitz, Niels Hooper, and Marsha Melnick. Two anonymous readers of the proposal, three of the draft manuscript, and two of the final manuscript saved me from numerous gaffes and helped to refine my approach.

I owe a special debt of gratitude to my "Left Coast" readers. Dore Brown gave this manual a thorough usability test from the vantage point of the in-house project editor. Sue Heinemann reviewed the text incisively as a self-professed "intuitive editor." Kate Hoffman helped flesh out the discussions of art and tables. And poets Evy Posamentier and Stewart Florsheim cheered me on while tactfully flagging tonal lapses.

The warm support this project has found at "the other UC Press" has been a high point of the experience. Special thanks to acquiring editor Christie Henry for her tact, professionalism, and collaborative spirit, to manuscript editor Mara Naselli for her perceptive line editing, and to Carol Fisher Saller for her guidance through the latter stages of production.

I am especially grateful to Karen Stough, ace proofreader, for offering to read these typeset pages. As usual, she made a number of spectacular catches. Any surviving deviations from formal grammar or *Webster's* style reflect my preference, not her eagle eye.

The sidebars in chapters 1, 4, and 7 are indebted to the lucid explanations in Madison Smartt Bell's *Narrative Design* (see "Further Reading"). The story of the death of Nanak, the founder of Sikhism, briefly related in chapter 10, is taken from M. A. McAuliffe, *Sikhism: Its Gurus, Sacred Writings, and Authors* (London: Oxford University Press, 1900), as quoted in the online Handbook of Today's Religions. The thesis for the case study in chapter 4 was inspired by a passage in Alan Lomax's *The Land Where the Blues Began* (New York: Delta Books, 1993), in which the legendary folklorist asserts the likely common ancestry of the African American "levee holler" and the *muezzin's* call to prayer (page 234).

That said, the character of Mezzy Walker is entirely fictitious, as are the authors, subjects, publishers, and editors in all of the case studies. The thesis statements and "research" underpinning them are intentionally bogus; the editorial problems are drawn from real manuscripts, but they've been transposed into different disciplines and then sliced, diced, and recombined.

Finally, for their unconditional love and support, I thank my family, Trudy, Fred, Steve, Eric, Heather, Lindsey, and Justin; dear friend Laurie Ferreira; our Glide family; and especially my life partner, Vincent Mason, who exercised the patience of an editor with this first-time author.

# INDEX

milieu, in narrative, 177
misreading, willful, 176
mission, publisher's, 221
mission statement, 23
Mitchell, David, 79
mixed metaphor, 169
"A Modest Proposal" (Swift), 178
modesty, false, in historical narratives, 69
motives, publisher's for development, 34
multiple personality disorder, in prose style, 182
*Murder on the Orient Express* (1934), 79
Murray, Bill, 16

narrative, 68–90; further reading, 224–25; thesis of, 53
narratives, rotating, as timeline strategy, 79
nested conclusions, unpacking, 153
nesting logic: in exposition, 96, in thesis selection, 58
niche publisher, in trade reference, 189
note, in table, 207
novelist, as historian, 69

omniscience, 15; and subheads, 192–93; third-person, 164
Onassis, Jackie, x
opening transition, 146–49; fused, 147
oratorical flourish, in title, 64
originality: assessing, 72–73, 96; of thesis, 55–57
ornaments, 194
outcomes, alternate: as argument strategy, 102; as timeline strategy, 79–80
overcriticism, 165; in prose style, 164
overfamiliarity, 165; in prose style, 164
overqualification, 166; in prose style, 164
overwriting, 165
ownership, of text, author's sense of, 130
oxymoron, 169, 171

pace: discursive, 123–41; editing for, 135–41; and plot summary, 136–37
packager, book, as client, 160–61
paradox, 169, 170
parallel lines of argument, 102
parallel storyline: in epigraph program, 198; in sidebar program, 216
parallel timelines, 79
part divisions, and rules of balance, 82–83
passages: drafting new, 130–32; flagging for deletion, 133; grieving lost, 133
passivity, 165; overuse of, 164
pattern of meaning, narrative as, 68
performance review, in-house editor's, 37
Perkins, Maxwell, x
permissions: costs, 205; fees, 202; further reading, 202–3; issues with epigraphs, 198
*Permissions, A Survival Guide* (Bielstein), 202–3
persona, author's, 164–66, 182
personification, 171
persuasion, three modes of, 225
pie charts, 209
plan, developmental, 112–22
Platonic ideals, in argument, 91
plot, and timeline, 81
plot summary, and pace, 136–37
poems, in epigraphs, 198
point of view: author's, 43; defined, 15, 52–53; finding, 53; in narrative, 69; in style, 182; and vision statement, 23
"post-avant," 92
posthumous editing assignment, 142
postmodern novel, use of subheads in, 192–93
postmodern thinking, 92
preacher, author as, 55
production packagers, 160
proofreading, learning, 36
proposal, shaping, 9–26

storytelling: discourse as, 72; templates, 68
straddle head, in table, 207–8
straight timeline, 76; repeated with alternate outcomes, 79
strategic interventions, limited, 113, 122, 222
structural issues, itemizing in developmental plan, 117–18
stub, in table, 207
style, 158–86
stylistic issues, itemizing in developmental plan, 117–18
subarguments. *See* supporting arguments
subheads: purpose of, 192; style, 193
subject: abstract vs. concrete, 72; culling concepts from, 14–15; tallying occurrences of, 42; transmuting into concept, 43
substantive editing, 1
supporting arguments, 91; and main line of argument, 98; order of, 101, 103
suspense: the art of, 78; via thesis splitting, 105
Swift, Jonathan, 178
syncopation, in discursive rhythm, 137
synesthesia, 171

table note, 207
table of contents, revised, in developmental plan, 117
tables: conjoined, 207–8; data, 207; list, 208; parts of, 208; title, 207
technical editing, 2
tension, and creating suspense, 78
tenure, and academic publishing, 93
text boxes, 215–16
text condensation, 136–37
text-to-art ratio, 203
thematic links: in *Cloud Atlas,* 79; in narrative, 68
theorist, as author, 92–93

theory boom and bust, 92
theses: culling concepts from, 15–16; culling from topics, 52–55
thesis, 48–67; borrowed, 55; of narrative, 53; splitting into halves, 147; working, 58
third-person omniscience. *See* omniscience
thumbnail sketches, in map development, 214
*Time's Arrow* (Amis), 78
timeline, 68–90; composing new, 80–81; finetuning, 81–85; vs. line of argument, 72–74; restoring bits of, 107–10; reverse, 78; straight, 76
timelines: parallel, 77, 79; untangling, 74; untangling from arguments, 72–74, 95–98
timeline strategies, brainstorming, 76–80
title, of table, 207
title: chapter, in exposition, 105–6; chapter, in narrative, 83–85; perfect, 62; working, 62–66
titling strategies, 63–64
tonal richness, conserving, 182
tonal shifts, flagging, 182
tone, as element of voice, 158; setting, 164–68
topics, culling theses from, 52–55
Track Changes feature (Microsoft Word), 128
trade houses: big, 29–30; reference, 189–90; regional, 125–26; small, 50; and university presses, 93–94
transition: closing, 149–52; fused, 149; opening, 146–49
transitional subheads, 193–94
transitions, 142–57
triage assignments, 122

*Ulysses* (Joyce), 144, 177
umbrella thesis, 58

Made in the USA
Monee, IL
15 January 2021

57668517R00152